Evidence of Arthur

Evidence of Arthur

*Fixing the Legendary King
in Factual Place and Time*

FLINT F. JOHNSON

McFarland & Company, Inc., Publishers

Jefferson, North Carolina

LIBRARY OF CONGRESS CATALOGUING-IN-PUBLICATION DATA

Johnson, Flint.
    Evidence of Arthur : fixing the legendary king in factual place and time / Flint F. Johnson.
        p.   cm.
    Includes bibliographical references and index.

    ISBN 978-0-7864-7681-7 (softcover : acid free paper) ∞
    ISBN 978-1-4766-0628-6 (ebook)

    1. Arthur, King.   2. Britons—Kings and rulers—Historiography.
3. Great Britain—History—To 1066.   4. Arthurian romances—
Sources.   I. Title.
    DA152.5.A7J64 2014
    942.01'4—dc23   2014000336

BRITISH LIBRARY CATALOGUING DATA ARE AVAILABLE

On the cover: model of a hypothetical construct of Arthur's home by Kenna Bjerstedt (photograph by Emily Adler); *inset* King Arthur of Britain, by Howard Pyle from *The Story of King Arthur and His Knights*, 1903 (Wikipedia Commons)

Manufactured in the United States of America

McFarland & Company, Inc., Publishers
Box 611, Jefferson, North Carolina 28640
www.mcfarlandpub.com

Table of Contents

Source Abbreviations

AA   *Archaeologica Aeliana*
Antiq   *Antiquity*
ASE   *Anglo-Saxon England*
Brit   *Britannia*
BBCS   *Bulletin of the Board of Celtic Studies*
CMCS   *Cambridge/Cambrian Medieval Celtic Studies*
EHR   *English History Review*
EC   *Étude Celtique*
MLN   *Modern Language Notes*
MP   *Modern Philology*
NMS   *Nottingham Mediaeval Studies*
PBA   *Proceedings of the British Academy*
PMLA   *Publications of the Modern Language Association of America*
S   *Speculum*
SC   *Studia Celtica*
THSC   *Transactions of the Honourable Society of the Cymmrodorion*
WHR   *Welsh History Review*
ZDP   *Zeitschrift Deutsche Philosophie*

Preface and Acknowledgments

While writing a thesis on several romances associated with Arthur, I came across an article written by Dr. Oliver Padel, "The Nature of Arthur." Even at that early date in my academic career, I was aware that the article's case of Arthur's historicity was not a balanced one, and thus I immediately composed a rejoinder that sought to rectify the inadequacy. I retained that paper in my files, but never published it. Throughout graduate school and since then, the paper has been improved upon and expanded as more ideas and better approaches have occurred to me. The product of all those ruminations is laid out below.

The present monograph is a sequel to my recent book, *Origins of Arthurian Romance: Early Sources for the Legends of Tristan, the Grail, and the Abduction of the Queen*. It employs the methodology developed in that previous work as an approach to a study of Arthur, and with it the exacting examination of all pertinent sources.

The current book is divided into three parts. Each has been designed so that, in part or as a whole, they are dependent on those preceding it. The opening group of chapters has been devoted to multiple approaches to the issue of Arthur's historicity. There follows a detailed examination of his possible area of activity and the years he flourished.

All three parts will make use of the same pool of resources. In moving forward from *Origins of Arthurian Romance*, that pool will include purely literary as well as pseudo-historical and historical materials. With their strengths and weaknesses known as determined by scholarship on each individual piece, each work will be employed only where its usefulness is credible. No source is used exclusively.

* * *

1

As this volume was formulated largely on the research and knowledge I collected during the construction of my Ph.D., I find that I must thank many of the same people. I greatly appreciate Mr. Warren and Mr. Schleh for their confidence in me and the support they have given me for many years. I wish to thank Dr. Wood and Professor Caie for their persistence and patience in helping me to develop my writing style. They have both proven generous friends long after I was officially their student. I would also like to note here the patience and persistence of my sister, Kenna. It is her offering which appears on the front cover, and it was only through many patient hours of discourse that I was finally able to relate what I was after in this hypothetical recreation of Arthur's home, Camelot. Only she knows how many hours of tedious work went into it. Thank you.

I have benefited greatly from several conversations with Dr. Thomas Clancy and Dr. Rachel Bromwich; they have guided me away from many pitfalls. I have often sought their advice pertaining to this volume. In the final stages of this book, I have enjoyed the insights and guidance of Professor Clyde Smith and the editorial patience of Michelle Klein. However, I take full responsibility for any misunderstanding or error in those dialogues. Many of the views that I have expressed here are not those of any other scholar. Most of all, I would like to express my gratitude again to my personal muse. Thank you, Marina. As abstract as your help has been, it has been essential to this and to me.

Introduction

In 825, King Hywel of Gwynedd died, and with him a dynasty that had included Maelgwn and Cadwallon came to an end. Hywel was replaced in the next year by his son-in-law Merfyn Frych, whose family was descended from Urien through the dynasty of Man. Merfyn was the first in his own Gwynedd dynasty, one that would last well into the Middle Ages. It is only natural that such an important change occurring within a powerful kingdom would have caused a great deal of internal unrest. That upheaval might easily have been taken advantage of by outside powers such as the Germanic kingdoms who had been pressuring the Welsh for centuries. It was not, however, and in this Merfyn was extremely fortunate. His accession took place during a period of disorder in Wessex. Their king, Cœwulf, would die in 821, to be succeeded by Ceolwulf. The new ruler would continue the aggressive policies into Wales that had been characteristic of the dynasty, but he would be killed in a factional conflict in 823. Beornwulf would be the next leader of Wessex and would live only till 825. When Merfyn assumed the Gwynedd throne, Wessex was in the process of trying to find its fourth king in six years. It would be some time before the kingdom would be able to solidify itself once again.[1]

Because of the respite, Merfyn would not only be able to stabilize his own dynasty, but he and those who followed him would initiate a change of policy. The kings of Gwynedd would, from this point on, actively engage in trying to organize the surviving British states into a united front against the English. This would be done through centuries of warfare, many marital alliances, and the recovery and transmission of northern British oral and possibly written literature from Strathclyde to Gwynedd.[2] It is this last accomplishment that will be the focus for the remainder of this chapter.

Merfyn was the first to attempt any of this, and his accomplishments were the most far-reaching. Much of the material that was gathered at his instigation was forged into prose form as the *Historia Brittonum*. This book had an agenda with two specific goals. First, he used it to strengthen the hold his dynasty had on the kingdom of Gwynedd. To forward this objective, the author shows the common northern heroic tradition which Merfyn's forefathers and Hywel's predecessors had shared. The author located the origins of both dynasties in the north. He then set about focusing his narrative on prominent characters from both lineages, and the prominent ancestors of the house to which Gwynedd was closely allied with at the time, Powys. *Historia Brittonum* so focuses on Urien and his immediate family, Cunedda and his descendants, and the Powysian hero Gwrtheyrn that it appears as if one is being given a family history of the two most prominent ruling families of Wales. One might consider the balance of the *Historia* as an attempt to set them in context with the major events of British history. In giving the other information, however, the *Historia Brittonum* author only highlights the importance of his main subjects and theme. This was most probably his intention.[3]

The second goal was that the accounts of British history would help develop a sense of British nationalism among the warrior class of Gwynedd.[4] Coupled with their newfound sense of Britishness would be a sense of unity, pride, and common culture with the other Welsh kingdoms. Nationalism was a second reason why stories pertaining to other British kingdoms were incorporated into the history. Whether or not they featured Gwynedd or Powys, all of the secular scenes and episodes depicted in *Historia Brittonum* consistently showed the British as the enemies of the non–British, and either friendly with or oblivious to each other. In this vein Urien again played a central role; he served as a symbol of what had been right with the British in the past. It was through him that the British had combined and brought a Germanic state to the brink of elimination.

His death highlighted the theme of unity. Though an alternative interpretation traditionally associated with Urien's cousin suggests that Urien died in combat, *Historia Brittonum* is clear. It states without a doubt that internal dissension and deceit among the Britons caused him to be killed.[5] The interpretation laid out by the *Historia Brittonum* has proven to be a vivid and powerful one through the centuries. It has remained almost to this day a perception that the British fought against the Germanic people on an ethnic level.[6]

Merfyn Frych's movement, and specifically the *Historia Brittonum*, was designed to validate his right to rule Gwynedd through a twofold process. First, it attempted to envelop Merfyn's ancestors in honors and prestige. In this, Urien of Rheged was given precedence over the other heroes of the past.[7] Second, the history provided the state of Gwynedd with a long and storied tradition of strong rulers.[8] Together, these were intended to paint Gwynedd as the greatest of the British kingdoms. And, along with the message of British unity triumphing over the German kingdoms and division resulting in chaos, demonstrated that Gwynedd was the natural leader of any British coalition.

In addition to the materials that made up the *Historia Brittonum*, several other extant literary works were also brought to Gwynedd as a result of Merfyn's movement.[9] These did not serve to promote any of the motivations listed above,[10] and therefore they did not find their way into the main text. However, they were written down. These additional materials included the *Annales Cambriae*, *Pa gur?*, *Preiddeu Annwn*, and *Y Gododdin*.[11] On balance, they highlight better than any knowledge of the period or absence of materials in the *Historia Brittonum* can the intent of Merfyn's literary activity.

For instance, it is of great interest that all the above named documents, including the *Historia Brittonum*, mention a powerful British war-chief, or *dux bellorum*, named Arthur.[12] Arthur's inclusion in these documents, especially given the intense political climate and specific needs of Gwynedd during the ninth century, demonstrates his widespread fame and his obvious importance to the Welsh people by this time.[13] Despite the fact that he is nowhere claimed to be related to the houses of Man, Gwynedd, or Powys in any records, the early literature pertaining to him is almost as great as for Urien.[14] Arthur's continued presence in the literature of the Welsh throughout the medieval period demonstrates his staying power and his ability to capture the imagination of the Welsh people. Arthur is the most popular British figure in Middle Welsh literature. He was clearly an unusually powerful personality who inspired a widespread body of oral literature. In the Gwynedd-derived literature regarding the North, there was simply little if any motivation for his story to be presented in its entirety.[15]

Arthur is not, however, well-recorded as a historical figure. Modern scholarship has only a meager amount of material pertaining to him.[16] One semireliable event exists for his lifetime, that of the battle of Camlann (537 or 539).[17] No archaeological evidence has yet been produced that would demonstrate conclusively that he existed, or where he may have been based; no coin or shard of pottery with his name has ever been found.[18] Cadbury Castle gave away no evidence of Arthur whatsoever.[19] In short, his very existence has been called into question.[20]

The absence of information regarding the British hero Arthur is disturbing and to some degree unexplained. However, it is not an unexpected state of affairs considering the general paucity of sources for the post–Roman British period. For example, to better understand the era, historians have been forced to enlist sources of information not designed to convey historical material about the literary Dark Age, and not informative enough to provide much significant data.[21] A *Life of St. Germanus* written some years after the notable's death, a condemnation of a fifth-century chieftain named Ceredig by St. Patrick (*Epistola ad Coroticum*), and a ruthless legal document addressed to several sixth-century kings (*De Excidio Britanniae*) are all commonly accepted fonts of information for the fifth and sixth centuries—in fact they are the only documents of the period. The situation is all the more frustrating for a scholar because even these are so highly specialized in the information they give as to be almost useless,[22] or so broad in scope or so littered with chronological incongruities and vagueness as to be untrustworthy.[23] Yet if one is to study the fifth and early sixth centuries they are the only historical sources available, apart from archaeological records.[24]

It should come as no surprise, then, that very little would be known of any figure from this period. In fact, it should be assumed that many significant people of the fifth century are still entirely unknown. For instance, the *Historia Brittonum* author considered a North British leader named Outigern notable enough that he would be well known. He is used to chronologically place the five famed poets he names. Unfortunately for the modern scholar, Outigern is otherwise entirely unknown to Welsh tradition.

Outigern is not an isolated individual. Almost nothing is known of the Pictish kings of this period except for some names and the length of their reigns.[25] For the kings of individual Pictish regions such as Caith or Fib, there is next to nothing. If one takes Gwrtheyrn out of the fifth century, one is left with no significant figure from the years 410 to the rise of Ambrosius around maybe 480. Yet with all these limitations, the evidence is there that Arthur did live. It is simply a matter of properly using all the sources that can be brought to bear on the problem. Looking at each source critically will be the first and most significant element of this book.

The Material

The paucity of knowledge about such an obviously popular figure as Arthur stands as a symbol of our ignorance of the British events following the Honorian Rescript. In the decades after the "Once and Future King's" presumed time, figures such as Maelgwn, Rhun and Brude, sons of Maelgwn, Urien Rheged, and Rhydderch Hael emerge into what is a progressively clearer historical focus. Our historical and literary resources steadily increase in number and value until we reach the lifetime of Bede.

Before 400 the history of Roman Britain is accorded better historical records than most other provinces of the empire. The personal letters found on *ostraca* near Hadrian's Wall, the wars and revolts catalogued by Tacitus and Ammianus, and the line of usurpers in Britain prior to 410 were a consistent reason for Roman historians to give news of the island. Because of their writings, the modern scholar has been able to reconstruct British history from the first through the fourth century. But nothing between 410 and the early sixth century had the benefit of so much or so honest reporting.

However, some of the period is recoverable, and perhaps it is best to start with its most striking symbol—Arthur.[26] The main reasons for the question of his historicity have been threefold. First, he does not appear as a subject in any contemporary poetry or historical documents. Second, he and his men seem to take on the characteristics of folktale characters soon after their appearance in the literature, implying this may have been their original form. Finally, Arthur has proven to be a figure without any dependable geographical location. These are serious arguments and have not been countered in the centuries that have passed. The following book is an attempt to rectify that situation.

Despite being unable to directly and authoritatively respond to the central problems, people of several fields have already done much work on the subject of Arthur and the questions of his existence and location. Geoffrey of Monmouth's politically inspired pseudo-history may have begun the movement, but hundreds of experts and authors have loaned their contributions to the question of Arthur. Adding to the problem, the results have varied widely. Among them, Geoffrey Ashe strongly favored Arthur's existence in Brittany around 470 in the disguise of the British leader Riothamus.[27] In sharp contrast, the literary specialist Roger Sherman Loomis spent his entire career portraying Arthur as a strictly literary character with mythological attributes.[28]

The mainstream of more recent studies, however, has focused on Arthur's probable existence, and his relationship to the world around him. In 1973, John Morris wrote an interdisciplinary, though not wholly discriminating, volume on the period.[29] He located Arthur in the Devon region, largely because of his main sources—the vitae. Archaeologically, Leslie Alcock's *Arthur's Britain* began a new age of more skeptical study, and he was wary of locating Arthur.[30] The Celtic specialists Thomas Jones and Kenneth Jackson simultaneously wrote articles asserting their belief in Arthur's existence. However, they both noted the untenable nature of his geography.[31] Their findings were later supported by Rachel Bromwich and Thomas Charles-Edwards.[32] John E. Lloyd, Rachel Bromwich, Thomas Jones, and Kenneth Jackson have all speculated as to Arthur's northern affinities.[33] The recent challenges to the stance of his existence have come from David Dumville and Oliver Padel.

Several studies peripheral to Arthur have been conducted as well. In Early Welsh literature, the work of Ifor Williams, R. Geraint Gruffydd, Kenneth Jackson, Patrick Sims-Williams, Alfred O.H. Jarman, Marged Haycock, and John Koch have contributed greatly. Through the efforts of these scholars, a good understanding of the probable development of Welsh literature and language has been developed over the past half century. It has been shown that the progression of the Welsh language and poetry between 400 and 900 is nearly unknown, despite the optimism of previous generations. The sixth-century *Y Gododdin* and Taliesin poetry can hardly be differentiated from the (possibly) ninth-century pseudo–Taliesin works, except by their tone and purpose. On linguistic grounds, it is nearly impossible to date an Old or Middle Welsh literary work.[34]

The Chadwicks have both made their strong contributions to our understanding of the heroic age phenomenon. Hector Chadwick's *The Heroic Age* (Cambridge, 1912) provided a societal context for the period, and an examination of various epics aided in developing some concept of how the king-based war-bands of the fifth and sixth centuries must have functioned within the larger culture of the period. It also introduced an interesting concept to heroic age literature: that an exceptionally prestigious historical figure would have a gravitational effect upon lesser heroes of the same heroic age. According to this theory, the literary war-band of a heroic age king would progressively attract warriors and other kings from a geographical and chronological area that would steadily grow as time went on.[35]

The Growth of Literature, by Hector and Nora Chadwick, referenced every major heroic age society and the literature it left behind. This study continued the work of *The Heroic Age*, making several points concerning the society and rendering the nature of origin of the heroic age more refined. Professor Nora Chadwick's *The British Heroic Age* (Cambridge, 1976) dealt specifically with the heroic period in Britain. She made use of the accumulated sociological knowledge of Hector Chadwick's research in applying it to the period 400 to 650. She was also the first to point out Carlisle as an area of some importance in this period, whether as a capital of Reged or a place of storage for oral history.[36]

In addition, Dr. Ker has made his own contributions on the heroic age phenomenon. It was his studies of how heroic age oral literature might develop into romance that allowed for the basic premises in *Origins of Arthurian Romance: Early Sources for the Legends of Tristan, the Grail and the Abduction of the Queen*.[37] That is, that many elements of the romance which seem purely artistic may have derived from original heroic age material and may therefore be relied upon as historical.[38]

Finally, literary scholarship and criticism of the secondary sources of the period have proven most valuable. The contributions of Geraint Bowen, Gilbert H. Doble, Arthur W. Wade-Evans, Stephen Baring-Gould, J. Fischer and Peter C. Bartrum have been beneficial for many reasons. The work of most of these scholars on the *vitae* has produced tremendous results—better acquaintance with fifth-century sites, some knowledge of specific rulers from less-distinguished lineages, and a glimpse at how fifth-century society might have functioned. In addition, Dr. Bartrum's work on genealogies has produced a compendium of people who lived during the era, and a very basic idea of when they flourished.[39] The coarsest idea of the political and social environment is being developed with their aids.

The opinions of these scholars and the general trend in Celtic studies and British archaeology have, however, become highly conservative over the past fifty years. A majority of scholars who are currently in the field constantly keep in mind what they do not know in looking through the material. This has proven a valuable approach; it has been shown that a great deal of what we thought was known in 1950 was based on a complex web of unproven assumptions. Many theories were prevalent before this movement that now seem ridiculous in context with the more critical studies of the past fifty years.[40]

However, this method of scholarship is not an inventive one, and little has been added to our knowledge of the fifth and sixth centuries by using it. Recently, a new and more creative, yet still careful, manner of approaching the material has been gaining support. The idea is to take one likely interpretation of the materials at hand and, using that interpretation, to devise an understanding of the fifth and sixth centuries. This is done with the full awareness that the interpretation may be wholly inaccurate. In all fairness, it often is. However, the exercise has often proven helpful, even when the experiment may have taken the scholar down the wrong path. John Koch has attempted a linguistic recreation of *Y Gododdin* as it would have appeared in the sixth century.[41] Because of this work and the implications of his findings, he has developed a likely theory that the men of Gododdin may have been fighting other Britons in the famous Catraeth battle. Kenneth Dark has had some measure of success in using the traditional regions of activity for the lesser saints to help define the kingdom boundaries of several Welsh regions in the fifth and sixth centuries.[42] Professor Higham has offered an alternate explanation of Gildas, Bede, and the *Tribal Hidage*, and has then used these sources to reconstruct the fifth and seventh centuries.[43]

It is in this frame of mind that this book is written. It is with the full knowledge that much, if not all, of the opinions and conjectures offered are controversial. The author believes, however, that it is better to propose the idea, and allow others to build upon what is learned here, than to remain with what is not known. As has been seen, the traditional course of action brings the historian no closer to the truth, only further from what is false. On the other hand, there is nothing to be lost in proposing a theory based on solid foundations, and a great deal to be gained.

With this in mind, my previous work has confirmed that much of the earlier Arthurian romances originated in a small number of basic and very old stories.[44] The effort has also shown that it is possible to reconstruct prototypes of these stories that date back to at least the ninth century. At least two of these prototypes are viable literary sources if used in the proper context. It is the evidence to be found in them, in conjunction with more precise and more critical approaches to the traditional material, which shall be employed in order to better understand the nature of Arthur.

The following chapters will begin by presenting a number of essays revolving around Arthur's existence. The evidence will be initially surveyed in the traditional manner. From there, two aspects of the arguments against his historicity will be scrutinized, his minimal presence and his comparison to the fictional characters, especially Fionn. From that point, more positive evidence will be employed; his possible presence in Gildas and his literary connection to Drutwas son of Triphun both place him in the proper generation, for instance.

A survey of all known British Heroic Age bards will serve to establish that the adulthoods of several known bards were spent in the years around Arthur's lifetime. This may be because Arthur, or at least the period in which he lived, inspired them to a rebirth of that part of the Celtic culture. This theory would explain the huge body of knowledge about Arthur in legend and history in comparison to many other early British heroes, among them the Ambrosius who is credited with initiating the war against the Germanic peoples.

Once evidence of Arthur's historicity has been presented, this volume will begin a study of the question of Arthur's geographic location. To do this, I will make heavy use of the literature from both the Welsh and continental sources. The information from pre–Galfridic Welsh sources will be studied for obvious reasons; they derive from the same culture as Arthur and survived in a Welsh oral environment for centuries. Works of this nature will be examined separately according to their reason for being and their style. First, they will be divided by type, and the context of each genre will be laid out. Then every poem and story in that group will be examined individually. The literary sources that do not pertain directly to Arthur but are associated with the more popular early Arthurian heroes will also be scrutinized. It will be found that the geography of the Arthurian heroes is much more consistent and therefore more useful in tracking him than the information on Arthur himself. Their geography is more useful because those individuals who were earliest connected with Arthur have retained more of their original geographical region than he has, even after their association with Arthur.

The continental romances will also be examined in detail and in accordance with the guidelines set out in *Origins of Arthurian Romance: Early Sources for the Legends of Tristan, the Grail and the Abduction of the Queen.*[45]

It was seen there that certain Arthurian literary works may have historical applications, if the patrons' and authors' motives are understood and taken into account as well as their source or sources of information. To that end and beginning with Geoffrey of Monmouth, I will assemble all the medieval romances and individually catalogue all of their known influences. With this information, it will be possible to identify and eliminate the locations which are a result of those influences. What remains will be one consistent location.

The study will generally locate Arthur in the North, specifically the Cumbric area and, in the case of the romances, precisely in what is now Old Carlisle. Independent archaeological, historical, and strategic evidence will be forthcoming that Old Carlisle was a prominent site during the period and may well have housed Arthur.

With his geography in place, the more difficult task of establishing his rough chronology will be attempted. To that end, a brief overview of the development of the traditional Arthurian dates will be useful introduction, revealing all established dates to be little more than guesses based on mistaken readings and unproven assumptions of previous historians.

Realizing that no extant historian has given the modern scholar any idea of when Arthur may have been active, the best place to start will be with basics. First of all, the level of *Romanitas* in his era and his probable region of birth will be studied. The results there will be supported by an overview of the archaeology for the period. A second look at the bards, this time focusing on their dates, will also be useful by showing when Romanitas might have ended and the British culture began to reassert itself. Logically, as the first of the British heroic heroes, Arthur most likely was around when they first became active—without kings such as himself there would have been no need for bards.

A chapter on the professional hagiographer Caradoc of Llancarfan will be useful in showing his unusual predilection towards the North and will suggest that his materials stemmed from some traditional materials in that region. If this is true, then when he names Gildas and Hueil as figures active in Arthur's lifetime he does it with more credibility than any other saint's life.

Showing that Gildas was possibly a contemporary of Arthur, it will be useful to follow this up with a study of Gildasian history as set forth in *De Excidio Britanniae*. His sequence of events within a few decades of his birth will be assumed to be historical. With that fixed point, the relative chronologies of several Gildas experts will be laid out and examined. Caradoc's sources will also prove helpful in looking through Arthur's men in the earliest sources and seeing where their chronologies might coincide.

Finally, several alternative histories will be examined for any useful ideas that might help with the study. It will be seen that, though littered with problems of their own, they did at some juncture stem from native and old materials and therefore have their own contributions to make.

It is most prudent to begin with the now-traditional survey of the evidence for Arthur's historicity. The review will be made without consideration of any influences they may have had upon them at the time of their construction, or at any other period anterior to the present century. These items may be dealt with more efficiently once all of the source materials have been introduced.

PART ONE: HISTORICITY

CHAPTER 1

The Historicity of Arthur: The Evidence in Traditional Form

The question of whether or not Arthur was a historical character is one that has occupied scholars for centuries; it is an almost obsessive distraction of the British people. Each year dozens of books are published in his honor. Every one professes to have found some new and hitherto hidden information or understanding that no other person had ever come across before even though they continue to tap the same small number of easily accessed books for their ideas. More importantly, each year these books sell. To them, and to all the world, Arthur is much more than a war-chief who fought against the English long ago. He is William Wallace, Hannibal, and Robert E. Lee. He was a national leader who fought the inevitability of fate with courage and honor. Though doomed to eventual failure, it is the way he carried himself in his struggle that is respected. His legacy is one of freedom and chivalry. It is for this reason that he is a source of pride and hope for all the British people.

It is unfortunate that his political and cultural importance is not much good in the court of historical evidence, and a scholar with an interest in the subject is forced to find an alternative means to verify Arthur's existence. There are a good number of literary, pseudo-historical, and historical sources for the period and place in question; all seem to have their own contributions to make. In the following survey, each will be listed and reviewed in the traditional way.

Our first witness is Gildas, writer of *De Excidio Britanniae*; it is primarily a diatribe against several contemporary British kings. According to his own testimony, the saint was raised in the period of peace following Badon.[1] This would place some of his life in Arthur's traditional floruit, and he would have been the beneficiary of Arthur's efforts. Gildas, however, does not mention

Arthur. In fact, he only refers to one Arthurian battle, that of Badon.[2] This is not necessarily an event that Arthur participated in, though. The text of his narrative actually suggests that Ambrosius may have been the leader of this battle, leaving Arthur excluded in our only first-hand account of early sixth century Britain. This has been a problem to anyone who has attempted to demonstrate Arthur's historicity, and one that has often been addressed.

Most obviously, Gildas' sense of time periods is atrocious. There is no indication of the number of years or even months that took place in this passage. There could very well be a generation between Ambrosius and Badon, making Arthur's battle appear in the history even if Arthur does not. Also, Gildas seems to prefer nameless people. In his entire account of British history he identifies only Maximus, (probably) Aetius, and Ambrosius. It has been argued that the absence of Arthur's name is simply another example of this tendency. While this may be true, using negative evidence to prove a point in a period of which we have so little knowledge to begin with is a hazardous exercise.

It is possible that Arthur was a beloved king whom the people of Gildas' time remembered fondly. Gildas may have left him out of his historical prelude simply because he did not fit into the theme of punishment and reward he had laid out for his letter. This seems a likely possibility; neither the usurper Constantine, nor Ceredig, Coel Hen, or any of the other known major personalities of the fifth century are listed in De Excidio Britanniae either. As with (presumably) Arthur, what is known of their floruits would have provided no unique additional support for the premise he was building in his letter as well. It makes good sense that they are excluded.

A third possibility presents itself in the traditional stories told of both men; Arthur and Gildas' family may have been feuding. Three admittedly questionable literary sources, the second Vita Gildae by Caradoc of Llancarfan, Culhwch ac Olwen, and a traditional story, all claim that Arthur and Gildas' brother Hueil fought each other during one of the latter's raids. Hueil was killed as a result. By custom, the incident of Hueil's death would have produced a blood feud between Gildas' family and Arthur. At the very least, Hueil's death would have generated a great deal of hostility between the families, which may very well have manifested itself in Arthur's absence from De Excidio Britanniae.[3] There is a great deal of circumstantial evidence to argue that Gildas and Arthur may have been at odds at one point in their respective careers. If this is so, Gildas' forty-fourth year would seem to be a likely point.

The legendary story of Arthur and Hueil may not be a historical account. However, it is a good indication of how many factors could have been involved in Gildas' exclusion of Arthur that we would not know about. The absence of Arthur's name in Gildas' historical prelude proves nothing. On the other hand,

Gildas' lack of detail leaves a pro–Arthur scholar without a firsthand piece of evidence for Arthur's existence.[4]

The other historical sources for the period are also quite useless. Procopius, Gregory of Tours, and the *Irish Annals* all fail to include the British hero in their histories. We may, however, excuse Procopius promptly because of his extreme distance from these isles (Constantinople). The other two may equally be pardoned. All the *Irish Annals* seem to limit themselves to Scotti successes when pertaining to Britain, and as Arthur was British they may be expected not to mention him. Finally, Gregory of Tours talks strictly of Gaul, not even deigning to mention St. Germanus' voyage(s) to Britain.

Y Gododdin is chronologically the next document that pertains to Britain in the fifth and sixth centuries. It is a compilation of elegies for those warriors who fought under a Gododdin king at the Battle of Catraeth. The poem was presumably created shortly after the battle it describes. The poem (or group of poems) itself was written down in its modern form during the early ninth century, though it is clear that the poem had an existence long before then.[5] It may well have been first produced within two or three generations of Arthur's demise.[6]

Y Gododdin mentions Arthur once, in stanza B38, an elegy to a Guaurður. Here it is simply stated that the man in question was a great warrior, "but he was no Arthur." The stanza has been dated by Professor Koch to "probably primary material (pre–638),"[7] and most other linguistic scholars would argue that the core of the poem dates to the British Heroic Age (c. 450–c. 650). The comparison to Arthur bears no mark of mythology or folklore, only of hero worship to a warrior of the past. It indicates an historical figure whose floruit was well known to at least some members of the *teulu* for whom this poem was created. It is safe to say that Arthur was a respected warrior of the past by 638.

The rejoinder to this argument is that neither the poem, nor any stanza, has specifically been dated by common consensus. Dr. Padel sought to disclaim *Y Gododdin*'s authority by assigning it to the tenth century.[8] If the document were this late, it would be useless in determining Arthur's historicity. A poem as late as 900 would have been influenced by innumerable parties, most conspicuously the same royal patronage that formed the *Historia Brittonum*. Also, if this later dating were accurate, Arthur's lifetime would have been well beyond living memory by the time it was written. Therefore the excerpt would be no more than hearsay to the body of evidence. All this is within the realm of possibility.

Next is the *Historia Brittonum*, ascribed to Ninnius. Ninnius was most probably a monk who worked in Gwynedd during the early ninth century. The work that claims him as an author attempts to harmonize into chapters a motley collection of stories about British heroes who lived between the end of Roman dominance in Britain and the late-seventh century. The document as we have it probably was originally produced c. 829–830 but was largely edited in the tenth century.[9] The source material for these sections has been dated back to the eighth century, and a source known as the *Northern Memoranda*,[10] a hypothetical source of indeterminate size, function, and form. As has been seen, *Historia Brittonum* was both created and altered for political reasons.[11]

In the *historia*, one chapter is devoted specifically to Arthur, preceding and probably a part of the northern history chapters which internal evidence suggests was recorded in the latter years of the seventh century.[12] *Historia Brittonum* assigns several battles to Arthur, most notably Tribruit.[13] None of these may be placed certainly in one location, and several may have been grafted from the battle lists of other heroic age kings.[14] *Historia Brittonum* also credits Arthur with defeating the English on several occasions.

In addition, *Historia Brittonum* contains an appendix known as *Mirabilia*. This is a list of miraculous events and objects in Britain. Among them, two are directly associated with Arthur. Both portray Arthur as a creature of fairyland. The argument has been made that one of our earliest references to Arthur describes him in a dual world, that of magical folklore and historical reality. Arthur was, according to this argument, as much a character of fancy as of history by the ninth century and therefore was more likely folkloric or mythical in origin.

Finally, there is the *Annales Cambriae*, whose early passages were probably written in the ninth century[15] but whose British sources most probably extend back another century to the *Northern Memoranda* we have just met. *Annales Cambriae* lists two Arthurian battles—Badon and Camlann. The nature of both battles and their connection with Arthur has been heavily disputed in recent years.

It should be remembered before any discussion that it is remarkable these two entries were made at all, as early as they are. Extremely little before 573 is recorded in the *Annales Cambriae*, and that information is primarily based on the traditional dates that could have been found in or derived from Bede and the *Anglo-Saxon Chronicle*.[16] None of Maelgwn's or Rhun's battles are named, and Urien and Owain are absent. In the fifth century only Ambrosius' battle of Wallop is listed. Yet Arthur is named twice, and Camlann is found in no source before this. His significance to his contemporaries and the Welsh of the Middle Welsh period should be measured accordingly.

As has been seen, Gildas is ambiguous as to the victor of Badon. Professor Jones has expressed the opinion that the Badon entry in *Annales Cambriae* is not written in the same terse style as other, proximal entries. For this reason, he believes it may have been a late entry, or at least one that was edited after its initial addition to the annal. This implies that the entry may not originally have been in the eighth-century prototype, and that Badon has no certain historical context except that it occurred in the year of Gildas' birth. Higham agrees, seeing in the entry an attempt to give the Britons a sense of national pride.[17]

However, the 537-9 Camlann passage in which Arthur is said to have fallen while fighting either with or against Modred has resisted similar arguments.[18] This passage has a strong claim for being historical by way of two factors. First, the terseness and phrasing of the line is similar to other early entries. It is therefore probably historical in that the event did happen.[19] As Arthur is named as a leader in this battle in every source that mentions it, he most reasonably was present there.

Also, *Annales Cambriae* is generally acknowledged as containing, apart from Arthur, only historical people in historical activities. It is therefore relatively safe to assume that this figure and this action are historical. In this case the terse, traditional entry would have been added quite early in the development of the Arthurian legend, perhaps well before the eighth century.

The two sources *Historia Brittonum* and *Annales Cambriae* have been the foundation for any theory that Arthur existed. They have been so integral because they so clearly derive from the same source and are the first pseudo-historical documents to name Arthur.[20] In addition, the information they contain on Arthur is consistent. Both texts corroborate each other and ensure that a large part of what they contain on Arthur was a part of British history well before 900 in their common original text (see drawing on next page).[21] Because of this, if one is to propose that the writers of *Annales Cambriae* and *Historia Brittonum* both contain information on Arthur that was added to give him historicity or for some political purpose, one must concede that this process was undertaken before the mid–seventh century, when their common source was most probably created.[22] This theory would also require that the process of historicizing Arthur began no later than two hundred years after his invented death at Camlann. This is no doubt possible according to the manner by which heroic age literature functions.[23] However, such a circumstance would be unusual. One must ask "Why?" Why would someone in the mid–seventh century, or before, want to historicize Arthur? What purpose would it serve? These questions have never been asked before, and certainly never answered. Yet they are fundamental in proving Arthur did not exist.

Admittedly, the time lag between Arthur's traditional death and the earliest provable date at which the *Northern Memoranda* prototype may have existed is cause for concern. Two hundred years is well beyond the range of living memory, and thus is considerably less credible than a first- or second-

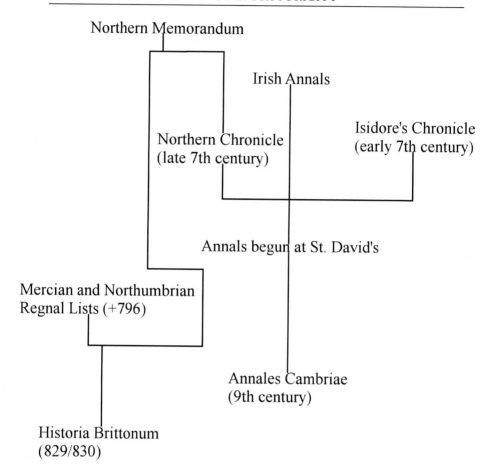

Northern Memorandum

Irish Annals

Northern Chronicle
(late 7th century)

Isidore's Chronicle
(early 7th century)

Annals begun at St. David's

Mercian and Northumbrian
Regnal Lists (+796)

Annales Cambriae
(9th century)

Historia Brittonum
(829/830)

THE NORTHERN MEMORANDUM. The lineage of the hypothetical document which
served as a primary source for the histories of the British and the English.

hand source might have been. On the other hand, the dearth of information
does not indicate or imply that Arthur was originally non-historical, either. It
cannot do so here for the same reason that it could not be used with Gildas'
letter.

It should be kept in mind that heroic age literature often has a long hiatus
between events and the written recording of those events. For example, the
destruction of Troy was not scripted till four hundred years after the event,
and even then not in a historical or even a pseudo-historical document. Our
main account of the war is in the form of an epic, a story that was already well-
developed orally before it was recorded. This is a literary stage through which
pseudo-historical and saga material regularly passes.[24] The actual destruction

of the city and end of the war is known from even later, though less developed, sources.

What has happened to our main source for the Trojan story is far more advanced from a literary standpoint and far less trustworthy from a historical one than the raw material we have access to in learning about Arthur. Despite the tangled data to be found in the *Iliad*, the Trojan War it gives has been proven to be at its core historical. The same may be said of the later myths and legends. The story of Arthur can claim a historical document with an assured past to the mid–eighth century at the latest, and it was never subjected to the workings of a master storyteller. Comparatively speaking, this makes the Arthurian documents perfectly credible.[25]

One must also approach the evidence directly. The theory that Arthur was a folkloric creature who was being transformed to a historical figure from 700 on seems an unnecessary manner of progression. The first sources that mention him, *Y Gododdin*, *Annales Cambriae*, and *Historia Brittonum*, treat him as a historical figure. He is a well-respected man in them, to be sure, but he is only a man. It is only the later sources that speak of a supernatural or superhuman Arthur. The reverse is not what happens. Even if that were the case, it seems more likely that a figure of tremendous military success would attract some legendary material to his name than it does that a mythical or folkloric figure would have had so much more historical than folkloric material associated with him.

There are other sources of information, which Professor Alcock and Professor Morris in particular have advocated, though with extreme caution.[26] These are the saints' lives. They have been used in the main for reconstructing the Early Medieval family trees of royal kindreds, establishing the rough floruits of Dark Age individuals and locating the domains of the saints themselves. Occasionally, archaeologists have used these economically inspired and deeply prejudiced biographies for reconstructing artifactual remains and architectural structures because the many details in them are often historical.[27] Those of (in order of creation) Goueznou, (1019), Cadoc (1100), Gildas (1120s or 1130s), Padarn, (twelfth century), Euflamm (twelfth century), Carannog (twelfth century), and Illtud (twelfth or thirteenth centuries) all deal with Arthur.

The very fact that Arthur is a part of the vita tradition testifies to his existence.[28] In addition, the *vitae* serve to point out Arthur's historicity because the protagonist of each *vita* was traditionally an adult around the turn of the sixth century. Their consistency here, despite the fact that many other figures are not always kept in a narrow range of dates, testifies for Arthur as well.[29]

This, then, is the historical evidence in the strictest sense. It contains four witnesses whose silence and chronological proximity to sixth-century Britain are disturbing—Gildas, Procopius, Gregory of Tours, and the Irish annals. However, the body of facts also contains one ancient poem and two ninth century sources that present Arthur as a prominent battle-leader and roughly date his presence to the same period. *Y Gododdin* would place him any time before the battle of Catraeth (540–600). *Historia Brittonum* places him after the demise of Hengest and the second departure of St. Germanus (c. 445) and before the death of Maelgwn (traditionally c. 547). *Annales Cambriae* puts a cap on his floruit at 537–9. Finally, Arthur is the butt of seven saints' *vitae*. All these religious men were persons of the late fifth and early sixth centuries. Taken together, these four sources seem to present a strong, consistent chronology and an argument in favor of Arthur's existence.

The rejoinder for this argument is a simple one. If, as seems possible, Arthur had been traditionally placed around 500 by the creators of his character (again, at some point before 700), it is probable that his floruit would have been generally known within the bardic community. From that point, it would have been a simple matter to incorporate him into certain of the relevant saints' lives. He would also have been placed in political contexts of the sixth century. It would then just be a matter of fortune, and perhaps time, that there have been found no folkloric stories involving his feud with a Viking king, or his battles with the Roman armies, or his argument with a British god.

This is the traditional evidence and the standard manner in which this evidence has been explained. The above data makes it clear that there is room for the possibility that Arthur existed, but no overriding proof that he must have. His is a gray area in British history. In the past, most scholars have simply presented this evidence and cast their educated guess as to which side of the fence they were on. It has seemed this is all that could be done.

However, there is much more and more compelling evidence that Arthur existed than traditional methods of research have yet revealed. I shall begin by discussing the question of why more was not written about Arthur in *Historia Brittonum*, and why no bardic poetry pertaining to him has survived.

CHAPTER 2

The British Arthur: An Elusive Hero

One of the most fundamental problems with the study of Arthur is his virtual absence in the literature that has been preserved from the earliest period of Welsh post–Roman history.[1] Legend and fantasy claim he impeded the Saxon advance for fifty years and managed to unite the Britons in common cause against them while under his banner. Yet Arthur is not present in *Armes Prydein* and appears in a mere chapter in the "Historia" portion of the *Historia Brittonum*. Apart from this, two battles in *Annales Cambriae*, and an allusion to him in *Y Gododdin* are the only fragments of documentation to prove (or rather conjecture) he existed at all. He is in none of the post–Roman era's poetry. Indeed, no genealogy is attributed to him, yet the period in which he supposedly lived was one in which a man's ancestors were the driving force behind society. These are truly critical arguments against Arthur's existence and have traditionally been the main pillars of the argument against him. Therefore, it is necessary to first account for these facts before it will be possible to put forward any evidence that that Arthur existed. This is the intention of the next few pages. Let us first begin by explaining why other figures of the period in question have more and often better historical evidence of their existence.

Urien is the most acclaimed hero of early Welsh history. He is given a great deal of respect in Chapter 63 of *Historia Brittonum*, where the reader is informed that he was the leader of the last coalition of British chiefs who were more powerful than the German kingdoms. The history does not linger much on accomplishments, moving straight to his death at the hands of one of his allies. This event is mentioned to make clear that the treachery that killed him had broken the British strength.

Unlike Arthur, however, Urien's presence is not confined to the references of later historians. He seems to have been a part of the bardic body of literature. He figures prominently in the twelve poems traditionally assigned to Taliesin, where he is the subject of eight of them. The poems traditionally assigned to Llywarch Hen speak in passing of Urien, the supposed author's cousin. Urien is also included in several versions of a genealogy that is historically feasible from a generation before him to its last named descendents.[2]

In sum, enough information is given to connect Urien with a consistent set of other historical figures that could, from a geographical and chronological standpoint, have been contemporaries. That Urien did exist in northern Britain before 600 is acknowledged by all. Looking at the information, one would think that Urien had dominated the British political scene in a grander fashion than Arthur himself in his own time.

However, Urien is not unanimously in all the literature of the period. He receives no word in *Y Gododdin*[3] or *Annales Cambriae*, while Arthur is in both. Curiously, these two works were created or compiled in Lothian-Strathclyde and Dyfed respectively.

The *historia*, it may be recalled, was collected and kept in Gwynedd. So were the bodies of poetry assigned to Taliesin and Llywarch Hen. It is interesting that these three particular bodies of literature are our main sources of our knowledge about Urien. As explained in the Introduction, some time in the early ninth century a Merfyn established a new dynasty in Gwynedd.[4] He claimed descent from Llywarch Hen. Because of his lineage's geographical origin in the North, the need to establish the family's royal lineage and later, under his son Rhodri Mawr, by desire to create a national conscience and unity against the English, both men evidently patronized all literature pertaining to the North. This literature particularly focused on their ancestor's more famed cousin, Urien of Rheged. The results of this patronage can be seen in *Historia Brittonum*, the Taliesin and Llywarch Hen poems, and other, minor pieces that were collected in this period. In the words of Nora Chadwick:

> It is in no way surprising that Rhodri should feel it necessary to draw together genealogical documents establishing his own and his wife's claim as a native Welsh royalty, and to expand them by notes in the form of annals and narratives. The interests of the dynasty on the male side would naturally be focused on the north, and on the genealogies of the *Gwr y Gogled*, "The Men of the North," and on such information as could be produced to supplement their testimony. The traditions and genealogies of the north were no less relevant to Rhodri's prestige than were those of Wales.[5]

This point becomes most apparent in a study of the two sources which detail Urien's death, *Historia Brittonum* and the poems of Llywarch Hen. As has been seen above, in *Historia Brittonum* Urien is said to have been assassinated at the instigation of Morcant. An alternate tradition is given in the body of poetry that was traditionally considered to have been written by Llywarch Hen. It describes a coalition against Urien headed by Morcant and Pabo Post Prydein. In that version Urien was killed in combat. Both *Historia Brittonum* and the Llywarch Hen poems are both unequivocally pro–Urien,[6] they simply differ in outlook.

Of the two, the Llywarch poems seem to contain the more likely information. Although they are probably only written in the Llywarch Hen persona and not by the historical character,[7] they likely do not date to the sixth century. Still, they demonstrate a more even respect for the other British chieftains.[8] This suggests historical tampering by the *Historia Brittonum* author and therefore a strong bias for those authorities that caused the book to be written on this matter. These authorities not only insisted that all positive information available on Urien was put into *Historia Brittonum*, but they were willing to edit his life's accomplishments to improve his status or follow a theme.[9] The way in which Urien's life is presented there does both perfectly.

A general pattern of the often disjointed chapters contained in the *Historia Brittonum* can be seen, and it focuses on Gwynedd's political interests in the ninth century. Under the alliance of Urien, the Britons were successful against the English and were able to halt their advance and even push them back to Lindesfarne. The same was true, to a lesser extent, with other war leaders such as Arthur, Ambrosius, and Cadwallon.[10] However, when the British fought among themselves or as individuals, they were unable to impede the advance of people with a Germanic culture.[11] The theme of invincibility in unity and ruin in separation is a consistent aspect of the book. Merfyn Frych and his descendants would attempt to unite Wales against the Germanic invaders throughout the ninth and tenth centuries. As they would prove, they were willing to do this through alliances, intermarriage, or conquest. In this respect, the *Historia Brittonum* served the purpose of giving its readers a political and social message.

As a result of Gwynedd's motivations, the materials related to Urien's floruit have been preserved better than that of any other time or place in the North. Thanks to Urien's legacy, the kings Morcant, Gwallog, Hussa, Pabo Post Prydein, and Theodoric can be seen interacting with each other, if only briefly. Still, even with just this the events of their careers can be better fitted together to get a perspective on the period that would otherwise not be possible.[12] We can see that Urien was much like Agamemnon in the *Iliad*, the first among ever-jealous equals. It can be gathered from Taliesin that he had no qualms about carving out a kingdom from his peers' lands.[13] Nor were his views unique; the Llywarch Hen poems imply that Urien's recent allies would have no second thoughts about dividing his territories on his death.[14]

It can also be seen that the balance of power between English and British was a consistently unstable one in the early centuries of the Germanic presence on this island. Not only were Ambrosius, Arthur, Rhun son of Maelgwn, and Cadwallon able to impose themselves on the Germanic tribes, but as late as the end of the sixth century the Northumbrians were one successful siege from extinction.[15] But with all that may be gathered and implied in the extant materials, the fact is that there is not much information. Even with Urien, having the most famous British bard of all time recording his activities and the most powerful British dynasty of the ninth century compiling all the information to be had on him for its own political elevation, very little of the details about his reign can be recovered. There were simply too many factors involved over too long a time to control how much of it survived.

After Urien, the most common individual of post–Roman Britain and the only prominent character preceding 500, is Gwrtheyrn.[16] Much like Urien, the survival of information pertaining to him over the centuries may be connected to the dynastic motivations of several powerful families. This may be seen in the development of his character in the historical sources.

Gildas is the first writer that alludes to Gwrtheyrn. He informs his readers that a *superbus tyrannus* was active in the period between the Hadrianic Rescript and the rise of Ambrosius, when Roman Britain was being threatened by the Picts, the Irish, and the Germanic raiders.[17] To counter the threat, he decided to invite several Germanic tribes onto the island as mercenaries or *foederati*.[18] Gildas goes on to state that it was his personal weaknesses which eventually allowed the *foederati* to revolt and conquer a good portion of the island for themselves.

Bede would take up Gildas' villainized name, anglicizing it to Vortigern and using the character to forward his own agenda.[19] Bede needed to somehow legitimize the Germanic overlordship of Britain, and the *superbus tyrannus* that Gildas had described allowed him to do this. Taking the suggestion he found in *De Excidio*, Bede portrayed Vortigern as the rightful heir to the former Roman province. Through a series of stories, he expanded on Gildas' intimations to show Vortigern's immorality and ineptitude. Demonstrating his unworthiness made the Germanic governments that replaced him divinely as well as politically appropriate.[20]

Meanwhile, the Britons appear to have had no interest in the Bedan vein of Vortigern history, nor in the information given by Gildas. Instead, it appears that the regional information on him was used. When Merfyn Frych married a Powysian princess, he had the history of his wife's dynasty added to his ancestors in the *Historia Brittonum*. We do not know what the Gwynedd version of the *Historia Brittonum* may have looked like, but we can gain some idea of how Gwrtheyrn (the British version of *superbus tyrannus*) might have been portrayed by carefully reading through the extant version. His descent from Gloiu and therefore his relationship with Gloucester, his descendants' occupation of the Powys provinces of Buellt and Gwrtheyrnion, and his own (apparent) authority to control *foederati* are strong indications of his widespread power in the fifth century. The regions that he and his near descendants are directly associated with in the extant version are greater than those of any other Welsh king for some time. All of this information would have served to support Gwynedd's claim to dynastic superiority.

In the tenth century, Hywel Dda, a descendent of Merfyn Frych's son Rhodri Mawr, came to the throne of Gwynedd's long-time rival Dyfed. Hywel Dda had the same kind of power as Merfyn had possessed and used that power to alter the contents of the *Historia Brittonum* to suit the needs of his kingdom.[21] He also had designs on expanding his area of control into Powys. His aims meant that Powys was once more of central importance, which meant that Gwrtheyrn needed to be re-treated.[22] The stories of the previous draft were probably mostly kept, but useful stories were added or expanded while unadulterated Powysian propaganda was cut. At this point the information to be had from Bede appears to have been accessed.[23] The result was the fullest version of Gwrtheyrn's exploits on record.[24] It is a fine example of the reinterpretation of history for political ends.[25]

As the above makes evident, Gwrtheyrn's very existence, not to mention the substantial information that is extant about him, is due to his usefulness for the various designs of Gwynedd, Northumbria, and Dyfed over the course of five centuries. Without his position as a crux for changing the histories of these three kingdoms, he might well have been no more than a footnote in *Historia Brittonum*, if he had warranted even that. He would never have been mentioned by Gildas or Bede.

Maelgwn is a third king who seems to have gathered about him a great deal of historical and legendary material. His name appears in *Historia Brittonum* in the synchronism that places Coel Hen in Wales during the fifth century.[26] He is also to be found in *Annales Cambriae*, where he is said to have died in 547 or 549.[27] He is present in the first of these sources because he served to place Coel in the correct temporal context. His powerful son Rhun does not appear there, nor does the Cadwallon who decimated Northumbria. They are only in the *Historia Brittonum* as part of their own accomplishments.

Maelgwn was included in *Annales Cambriae* because he had the good fortune to live after 488 and before 613 and was associated with the Irish materials which found their way to Britain.[28] During this period, all but three of the entries in the *Annales Cambriae* were derived from the Irish Annals. Even here the date is unreliable. As has been conjectured often, Maelgwn may only have been known to have died of a plague. An annalist may have simply connected a plague with the most famous one of the time.

Again we have luck as the most important factor in a king's retention in the strictly historical records. And again, we know that Maelgwn was a powerful king despite this. Gildas seemed to think he was the strongest ruler of his time, and the *vitae* mention him nearly as often as they do Arthur.

In addition to these three British heroes, the memories of Ambrosius and Coroticus (British *Ceredig*) are also impressed upon the minds of early British historians. They have been remembered for one reason: they are listed in firsthand sources. Ambrosius is the only native whom Gildas directly extols in his literature, and Coroticus is the subject of St. Patrick's tirade against the kidnapping and selling into slavery of his Irish Christians. Chance has made these two men the subject of literature that survived to be used as our sources for fifth-century history. If a Pictish king had been the culprit of the raids and thefts Patrick complains of, Coroticus would be known only from the Strathclyde genealogies.

If Ambrosius had not been the point of comparison for Gildas' attack on contemporary kings, his presence in Chapters 31 and 48 of *Historia Brittonum* would no doubt have been less prominent. In the former chapter, he is given his kingdom by the most prestigious of the Powysian kings, Gwrtheyrn, thus earning a great deal of credibility for his line and Gwynedd. In the latter, he gives the Powysian king Pascent rule over two provinces. As Gildas' hero, the act would have increased the stature of Pascent lineage as well. This leaves the historian with one annals-like entry in Chapter 66 about Ambrosius' conflict with Vitalinus and leadership at the battle of Wallop (c. 437), an event that remains of questionable historicity.

Apart from these characters, there is only one more body of literature that contains a large assortment of names that pertain directly to the sub–Roman period, the king-lists and genealogies of those kingdoms that survived until the ninth century. The reason for their preservation is clear—they recorded each kingdom's traditions. As is well known, these sources of information not only would have remembered the most famous kings, but would have had a tendency to absorb the most powerful kings of their region as well.

There is one commonality of all these sources for fifth- and sixth-century information. Those who preserved the genealogical lines, catalogue of rulers, or other historical information had a vested self-interest in the maintenance of that particular data. This in itself is a *very* common motive. In understanding this common theme it is also necessary to see one potential problem with it. Only the kingdoms that survived until the ninth century were able to consolidate the memory of their respective dynasties. This implies, in turn, that those dynasties that did not survive, or whose dynasty's members were not intimately intertwined with a surviving dynasty, had no voice and their existence had no certain means of preservation.

Due to poor fortune, Arthur's name does not appear in the most historically acceptable sources with any regularity. He is not as constant a figure as Gwrtheyrn, Urien, Urien's allies, Maelgwn, Ambrosius, Coroticus, or the royal families of kingdoms who ruled up to at least the ninth century. No family before the year 1000 claimed him as an ancestor,[29] and there never has been a royal family who did. He was by legend related to no person who was royal or noble either.[30] His name did not serve a political function to any of the royal families of the ninth or tenth century and therefore he has made his way into no genealogy. He was simply a legendary war-hero. All that remains of him are legends and folktales.[31]

In this Arthur is not alone, for it is known that the figures Coel Hen, Outigern, and Pabo Post Prydein must once have stood at the head of vast bodies of lore as well.[32] These are now all but vanished. Further north, the only evidence of the Pictish political system in the fifth and sixth centuries is to be found in the king-lists. A very few subkings of any of the Pictish provinces are known from pseudo-historical sources prior to St. Columba. The same could be said of nearly all those British kingdoms which had been swallowed by the Germanic kingdoms up through the ninth century.

When it has been seen how the records of various kingdoms and royal families have survived only through the haphazard fortunes of geography and war, it is easy to understand why the family of Arthur and the memory of his historical encounters have not been remembered in a historical context which is more satisfactory for the student of the period. He cannot compare in residual evidence to other people of the fifth and sixth centuries such as Urien or Rhun, nor should he be able to.[33]

Even then, history only reveals itself because the political climate of the ninth century allowed Gwynedd access to information about them, and Gwynedd's political climate made the materials on them desirable.[34] On the other hand, there was simply no practical reason for Arthur's name and reputation to have been preserved as anything more than a standard of excellence for other kings and warriors.[35] Despite this, he did survive in the literature; he is granted a chapter in the Ninnius compilation, and he is to be found twice in *Annales Cambriae*. To this latter chronicle not even the widely famed Urien may claim an entry.[36] Clearly Arthur was an important figure, and his repeated inclusion in *vitae*, legends, folklore, and the later romances is testimony to his prominence among the common people in the Middle Ages. It is an unfortunate turn that the same respect and love for him was not to be found in the kings of the Welsh states during the same era. Their indifference has caused the modern scholar of the period a great deal of trouble.

CHAPTER 3

The Heroic Age Phenomenon

In the previous chapter, it was seen that Arthur's near-absence in the historical record is a result of the limited political interests of the ninth-century Gwynedd and tenth-century Dyfed kings. This chapter will develop an explanation as to why the sources used to create the *Historia Brittonum*, and similar documents, may have overlooked him: the timing of his reign predated their concern. The remainder of this chapter will be devoted to explaining why the period before about 500 imposed an environment upon the Britons that led to Arthur's rare presence in the historical record. Further, it will explain why his superimposed presence in the middle of a number of Welsh legends and popular tales may in fact be used to confirm his historicity. Arthur lived at the beginning of a heroic age, a period which normally and necessarily retains the identity of a very small number of personal and place-names. Of those, it rarely has any specific information. However, as the next pages will show, those early figures who are influential enough to be superimposed on other legends are generally all historical figures. Those heroes who become the center of a cycle are nearly always historical as well. The oral storyteller is at the core of these peculiarities.

To see this, however, it is necessary understand what a heroic age is, how and by what stages it comes about, and approximately when the British Heroic Age took place.[1] It will be helpful to discuss the latter aspect first.

It has been argued that the date for the battle of Ardfyredd, around 573,[2] should mark the beginning of the British heroic age, which ended in about 650. Leaving aside for the moment that most of the non–Romanized Britons appear to have been in a heroic age long before the Romans departed and focusing entirely on the Romanized Britons, there are still several problems with this suggestion. These boundaries would be inclusive to much of Urien's career and possibly the battle of Catraeth.[3] However, such a late horizon fails to account for several other figures whose treatment in the literature is clearly heroic in nature.[4] In addition, the process by which a heroic age inception as late as 573 is derived demonstrates a lack of understanding of the development of and motives behind a heroic age's beginnings.[5]

A heroic age is often a period that is poorly defined in chronological terms. It would be as difficult to name a date for one's inception as it would be to precisely name the day the Roman Empire fell. Therefore 573 is at best an arbitrary date, and Dumville also uses a more rounded 575.[6] Even though the exact year at which one could first call a society heroic is impossible to determine, the sociological stages by which a society finds its way to a heroic age are easily traced and consistent. From here a date may be broadly determined.[7]

One may be so certain of these preliminary stages leading to a heroic age due to the work of Hector Chadwick. His researches discovered that two contemporary cultures had transformed to heroic age societies just after anthropologists had begun studying them. The result was that the entire metamorphosis from one society to another had been fully recorded by the scientists, and could be studied. This was an amazing stroke of luck, which was matched only by the nature of the two peoples involved. The two relevant cultures were the Lango of Uganda and the Tonga of the Pacific Islands. Their tremendous distance, cultural, climatic, ethnic, and religious differences meant that any commonalities between them could be assumed to be universal truths for developing heroic age societies.

And certain basic cultural elements did emerge, elements that were complementary to other known pre-heroic societies; both peoples were rural, agrarian, and loosely democratic when discovered by western civilization. Their societies were also quite poor. It is known that the pre-heroic Greeks and Sumerians had all of these attributes. With the departure of Roman government and the abandonment by the rich of the island, the Britons would have found themselves in much the same situation.

As a supplement to their income, the young men of the Tonga and Lango tribes found employment serving as foreign mercenaries to two other nations who were themselves enjoying a heroic age. In time, veterans of this service returned home and participated in transforming their own society into one of a heroic age character. To quote Professor H.M. Chadwick: "It would seem that the militarisation or 'heroisation' of barbaric society sometimes arose from a kind of contagion, much like the militant nationalism of modern times. Economic and geographic conditions are doubtless to be taken into account, but in such cases as these the primary factor is apparently a social disease."[8] This seems a feasible hypothesis, and workable in an everyday environment. In Depression period America, youths of poor big city families that had no jobs would have found it simpler and easier to become members of the mafia and learn to live that lifestyle rather than face starvation.

In a broader context, what this means is that heroic society is created as a result of contact with another society with heroic character. The victim culture is contaminated with heroic values by having its more militant elements learn them from outside, and then integrate those values into their culture on their return. There is also probably a degree of self-preservation involved as well; the victim culture is better able to defend itself from the heroic culture if it also becomes heroic in nature. Access to a culture that is having a heroic age is thus a primary ingredient for the beginnings of a heroic age.[9] It must be assumed that the sending of young men to the heroic age culture is necessary for a smooth transition. In effect, these young men are being trained for their future roles. All this seems plausible, but it cannot be demonstrated for any period before the twentieth century. Unfortunately, our historical knowledge of other pre-heroic cultures is too incomplete to complement these observations with reference to the Sumerian, Greek, Irish, British, or Germanic cultures.

These findings imply further ingredients exist as well; clearly a strong and well functioning government would not allow a significant number of its young men, the backbone of any patriarchal economy, to go to another kingdom or country. The tribal societies of the Greek people were certainly weak at the end of the Bronze Age, as well as those of the Germanic people during their migratory period.[10] For the Lango and Tonga tribes the decentralized government, or a society of multiple chiefs similar to many pre–Columbian Native American tribes, may be assumed as well.

All of these requisites can be matched when we turn to Late Roman Britain. A number of circumstances combined to help weaken the entire economic base and political structure of the Roman Empire in the fifth century. This process began with Trajan, an expansionist emperor. His activities in Britain helped to unite the Picts against Rome in defense. His successor, Hadrian, was unable to hold the new borders and moved his legions back to more defensible positions. In Britain, he would build a wall in his name that was lined with defensive forts. His actions would leave a good deal of territory without any of the political and economic stability it had already come to depend upon with Rome.

In the next century, the Germanic tribes began to penetrate Europe. As a rule they seem to have accepted Roman authority, but they brought with them two pieces of unwanted baggage. The first was an inadequate understanding of agriculture. The second was an ongoing internal power struggle. The losers of the latter were left to either follow the victor's banner or turn to Rome for food and protection.

By the time the Germanic tribes appeared on the borders of the empire, the dynasties of Rome were becoming weaker, a fact which was only exacerbated by the massive size of the empire. This led to challenges by the Germanic, Pictish, Irish, Parthians, and other political groups. These situations in turn called for the best generals, who with their training and the discipline of the legions were always able to secure the borders. However a number of factors often led to their soldiers electing them as emperors. These generals would accept their new title and return to Rome to be crowned, fighting against loyalist armies along the way. Recurring scenarios like this would cripple the political system, but on a more obvious level the civil wars would reduce manpower in the Roman army and lead to fewer soldiers garrisoning those very same borders that were already being attacked.

The empire's response to reduced numbers in their military was to hire barbarians to serve in place of professional soldiers; these amateur recruits were known as *foederati*. Despite their efforts, the raids of their cousins would periodically cut the island off from communications and long-range trade with the continent thus weakening the political structure from the inside.

Still, the steady decline of regular soldiers would force modifications in the government of Britain. The governors regularly shrunk their area of control in order to effectively protect the province. Soon much of what was Romanized Britain was left to the non–Romans. By 400 Wales, Cumberland, and Northumbria—in fact little more than England below the Umber River and East of Cornwall—was still in Roman hands.

By the time the Roman presence was finally dissolved around 411, the economics of the entire island was likely a shambles. Many of the wealthy had gone back to the security of the continent, and the Romans who were left had no means of generating their own wealth. In short, in a matter of years Britain metamorphosed from an important part of the most powerful empire on the planet into a poor and politically broken area.[11]

These factors combined to transform the Late Roman cities of Britain into what Dr. Dark has termed a "polyfocal administrative center."[12] That is, "only élite residences, and religious buildings need survive. The town has lost its productive role and has ceased to be a population concentration of exceptional size. It is, once again, closely integrated with its agricultural hinterland." In other words, the economy in which a polyfocal administrative center was created would be one which had taken a step backwards. Such was clearly the case in Late Roman Britain.

The population of Late Roman Britain, therefore, suffered from a variety of difficulties which led to its becoming much more rural, agrarian, and poor. Every diminishment of privilege would have given the Romanized Britons that much less confidence in the Roman Empire.

We may only speculate what happened next, but by using the Tonga and Lango as references, we may be sure we are not far off. The economic and political changes discussed above eventually caused a need for a significant number of the population to find non-traditional employment. Eventually, some young Romanized British may well have become raiders themselves. Years later, these men would return home. A situation would present itself (or be made to present itself) in which the unstable government they worked under was ready for change, and these men, those who had worked in and understood the dynamics of the brutal situation they were in, would easily have taken control of the government by force. They would have stabilized their positions by making promises of protection to the farmers on a model similar to the promises of their former military employers.

By the first quarter of the fifth century the politically unstable and economically weakened Britons of the Roman province had all the major symptoms prerequisite to a heroic age. Thus the period 411–425 is the most reasonable estimate for when it might have begun.

This process of converting from one societal model to another would have taken a great deal more time than is apparent, however. It could not have happened immediately. After the socioeconomic factors were in place and the influence of another heroic age society was present, there were still several more stages through which the British would have to pass, unhindered, before the transformation was completed. Those stages could account for decades. By around 425, however, it was inevitable that these junctures would follow if allowed to continue without any outside force interfering. To recap, this is what could have happened in Britain as the power of Rome faded.

First, within a few years of the Honorian Rescript groups of young British men from the economically broken *civitates* joined Pictish, Irish, northern British, or Anglo-Saxon raiding parties in pursuit of money. The island-wide raids of Gildas and the *Gallic Chronicles* would have served as an anima. After this phenomenon had occurred, the integrity of the Roman-based government must have been greatly strained, and the warriors would have taken advantage.

On a regional level, charismatic leaders would have emerged among the now powerful warrior class. Alternatively, a wealthy landowner may have adjusted to the new social conditions and transferred his status and wealth into the organization of a small personal army and a reputation for generosity.[13]

This new order would have been based on the militaristic culture that the warriors had seen in their former employers. It would have had its foundations in the martial awe that an individual chieftain was able to invoke from other men.

This change in leadership would naturally lead to both general political instability and likely to uncertainty among the new leaders as to their position.

If a man had come to power only by the strength of his arm, the intimidation he could invoke, and the men he was able to maintain in his band by his personal charisma, he was in a precarious situation. Who was to say that one day another man would not come along and oust him, killing all of his sons in the process? The fact was that this hypothetical new man would have just as much right to the throne he would occupy as the present man had. In fact, he could argue that he had more right, because he would have overthrown a weaker warrior. There simply was nothing to stop another man from murdering him and taking away his leadership; there was no tradition, no divine aura about the person who was king beyond his accomplishments in battle and the impression he could leave on those who followed him.

For this reason, these newly-made chieftains would have been as politically awkward as the very concept of kingship from which they had derived. Fundamental to establishing themselves would have been legitimacy.[14] Authority would have been accomplished in several ways, all mutually inclusive. The most basic technique was simply by continuing the behaviors that had won them their power. The cattle raids that appear to have been regular activities among the early kings bonded them to their men as it helped them gain a reputation with friend, foe, and potential members of their war-band for savagery, success, and wealth.

The second means was through bards. Retaining a bard of some ability and reputation allowed for a chieftain to directly influence the political persona he was creating. A bard in permanent residence at one court could be impressed upon to turn simple cattle raids into evidence of a king's superiority as a warrior and a leader of men. In creating a solid foundation for kingship, these bards could be fundamental in developing a tradition of a royal family's past.[15] They could artificially formulate a ruler's family history, incorporating vaguely remembered warriors and even chieftains whose reputations had been strong and positive. Evidence that this was going on may be deduced from Gildas, who complains of the flatterers Maelgwn kept about him.[16]

A bard's diverse and intense education also made him capable of adapting to new needs. As the chieftains' unofficial followers became more stable and developed into more of an extended household, the bards could also double as entertainers to the restless youth who found themselves tied permanently to their chief by economic and social bonds. In time, as the bards learned more about their audience and the warriors' accomplishments grew, these entertainers would be able to produce more detailed and better tailored poems about them.[17] With warriors being praised regularly by an individual trained to add art to his words, a further degree of bonding would be allowed.

Those praises would be heard by other bards passing through, and by that means would be spread throughout the neighboring areas. These demonstrations of a king's leadership abilities and his gift for attracting great warriors would have served to further strengthen his position in society and his standing with other chiefs.[18] The above series of developments can be seen to begin before the departure of Roman troops and was probably finished within fifty years of the 410 Honorian Rescript.[19] Such is my progression of the heroic age culture of Britain[20]:

367–410	British suffer through famine and raiding caused by progressive troop departures and the overturning of government
409	For all intents and purposes, Britain is independent upon the departure of Constantine for continental Europe
410	Honorian Rescript, the emperor informs the British that they will receive no Roman aid
410+	British governments becomes more and more unstable as contact with Rome weakens and citizens begin to see themselves other than Romans
420+	British men go for foreign service
430+	First mercenaries begin returning
441–446	The devastating Germanic raid of the Gallic chronicles
441–450	Takeover of military dictatorships[21]
445–470	Establishment of first British heroic kingdoms,[22] and the reinstatement of the bard.

During this preliminary phase of heroic society most cultures have very poor and sketchy memories, and the names of early heroes are often forgotten, or they are remembered more as mythical than real. For example, the *Prose Edda* intimates that Odin, Thor, and the other *Æsir* may originally have been historical people who lived in the second or third century. Among the Greeks Heracles, Perseus, Bellerophon, and a host of others walk the line between godhood and human. Tradition assigns them potentially historical dates, yet myth is convinced they are the sons of gods.

The problem is apparent even of such recent peoples as the Lango and Tonga, who were mentioned above and have so far served as guideposts in better understanding what was happening in early post–Roman Britain. Of the two, only the Lango managed to preserve the name of their original revolutionary leader. His name was Akena.[23] The Tonga have no memory of a person who brought them to a heroic age. This latter tribe seems to have followed a more common route to the militaristic culture; no other heroic age literature contains the name of its founder. In Britain, Arthur is one of the few names that have been recovered from this period in British history, and tradition has assigned him a date well after the theoretical dates suggested above for the beginnings of the British Heroic Age.

The history of the fifth and sixth centuries was almost exclusively in the hands of bards, and these men were under the control of the various kings and chiefs who patronized them. Because of this fact of economics, it was their vested interest to disguise history with royal policy. This imperative was followed in every possible circumstance. Undoubtedly there were many men who were feared and respected in their lifetimes who have been forgotten. They did not have the foresight to hire bards, or the good fortune to have a family that could retain control of their kingdom or the bards who told their stories after their deaths. When this happened, the next man to rule his area would have taken the same precautions as his predecessor. His own *bard teulu* would have been made to excise his predecessor from the oral records, or better, to add the old king to his lineage, to strengthen his own position and hide the fact that he was only as legitimate as his sword.[24]

Even if a lineage was able to survive for several generations and establish an oral history which complemented themselves, there was no guarantee it would be preserved. There were severe language shifts from the mid–sixth century on, so that the original praise poems of the fifth century would have been unintelligible within a few generations. It would have been all but impossible to keep a praise poem updated with the transformations up to the emergence of Middle Welsh around 900, even if there had been a reason to.[25]

If Arthur had been a northern figure, the Anglo-Saxons eventually managed to suffocate and silence the Cumbric dialect by perhaps 1000,[26] so that even regular modernization would not have allowed poems of him to survive past that point unless they had already been transferred to Wales. Despite all these difficulties, it is important to remember that Arthur was remembered. From *Culhwch ac Olwen* on, he was put in the center of each story he was a part of. As Hector Chadwick pointed out long ago, such figures are always historical where corroboration is possible. Gilgamesh, Siegfried, Hrolf Kraki, Beowulf, Vladimir I, and Conchobar were all in the middle of their own group of stories, and each of them was undoubtedly a real person.

It is clear, then, that the British Heroic Age began somewhere in the middle of the fifth century. It is also clear that if Arthur did live, his life was spent in the early part of that era.[27] Cross-cultural study has shown that heroic age culture would in fact impede the preservation of the very same literary and historical records that would be required to positively establish Arthur's historicity, location, accomplishments, and chronology. However, study of the development of heroic age literature has introduced additional information as well. It has been seen that any figure placed in the center of a heroic age cycle is historical. Taken together, this is negative and complementary evidence for Arthur's existence is useful in understanding the difficulties involved in the study of Arthur.

The fundamental role of the bards in this society has also been established. Their presence represents the full maturity of a heroic age society. It was their poems that established a ruler's hereditary right to rule, his victories and therefore his personal right, and his generosity. It was also the bards who inspired fear among other chieftains. More pertinent to the present essay, they were the recorders of history in heroic society, the pseudo-journalists of their day who were the only individuals interested in the day-to-day activities of the kings.

Because of their duties and unique place in society, it is reasonable to assume that those areas where known bards were from would be the same places from which most of the material pertaining to the early kings would have originated. These are significant points that will be touched upon below.

CHAPTER 4

Fionn macCumhail and Arthur[1]

The forms of evidence that have been used to prove Arthur existed are not the most desirable. The only direct evidence for the period comes from Gildas, and he clearly was motivated by a purpose other than historical accuracy. The *Historia Brittonum* author wrote three centuries after Gildas, and there are strong indicators that by this time Arthur was as much a product of fable as history, perhaps more so.[2] In actuality, the balance of the material pertaining to Arthur for the next few centuries is decidedly more based in fantasy than fact. Only the *Annales Cambriae* entry for Camlann and the *Y Gododdin* passage offer early pseudo-historical support for his existence.[3] Because of this development of his persona, it has been recently argued that Arthur was quite likely a folkloric character whose historical attributes were secondary additions to his original nature.

This argument has been made with a direct comparison to the Irish folk-hero Fionn macCumhail.[4] Fionn's death is recorded in the *Annals of Tigernach* in the year 283. Because there is no supplementary material or historical context for the battle's existence in the Irish traditions, it has properly been seen to be an attempt by a later scribe to historicize him. It has been argued that, as the comparison to Arthur is a valid one, Camlann must also be seen as a later addition to the *Annales Cambriae*, and is therefore not valid as evidence for Arthur's historicity.[5] Building on this premise, the less substantial arguments for Arthur's existence have been argued against or simply ignored.

However, the literary-historical tie between Arthur and Fionn is flawed for several reasons. Chapter 1 presented the strongest argument thus far. Two pseudo-historical sources that have a common source dating back to at least the eighth century both agree on Arthur's existence and provide him a rough, though consistent, chronology. This chapter will seek to elaborate on additional criticisms with the comparison. The Fionn character and Arthur did not develop along similar lines during their respective pre-histories, and therefore the extant evidence for their respective historicities cannot be used to undermine one another.

First, the manner in which Arthur and Fionn are drawn together is weak; they both have supernatural elements in stories pertaining to them. It should come as no surprise to the reader that there are many fantastic aspects to the Arthurian persona. The entire body of literature around him was in an oral environment for centuries. During that time, it was subject to the literary devices of the Celtic storyteller. It would be preposterous to believe that such a thing would not happen in an oral society. Even in the modern world such things happen to historical figures. George Washington's famous honesty, Paul Bunyan's prodigious size, and Davy Crockett's ability to outwrestle bears are only a few examples from my country. There is no doubt that all three men were historical, though. One served as president and another as a senator. Less outstanding records prove the famous lumberjack lived in the 1800s.

Second, there is the argument of tradition. The Battle of Camlann is recognized throughout Welsh literature as the site of a great tragedy. Camlann has the same meaning to the Welsh as does Waterloo to the French and the Armada to the Spanish. It was a catastrophe of immense proportions, remembered by their bards as synonymous with the worst possible calamity.[6] In addition, Camlann is specifically Arthur's battle in all the legends,[7] and no tradition runs counter to the fact that this was his last battle.

In contrast, Fionn's entry in the annals is isolated. It is not associated with any great disaster in Irish lore or history. It is instead listed only in the *Annales of Tigernach*, and as a battle between Fionn's *fiana* and the Vikings, a historically improbable scenario given the third century date. More than that, this battle is in direct contradiction with other Irish lore, which says Fionn died in old age trying to repeat the feats of his youth. This alternative death brings into question the official annalistic record of Fionn's death; it means that there is varying external corroboration on the subject. The same may not be said of Arthur's Camlann, which has the unanimous support of a large body of Welsh literature.

Third, the earliest references to Arthur make him contend with historical Germanic enemies as a battle-leader at some time after 410 and before the rise of Urien. He is consistently portrayed as a Briton who fought and defeated the English. Arthur is a figure specifically of post–Roman Britain, and I think that no respected scholar in the world would argue differently. Fionn has no such historical perspective; his own deeds are achronological. The king who first raised the *fiana* and made Fionn their chief was Cormac, traditionally a third-century king. Fionn's men speak with St. Patrick and he himself is reputed to have fought the English and Norse in the eleventh century. This would make Fionn a figure active for an improbable 800 years.[8]

There is also a fourth, related reason why the correlation of Arthur with Fionn is not valid. Because Arthur is associated with a specific era, he can be tied to a clearly defined heroic age. This statement may be supported by some of the older remains of Welsh poetry pertaining to him, which contain heroic qualities.[9] Fionn is, to my knowledge, mentioned in no paragraph in all of comparative literature or historical writings in conjunction with the Irish heroic age. This is because he was attached to no one era. He is a purely folkloric character who could be attached to any period. Likely, this was a part of Fionn's attraction.

Because of Arthur's connection to the British Heroic Age, certain other apparent correspondences to Fionn may very easily be explained by alternative means. First, as Arthur's floruit occurred in a period of heavy oral activity, in a culture where its storytellers moved around a great deal, it is only reasonable that one would expect his name to be found in the natural geography of the entire British-speaking world. As Professor Chadwick often pointed out in dealing with heroic ages, a figure who attained great fame in life would likely be remembered after death by all culturally related peoples. For instance, Beowulf's life was not recorded by the elusive Geats, but was first found on English soil.[10] The Greeks respected their enemy Hector, and his name is still considered to represent true nobility in that culture. This was all a part of the hero worship which heroic age cultures held for great warriors.

Fionn also had the good fortune of being attached to place-names, as Dr. Padel has painstakingly demonstrated.[11] As he was a favorite figure of the Irish people, this development is a natural one. However, if one is to build a comparison between Arthur and Fionn on this point, one need also mention that George Washington and St. Peter have been attached to place-names. This phenomenon means nothing more than that all four were widely famed figures.[12]

In heroic age society, the king and his men had a different set of priorities than farmers, artisans, and even their own servants. Bonds of blood kinship held little or no value inside a *teulu*, or war-band. In fact, the *teulu* was intended to replace an extended kindred, and the name itself is translated as "family." In this way, the *teulu* operated outside of society and therefore had its own set of rules. Dr. Padel has pointed out that Fionn and his men also live outside of society.[13] Because of the strong ties to nature and away from society as a whole that are endemic to the Fionn cycle, Fionn's band also happen to contain this aspect of the heroic age. It should be emphasized that both Fionn and Arthur have this common trait by coincidence alone. As has been seen, Arthur is consistently attached to a heroic age, whereas Fionn is nowhere connected to one.

There are also more general problems with the connection of Arthur with Fionn as similar figures of literature and folklore.[14] Fionn is invariably an extremely tall individual in the range of forty or fifty feet in height. A local northern Irish legend has it that he and a Scottish giant sought each other out as opponents when they realized they were the only two people in the British Isles of such stature.[15] In the literature, Arthur is described as rather larger than his contemporaries, but he is nowhere given credit for superhuman height.

Further issues abound. Fionn is innately tied to magic. Because of good fortune Fionn's thumb was magical, and when he was in trouble he sucked on it to have access to supernatural powers. Arthur is a better fighter than his men, and has the same fantastic war-band and possessions as Fionn in some of the British tales, but he is definitely not magical,[16] nor does he have access to supernatural wisdom. Both these differences are key. With Arthur, one may see that the gradual process of exaggeration that affects all heroes has begun as the extant literature goes further and further away from its point of origin, but Arthur is clearly a human figure. On the other hand, many of Fionn's abilities are nearly godlike. In fact, there is strong evidence to support the theory that Fionn may at one time have been a deity of the Celtic pantheon.

The name Fionn derives from Celtic *ûindo* (white or bright), implying Fionn may have been a solar name. Supporting evidence can be found in derivatives of *ûindo* from France, where Vindonnus and Vindos represent solar gods.[17] Another variation can be found in Wales as Gwyn,[18] a euhemerized deity in the *Mabinogion*. Ireland itself contains two further examples of the name in Irish myth.[19] In total that makes five additional examples of the name Fionn in Celtic, and every one is a god or humanized god of the Celtic pantheon. Taken together with Fionn's supernatural height and wisdom, it seems highly likely that Fionn was also a solar deity at some time in the past. Irish legend has it that Irish Lugh replaced the old sun-god upon his entrance into the pantheon of gods. It has been suggested that the replaced god may have been Fionn.[20]

If this were so, much could be explained. Gods are not displaced on a whim, but as a result of conquest or social transformations. The result is that a deity's old followers are not dead and have not necessarily renounced him, but are no longer able to worship him as a part of the state. Such may have been the case with Fionn. Deprived of the following he once had and no longer sanctioned by the ruling class, he was diffused into several figures of lesser stature. Among these would have been the folkloric figure Fionn macCumhail and the other two Fionns which are extant in the records. However, the change was not seamless; they never are. Each of them retained some godlike qualities. The other two retained most of theirs and are still easily recognizable as such. As time went on, Fionn macCumhail would have become more and more human. Because of his enormous popularity, he was gradually associated with historical characters. This would have been a haphazard process, however, without a controlling entity to make sure he remained consistently tied to one era. This would explain his associations with the Vikings and Cormac as well as the related obit.

Arthur went through no similar renovations that may be found in the historical or literary record. His name indicates no deity and suggests no comparison to deities.[21] His actions contain no indications of a euhemerized deity.[22] He is clearly a figure who has been given associations with some supernatural phenomenon, but he also has a historical persona with historical qualities. In this, *Y Gododdin* is the most valid evidence that he was seen in living memory as a man.

In conclusion, there are several documents that record a historical Arthur, and every piece of obtainable historical evidence that accepts Arthur's existence places him in the same post–Roman era. By all accounts, he lived long after the mid–fifth century and well before Urien of Rheged's rise to prominence. Two sources, whose progenitor one can be sure was in existence before the late eighth century, confirm Arthur's existence. The social orientation of heroic society explains the dearth of more plentiful historical references to him. There are no discrepancies about his life or death.[23]

On the other hand, Fionn cannot be connected with any one era, and thus to any heroic age; nor did any scribe make such an attempt. His obit entry in the *Annals of Tigernach* does give a date of 283. However, it records that he died impossibly fighting the Vikings. The site of his battle is not given, and there are no local legends about the event. Further, the annal's statement contradicts common folklore about his death. Finally, Fionn's name is cognate with several recognized deities among the Celts, and his superhuman height and supernatural wisdom are two signs of his original godlike qualities. He is most probably a sun-god that has been euhemerized into a popular figure of folklore and legend.

Attempting to prove that Arthur did not exist by relating his literary career to Fionn's development as a figure of folklore is unwarranted. As has been seen, some of the comparable qualities may be shown to be the result of fortune, while most simply fall apart under closer scrutiny.

CHAPTER 5

Arthur and the
Superbus Tyrannus

The previous chapters have gone a long way in showing that many of the arguments that have traditionally been raised against Arthur's historicity are invalid. It is true that Arthur is much rarer in the extant literature of the period than Maelgwn or Urien, but it is also true that these two lived crucial decades later in the period, when there was more stability and a better chance for recordkeeping. They both also had descendants in the ninth century, when the records we now have were being formed into their present state. It is true that Fionn and Arthur are both recorded in annals, both are associated with the supernatural at times, and both live apart from society. However, these similarities are due to coincidence, not similar paths of development. It has also been argued that Gildas, the one contemporary who wrote of British history during the fifth and sixth centuries, does not speak of him. This has seemed an insurmountable objection to many, but there is a valid response to this argument as well.

In the early to mid-sixth century Gildas wrote, in classical Roman oratory,[1] a lengthy condemnation against several kings of Britain along with many religious individuals he felt were not living up to the ideals of their faith. For both parties, he argued that their continued drifting from their duties would result in God's wrath in the form of barbarians destroying them. As part of his prosecution argument, Gildas opened his book with a historical prologue; it served to introduce and illustrate the theme of punishment of sins by God. This approach was key to his writing as it would be the hammer for his arguments in favor of reform by all parties. From a historical standpoint, this element of the diatribe has proven the most valuable. Over the centuries, it has also proven intriguing and tempting. Any good scholar can see even at a glance that there are several glaring historical inaccuracies. On the other hand, Gildas was traditionally born around the year 500 and thus would have had access to perhaps a century of living memory before that, the very century after the end of Roman rule during which the greatest and least understood changes of post–Roman Britain took place.

The inaccuracies are troublesome, but even where there are none he is difficult. In all places he is chronologically vague because his purpose was not served by clarifying himself. His motivations have meant that the horizon of living history has proven difficult to establish. The result is that certain historians have simply thrown his entire hazy prologue out as a document without any historical worth.[2]

There are several other problematic aspects of the writing as well. The original motives of Gildas' characters have been altered to suit his purpose, and the personal names are almost nonexistent; Gildas mentions only Magnus Maximus and Ambrosius Aurelianus in unmistakable terms. And yet he remains tantalizing to historians. As far as one can see, the order in which he lists his characters and events is generally accurate. It may also be assumed that Gildas wrote for an audience that had some idea of the course of events over the past century. He would have known that anything he wrote could easily be corrected by an individual as old or older than himself. Consequently, he must be considered a competent primary source in the region or regions he wrote about. He must have been reasonably accurate for as far back as living history went in his childhood as well.[3]

Therefore, when Gildas places a man he calls *superbo tyrrant*[4] between Honorius and Ambrosius in his history, it can be assumed that this figure was historical and active sometime between the Roman Emperor and the British freedom fighter unless it can be shown otherwise. On this premise his career was between 410 and perhaps 493–517.[5] This is all the information which may be drawn from Gildas. The title's regular association with Dyfed Gwrtheyrn is both alarming and unfounded, being introduced only in the ninth century.[6]

The evidence as we do have it makes it unlikely that Gildas' title and the king he has been connected to are the same person. As has been noted above, it is the eighth-century Northumbrian historian Bede who first connects the title of *superbus tyrannus* as found in Gildas with the name *Vortigernus*,[7] and he does so some two hundred years later. Add to this the personal biases that Bede brought to his writing. His religious, political, and ethnic viewpoints were diametrically opposed to those of Gildas.[8] Their respective positions meant they had very different goals in writing, and therefore different uses for the *superbus tyrannus* character. He might or might not have been a historical character that Gildas could conveniently blame for the coming of the Germanic peoples, but for Bede to connect him to a historical person with a real name, Vortigern, meant that a real person had given his predecessors land in Britain. In turn, the character could be used to show that his people had legitimately been given sovereignty in Britain.

Nor can the argument be made that Bede might have had a better source than Gildas that is now lost. It seems that Bede was fully dependent on a Kentish source when discussing the origins of the Germanic people in Britain. This is indicated by the prominence which Kent is given in the early chapters of *Historia Ecclesiastica*.[9] Exploring the Kentish history as laid out by Bede and its significance to Kent will serve to better explain the Vortigern character.

In *Historia Ecclesiastica*, Kent was the first British area to be settled by Germanic tribes, and therefore Kent had primacy over all later settlement areas.[10] Bede would easily have understood the underlying message that the kings of Kent were the rightful rulers of the island. However, Bede was not in a position to rewrite the history he had in front of him. Despite his personal interests, he apparently had no source that countered Kent's claim in favor of his home kingdom. Likely the fact that Kent was Christianized first meant that their historical records had been composed early enough that there had been no competing claim and with the full support of the church. No other kingdom would have been able to make an alternate claim before Kent's history had become an accepted fact of English history. Bede may have wanted to create his own account of the settlement of Britain, but he was not a historian writing for the sole purpose of extolling Northumbria. First and foremost he was a man of the church, and when records came from Kent that it had been settled first, his own personal motivations would have been set aside.

According to his (and therefore Kent's) account, the leaders of that initial settlement group had been the brothers Hengest and Horsa. Their ancestor was listed as Woden, Norse Odin, and the chief god of the Germanic pantheon. However, by the eighth century that would no longer have been the case. In fact, likely by the middle of the seventh century he would have been no more significant than any other name in the pedigree. This fact speaks to the age of the original family history. To the Germanic people during the pre–Christian and Conversion period, Woden's name would have been a symbol of authority and legitimacy for the house that claimed him.[11] His presence in the Kentish pedigree, coupled with the tradition that the Kentish settlers Hengest and Horsa were the first Germanic-speaking people in Britain, would have made the strongest possible claim to political primacy for their kingdom.[12]

Once Vortigern had been introduced to the story, certain details necessarily had to be added. To have the authority to give away what amounted to a substantial portion of Britain, Vortigern had to be a man of great power.

Gildas' title of "great tyrant" allowed a good deal of latitude in that regard. To lose any of that power, he had to be proven unable to rule. At the same time, those who took power from him had to be shown not as liars or thieves, but as men who were craftier and more capable than he was. Thus was born the legend of Vortigern.

Understanding this, it becomes clear that what Bede presents us with is a foundation myth; it is not something the pro–Northumbrian writer would have created, but it is a creation that forwarded the political aims of Kent. It cannot be wholly historical simply because of Kent's goals. Every episode apart from the one borrowed from Gildas has the single-minded purpose of showing Vortigern to be an incompetent ruler and Hengest to be his rightful usurper.

Because of this fact, there can be no hope that any of the Vortigern-Hengest scenes first mentioned in Bede are in any way historical. There is no traceable origin for the information in any event. The kingdom of Kent was converted in 597, with a religious house established shortly thereafter. To believe that the name of a foreign leader who was nothing more than a tool would be remembered some hundred and fifty years after the fact and in an atmosphere of purely oral memory would be to go on nothing more than blind faith. To believe that any of the stories attached to him were historical, given the circumstances of where the impetus for the foundation tale came from and Kent's specific goals would be preposterous.

Nor does it seem likely that the nature, and the rough chronology, of the initial Germanic settlement would have been known as late as 600. What seems much more plausible is that the first historians of Kent, the religious men who came over with Augustine, went to Gildas and used the dates they could derive from him to derive a framework of early Kentish history.

The fact is, Vortigern and all the materials associated with him through Bede are not historical. It is possible that Bede himself made the connection between the *superbus tyrannus* of Gildas and the "great king" of Kentish legend in 729 based on a similarity of circumstances. It seems more likely, though, that Kent did so at some point between the foundation of Canterbury and the time of Bede's request for information on early Britain.

With *Vortigern* understood as a misunderstanding or at least a misinterpretation suggested by Gildas' elusive choice of words we must ask ourselves again, who is the fifth-century *superbus tyrannus* whom Gildas accuses of inviting the Germanic-speakers to Britain? I would like to suggest that he was Arthur, one of the few known prominent figures of the fifth century.[13]

This connection does not mean that the author believes Arthur did make the invitation, or even that he was active in the era Vortigern was. It cannot be overstressed that Gildas had an agenda of his own, and this agenda did not depend on any level of historical accuracy beyond what his audience believed.

Gildas names a superbus tyrannus

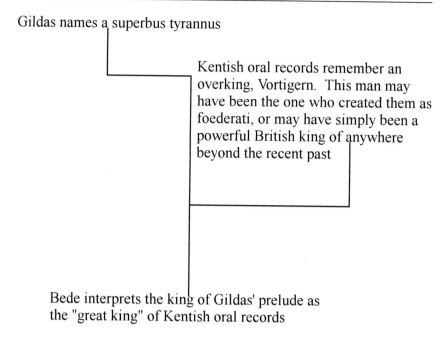

Kentish oral records remember an overking, Vortigern. This man may have been the one who created them as foederati, or may have simply been a powerful British king of anywhere beyond the recent past

Bede interprets the king of Gildas' prelude as the "great king" of Kentish oral records

FIRST THEORY OF VORTIGERN'S DEVELOPMENT. A potential means by which happenstance and interpretation may have led to the connection of the historical king Vortigern with Gildas' *superbus tyrannus*.

His primary concern was to illustrate the correlation between the political dilemmas of the British people and their actions regarding God.[14] Any name or event that did not somehow forward this argument was unnecessary for his letter. There is no evidence any aspect of Gildas' preliminary historical survey contains a single item that weakens the force of his views on this point. On the contrary, he has overlooked much because it did not directly bear upon his theme.[15] If Arthur was a major figure in the fifth or sixth centuries and Gildas found him to be unhelpful, he would have ignored him as he ignored several other important personages.

Yet his *superbus tyrannus* is present and prominent. One must ask why this is so. His presence within living memory of Gildas' writing implies that he was a historical figure, and that he did invite people of Germanic culture to the island. However, nothing in Gildas' narrative gives any indication of who this *tyrannus* may have been. Further, no historical or pseudo-historical tradition independent of Bede offers an alternative to Vortigern. No other source of the fifth century exists which might provide some insight on the subject, either. Yet clearly this man's actions were despised by Gildas, as much or more so than the five kings who were the main subject of his paper.

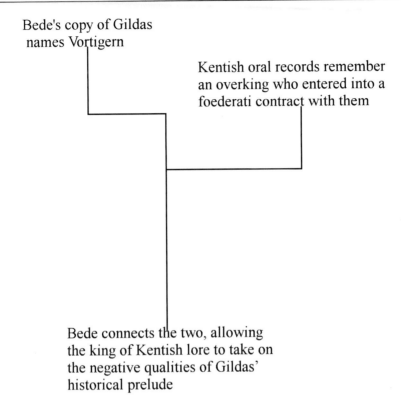

Bede's copy of Gildas
names Vortigern

Kentish oral records remember
an overking who entered into a
foederati contract with them

Bede connects the two, allowing
the king of Kentish lore to take on
the negative qualities of Gildas'
historical prelude

SECOND THEORY OF VORTIGERN'S DEVELOPMENT. **Bede may have connected the Welsh king Vortigern with an overking, translated into Latin as** *superbus tyrannus*, **resulting in the formation of the medieval Vortigern character.**

There is also some suggestion that Gildas may have had more secular objectives in mind when he edited his historical prelude. As mentioned in the Introduction, oral tradition indicates his brother Hueil was killed by Arthur. This legend is mentioned in the *Vita Gildae, Culhwch ac Olwen,* and *Trioedd Ynys Prydein,* so it may well have been part of the large body of oral knowledge that was in Wales during the Middle Ages. If the core elements of the shared tales were based on history, they would explain Gildas' added reluctance to mention Arthur by name and his willingness to exaggerate and make Arthur the scapegoat for the English presence. If the story is entirely fictional, its existence at least suggests a tradition of hostility between Arthur and Gildas' family and, again, suggests a motive for not mentioning Arthur.

In addition, if Arthur may be described as the *superbus tyrannus* or great king, one problem area in British history may be resolved rather neatly. For instance, the Ninnius text states that Arthur "pugnabat contra illos in illis diebus cum regibus Brittonum," that is, he "fought against them [the Germanic chieftains] with the kings of the Britons."[16] Arthur is clearly described as the first among equals. This description is similar to the one we find in Gildas about the *superbus tyrannus*: "omnes consiliarii una cum superbo tyranno cae-cantur": "all the members of council, together with the proud tyrant."[17] This, as Dr. Bromwich has suggested, seems to indicate that the *tyrannus* here spoken of "acted as the chairman of a council or perhaps a 'high king' in something like the Irish sense, rather than absolutely on his own initiative; he acted in conjunction with kings."[18] This would have been an unusual situation. No other kings or over-kings are referred to as taking counsel, not even Urien.

There is also the negative evidence. *Superbus tyrannus* is merely a title, which means the man Gildas spoke of must also have had a real name. In all the British historical literature only two people who may be connected to the mid- or late fifth century were renowned by the British for their widespread powers and influence—Ambrosius and Arthur. Of these two, Ambrosius could not be the great tyrant by the next few lines of Gildas' history, when he is described as the leader of the resistance who first emerged after the English revolted. Ambrosius was a figure to be admired and mimicked in Gildas' eyes. In his entire letter, he is Gildas' only hero. A Gildasian hero would never have done such an act of treachery as to invite the Germanic tribes to Britain. Certainly Gildas would not have mentioned the event if he thought it might be tied with Ambrosius. That leaves only one traditional figure who may claim to be the *superbus tyrannus* of Gildas, Arthur.

It may be rightly objected that a man whom medieval and modern tradition have given such a healthy presentation seems awkward in such a position as the one *Vortigern* has heretofore occupied. However, it has often been noted that the invitation of the Germanic chiefs Hengest and Horsa followed the tradition of the Romans. The leaders of the Late Roman Empire often hired Germanic tribesmen as *foederati* and paid them with food and supplies during their service, and eventually with land inside the empire. The action was a common and generally trustworthy one on the continent during the fifth century. If Arthur had invited Germanic speakers to Britain, he would have been following a proven custom and, by contemporary standards, would have been considered to be making a wise move. Only after the full aftermath of the revolt had been seen would this act have been seen as a mistake.[19] So, while Gildas might labor that his tyrant had made an error in judgment, Arthur's contemporaries would have thought differently.[20]

Some support for the development of two traditions pertaining to Arthur may be seen in the literature of Medieval Wales. The strong king who held back the Germanic invasion is the best known, being seen in *Historia Brittonum*, but also in most of the literary references to him.

However there is a second tradition which sees him as too prideful. The *vita* tradition seems to have exaggerated this. However, there is also the less biased reference in Triad 37R, where Arthur is said to have dug up the head of Brân so that his strength alone could protect Britain. It is said that he was one of three men whose foolish, prideful acts allowed the island of Britain to be conquered. That sounds like an apt after-thought of the *superbus tyrannus*.

As has been seen, Gildas made no attempt to write his historical prelude as a historian. If he could exaggerate within the known facts to make a point, he did.[21] The main purpose of his abridged history was to demonstrate how God punished and rewarded the British in direct proportion to their actions. Anything that hindered his purpose, and often much which simply did not directly complement it, was excised. In the latter category, a war hero of Arthur's repute would fall. In making Arthur an example of what not to do as *superbus tyrannus*, he would have been forced to pass Arthur's successes over in silence for the sake of consistency.

If Arthur was the *superbus tyrannus* of whom Gildas speaks, then there is a firsthand source that names Arthur, and this source gives a very rough idea of his floruit. Professor Dumville has already provided a rough chronology for his career. For him, the *superbus tyrannus* (Arthur) would have come to power around 480 and after the long period of peace. He would have been dead or his power greatly weakened by the time Ambrosius came to power around 495.[22] Thus Arthur could be seen as, in Dr. Bromwich's words, "the first and the most prominent of the many North British heroes concerning whom traditions were brought south from *Y Hen Gogled*, and were freshly localized and elaborated in Wales in the early Middle Ages."[23]

CHAPTER 6

Drutwas

The previous four chapters have shown evidence that if there was an Arthur he existed in a heroic age. Evidence has also been presented to suggest that Gildas may have used the title "great king" to identify him. Chapters 2 and 4 have provided evidence for believing that if Arthur did live it was in the last two decades of the fifth century. The purpose of this chapter will be to present evidence that, on historical, literary, and perhaps chronological grounds, the character Drutwas son of Tryffin might have been a member of Arthur's *teulu*, possibly a rival, but in all likelihood a contemporary of the British king.

The character Drutwas son of Tryffin first appears on line 200 of *Culhwch ac Olwen*, in the catalogue of people which the hero Culhwch names off as sureties to his request of manhood from Arthur. This catalogue is commonly known as the court list. Drutwas does not appear again in the tale. Instead, it focuses on the activities of the main Arthurian heroes—Cei, Bedwyr, and Caw of Prydein, and their achievement of the various tasks assigned to Culhwch so that he might earn the right to marry Olwen.

Drutwas next appears in two related but later traditional sources. The first reference is to be found in the group of poetry traditionally assigned to Llywarch Hen and is clearly a mere hint of an older traditional story.[1] The poem uninformatively mentions the birds of Drutwas son of Triphun. This reference is found more fully elaborated in the *White Book of Hergest*, though here a touch of the fantastic has already overtaken the details.[2] Now Drutwas is able to speak with them, and the three flocks of birds he owns are capable of killing a fully armed warrior.

The two allusions together indicate that Drutwas was a character remembered in popular folklore. The latter tale strongly suggests that he may have had some ties with Arthur. However, the inclusion of the magical birds in a role integral to the story implies the legend had spent a long interval of time in an oral state before first being written. The degree to which the relationship between Arthur and Drutwas can be trusted is therefore limited.

The genealogies, on the other hand, are more credible. They may not indicate a true father to son relationship, but kingships stayed within a cousinhood, and up to the historical horizon the genealogical records generally name only members of a kingdom's royal family.[3] This is an especially safe assumption if multiple genealogies are consistent on the persons or person being studied. The *Harleian 3859* and *Jesus College MS 20* are the two best sources for genealogical records, and they both have a version of a Dyfed pedigree. They name Drutwas' father as Triphun[4] and Tryphun,[5] respectively. Tryphun, rectified as Tryffin, is a historical figure who is mentioned elsewhere and whose floruit has been well-studied.[6] He was likely active during the middle of the fifth century.[7]

There are, then, some reasons to suggest that Drutwas did exist during the period before 500 and no real evidence to deny it. To recap, Tryffin's floruit has been placed in the mid–fifth century. A son of this king would likely have been active in the latter half of the century. Drutwas is listed in Arthur's *Culhwch ac Olwen* court and folklore holds a tale of his dispute with Arthur. As has been seen above, Arthur has been tentatively placed in the late fifth century as well, making them tentatively contemporaries. Admittedly, of all this coincidence nothing could be used as concrete proof for claiming either Drutwas' historicity or that he lived at the same time as Arthur. However, the three facts are perfectly congruent to and in fact do corroborate each other. However, the evidence seems to point both to Drutwas' existence and his association with Arthur.

The dilemma that these correspondences produce is that Tryffin, and therefore Drutwas, are Dyfed personalities and presumably persons of ultimately Irish origin.[8] On the other hand, Arthur is indisputably British and most probably northern.[9] The discrepancy would seem to imply that the regions of activity for the two figures are mutually exclusive. On the surface, it appears as though the presence of Drutwas at Arthur's court was more a matter of Arthur's orbit expanding to include Dyfed than of a historical Drutwas presenting himself at Arthur's court. Drutwas has apparently been geographically misplaced and reoriented to the most dominant king figure of the era. Surely an Irishman of Dyfed would be out of place in Arthur's *teulu*, except under the most bizarre circumstances.

However, as Arthur's period was a part of the British Heroic Age that continued until roughly the Battle of Winwæd or Maes Gai in 655, there is another possibility. In a characteristic historical *comitat* of the heroic age, not all the young warriors were the sons of men who had previously served the tribal chief or his predecessor. Most often foreigners, or at least men of diverse cultural backgrounds, were additionally to be found in the war-band of a successful chief or king. Hector Chadwick gave two reasons for this phenomenon. First, those sons of a chief who were not in line to obtain a throne would be likely to enter the *teulu* of another king in hopes of inheriting some portion of the patrimony. Second, often the sons of a chief or his nobles would be given to a more influential ruler as a hostage in return for a semi-independence, or for protection from attack.[10] To these possibilities something unique to the Celts might be added. Both the British and the Irish allowed inheritance from a distant cousinhood. When a ruler died, those individuals who had best proven themselves as leaders were considered the most eligible to succeed him. Serving in a foreign king's court would have given Drutwas just such an opportunity to prove himself.

Members of significant families serving in the war-bands of other kings can be seen in the legendary Celtic courts. In *Táin Bó Cuailgne*, it is explained that the Cú Chulainn is not from Ulster (ll. 524–539). It is further learned that Fergus and his troop, and many heroes who were originally members of Conchobar's Ulster court, now reside with Aillil and Medb in Connaught. Nearer to home, there is limited evidence of an Elmet and Irish mercenary in Wales,[11] and that Cei's father may have been Irish.[12] Late Roman writers know of British mercenary war-bands on the continent, most notably that of Riothamus. Archaeologically speaking, Germanic remains found in decidedly British settlements intimate these foreigners may have been originally hired mercenaries of the British chiefs.[13]

In understanding the unique mores of heroic age society, Drutwas can easily be seen as a later son of Triphun. He would have been forced to make his way to Arthur's court in hopes of finding a more happy position for himself, or under the best of circumstances of winning enough renown to go back to Dyfed and claim his father's kingdom for himself. Of course he remained proud of his royal ancestry and unquestionably was persistent in being known as a prince in his own right. It is probably for this reason that his lineage was preserved even in stories that were confined to the Arthurian orbit.

And all references to him are limited to the Arthurian orbit; there is no reference to a historical figure named Drutwas in the Welsh records that have been preserved through the centuries, let alone of an individual from Dyfed by that name. This lack of evidence means there is no way in which to effectively validate all the conjecture of the last few pages.

However, the absence of supporting evidence cannot disprove the possibility, either. The general paucity of records for this period and the fact that the extant genealogies have retained only the names of kings and at best the relationships between them means that many other members of the royal lineages may have been active outside of their home kingdoms and important men in their own right. In this, a son of a king whose major accomplishment was joining the household of another king would have a poor chance of being preserved in any record outside those of his adopted king. The harsh reality is that the politically-minded historians of the ninth century had no reason to remember Drutwas, and so it should come as no surprise that he is not in any non–Arthurian document that has anything to say about the fifth century.

On the other hand, it has been seen that there is a small body of positive evidence to support the argument. He does appear in several legends, and unanimously in conjunction with Arthur.[14] Genealogies confirm his contemporaneity with Arthur. These may be coincidental facts, but it seems more likely that they are not. The fact is that neither Cei nor Bedwyr have so much corroboratory evidence.[15] It is also conceivable, though hardly probable, that Drutwas was originally a rival of Arthur as the folkloric account in *The White Book of Hergest* implies.

With Drutwas, literature, heroic age culture, and genealogies all seem to come together in agreement. Arthur and Drutwas may have been combatants during their lifetimes, or Drutwas may have been a part of Arthur's *teulu*. Either way, the evidence points to Drutwas being a historical character and Drutwas is only associated with Arthur. These facts would suggest that Arthur was historical as well.

A historical Drutwas being a part of a historical Arthur's *teulu* would also go a long way in explaining an intriguing anomaly in the Dyfed pedigree. Date-guessed to the late sixth century is an Arthur.[16] The name is surrounded on both sides with names unique to Dyfed, and there are no legends regarding an unusual marriage, an invasion, or even his father's interest in the legendary king; it is simply there. The sudden appearance has occasionally been seen as a counter to the general onomastic trend of several northern lineages having Arthur in their pedigrees at around this time.[17] However, if Drutwas was a member of Arthur's war-band it would explain much.

On a larger scale, the conclusion that Drutwas had some historical relationship with Arthur is significant because it again demonstrates that some of the historical record for the fifth and sixth centuries can be tenably reconstructed through the critical use of folkloric and legendary tales, supplemented by the traditional tools of Gildas, Patrick, the *Vita Germani*, the genealogical lists, *Annales Cambriae* and the Ninnius compendium.[18] This has already been done with heroic cycles of other nations.[19] It has also been initiated in a Celtic context.[20] It is hoped that this process will continue.

CHAPTER 7

The Bards of the Fifth, Sixth and Early Seventh Centuries

The bards of Medieval Wales were prized scholars and poets until only a couple of hundred years ago in their function as keepers of the lore of the British people. It was a position they had well earned. From a time before memory, they had served in multiple capacities for the thousands of chieftains who had ruled their tiny kingdoms on the island. They had served as seers and were feared and respected for their ability to praise or ridicule a warrior and to foretell and in some cases create the future.[1] Heroes such as Cú Chulainn preferred to walk into imminent doom to avoid their sarcasm. Their art was used to craft pedigrees and enhance the reputations of warriors and kings who served as their patrons. Their presence was constantly renewed in the nightly stories kings and their warriors enjoyed through the storytelling abilities of these poets.

The evacuation of the Romans helped set in motion a series of events that helped to revitalize their profession in modified form.[2] In a relatively short time, their cultured poetry had once again become the entertainment and intellectual epitome of the British people. It is for this reason, and the reverence with which these poets were cherished, that some of their earlier works were considered valuable enough to put to paper and copy in multiple centers. Because of the reputation of this group, some of their poems have been fortunate enough to survive to this day.

Because of their standing among the post–Roman Britons these early poets are of great interest from a historical standpoint. It is this group whose rebirth signaled the end of Roman influences and the beginnings of the British Heroic Age. As has been seen in Chapter 2, the bards of the fifth century soon became the genealogists and record keepers of the chieftains; they were the local historians, whose ability to color their knowledge with references to Celtic mythology and island-wide history would once again make them popular entertainers among their people. It is also most likely they who created many of the surviving legends of the known fifth- and sixth-century personalities. For this reason, a better understanding of this group, and the individuals who composed it, can only enhance our understanding of the period. Many of the answers to the fifth century may eventually be found in a close study of these people. Therefore, the questions "Where did they perform?" "For whom did they create?" and "When in this period did they live?" will be posed of all seventeen known or likely bards of the fifth, sixth, and early seventh centuries. These will be met with varying levels of success. The information acquired from the general study will then be applied to those bards of whom relatively little is known. This will be for the purpose of forming as complete a picture as possible of these artists' floruits and regions of activity. It will be the collation of all this effort which will then be applied to the British chieftains of the period, and Arthur in particular. The study will begin with the earliest known mention of bards for this period, in the *Historia Brittonum*, and conclude with the final known poets of the seventh century.

The *Historia Brittonum* has already been introduced. It is a collection of fragmented stories and historical anecdotes which was formed into a semicoherent history by a monastic editor of c. 829–830 in Gwynedd. The extant form of the history is thought to have been composed in the next century, probably by a monk and definitely in Dyfed.[3] The sources for this conglomeration appear to have come from local legends as well as historical, pseudo-historical, and literary sources.[4] For this reason, *Historia Brittonum* does have some potential merit as a source of knowledge for the early post–Roman centuries, if used with extreme caution.[5]

Chapters 56–65 of the work form what is known as the Northern British section.[6] These have been so termed because they are concerned solely with the characters and activities which took place north and east of modern Wales.[7] Everything mentioned there is known to have taken place between the late fifth century and roughly 700. This information is noteworthy because Chapter 62 lists five bards. Because of their context, they must all have flourished in *Y Hen Ogled*, the Old North, before about 700 as well. The names of these poets are Talhaearn Tat-Aguen, Neirin, Taliesin, Cian, and Bluchbard.

The precise dates for these poets have been traditionally based on the context of two figures that are placed in a chapter before and after them. These are Ida, a Northumbrian king whom Bede and *The Anglo-Saxon Chronicle* put in the twelve years anterior to and including 547, and Maelgwn, whose death is listed in *Annales Cambriae* at 547 or 549.[8] Therefore, the reasoning has gone, all five poets would have flourished between about 535 and 549.

However, the simplistic approach that the poets' floruits all took place in the mid–sixth century is not necessarily accurate for several reasons. First, it is now known that Maelgwn did not necessarily die in 547 or 549, as the *Annales Cambriae* claims. As Dr. Miller conjectured, it was probably known that Maelgwn died of a plague but not exactly when. *Annales Cambriae* and its source had listed 547 or 549 as the year of a great plague.[9] At some stage in the growth of the *Annales Cambriae*, the connection was made between the two, and Maelgwn's year of death was tied to it in the record. His year of death is still unknown, though it was certainly near 549 and probably before. Considering the information to be derived from *De Excidio Britanniae*, Miller and Dumville have both extended Maelgwn's potential obit to 534–549.[10] If the *Historia Brittonum* is to be regarded as a valid source and its relative dating accepted without question, this would be the *terminus* for the poets' floruits as well.

Even this broad margin of error is not a secure one. The editor of *Historia Brittonum* has simply thrown these five poets in one place, and nowhere else mentions any other bard in his entire composition. This is cause for some hesitation about so specific a chronological setting. Putting oneself in the editor's position, it seems most likely that here he conveniently grouped together five of the Britons' most respected early muses from a broad chronological area. It is unlikely that five individuals of that stature would all have lived in the same fifteen-year period.[11] In a section devoted roughly to *Y Hen Ogled* and the period 470 to 700,[12] they must be seen to represent the entire period too.[13]

This is all that may be deduced about the group of bards as a whole. However, of the individual poets something more can be learned, and much confirms the above deductions. Talhaearn Tat-Aguen has commonly been associated with a king named Outigern of *Y Hen Ogled*, and thus possibly to the mid–sixth century and Powys. A simple transposition of letters would give Uotigern, and the "V" was often mistaken for a "U" in transcribing manuscripts. This would give Votigern. Vortigern is the most famous of the Powysian kings, and was revered by Powys at the time *Historia Brittonum* was being written. Powys was related to Gwynedd by marriage at that time. It would make perfect sense to have assigned their greatest king's bard the title of greatest bard.

However, his title may be the key to understanding more about him; it means "Father of Inspiration." It is indeed a high compliment to treat Talhaearn so in company with the greatest of the British bards. In the context of what has been deduced of the *Historia Brittonum* over the past forty years by scholars such as Nora Chadwick and David Dumville, however, this obvious favoritism is probably another indication of his affiliation with the early House of Gwynedd.[14] In this case, Talhaearn may well have been placed at the head of the list of bards simply for nationalistic reasons. As the book was written in Gwynedd and patronized by the Gwynedd king, he would have been a Gwynedd bard. Support for this theory can be seen in place-name evidence; it has been noted that several place-names around Din Orben, Gwynedd, contain the rare personal name *Talhaearn*. If the connections to Gwynedd are legitimate, his primacy in *Historia Brittonum* would thereby be explained, as well as the list's nature, which is to further gratify the Gwynedd kings.

On the other hand, the borders of Gwynedd and Powys were in a state of flux throughout the fifth and sixth centuries. Though Din Orben was clearly inside Gwynedd territory by the ninth century, it may well have been Powysian while Talhaearn was active.

From the above evidence it is impossible to narrow Talhaearn's floruit further than sometime within one of two Gwynedd periods, c. 450 to 580 or c. 625 to 635, and one Powysian era, the mid–sixth century. Four hundred and fifty would be a generously early guess for the initial rise to kingship of Maelgwn's family. The period to 580 marks the end of an era of the great Gwynedd kings, as does the ten-year expanse in the seventh century. To accept Powys as the bard's native kingdom is to accept the lord assigned to him until a better explanation is put forth, and Vortigern was active during the middle of the sixth century.[15] My opinion would be that Talhaearn in fact was Powysian, with the alteration of his name aided by the later villainy associated with it. If Talhaearn was a native of Gwynedd, then he lived during Cadwallon, Maelgwn, or Rhun's reign. It is they who have the most saga material attached to their names, and most likely an extremely good bard inspired it.

Of the other poets, *Historia Brittonum* provides no information. Fortunately, however, there is a small degree of independent data which may be called upon. Neirin, in the form *Aneirin*, is generally credited with the creation of *Y Gododdin*. Most probably he was in the service of Uruei of Eidyn[16] and composed somewhere in the period 540 to 600.[17] Neirin was possibly the son of Dwywei and nephew of Gwallog of Elmet, as later genealogies claim.[18] He is associated with the kingdom of Gododdin.

Taliesin is the third of the bards and is also well remembered in Welsh tradition. Twelve extant praise poems are regarded as his and indicate his patrons. Two poems without the subtleties of the other ten are regarded as his earliest. They compliment the bounty and wisdom of one Cynan, king of Powys. Later, it would seem he took up residence with Urien and spent the majority of his career in Rheged. Eight of the remaining ten poems praise him. At some time during his stay with Urien, it seems he allowed Gwallog of Elmet to give him patronage. Gwallog is addressed in two Taliesin poems, followed by at least one more to Urien apologizing for his lack of loyalty and assuring his lord that the poems he had written for Gwallog meant nothing. There is no doubt that Taliesin was a bard of *Y Hen Ogled* who was active during the mid- to late sixth century.

Cian and Bluchbard are both unknown in Britain outside of the *Historia Brittonum* reference. However, Cian has one additional clue to offer regarding his origins, his name. It is distinctly Irish and first appears in legend as the name of the founder of the *Ciannachta* of central Ireland. This implies that Cian was either Irish or was born to a British family that was influenced by the Irish. The Irish were heavily settled on the west coast of Wales, southern Scotland, and England during the late fifth and early sixth centuries. However, it seems most likely that he was from what would become Gwynedd. Though the west coast from Dumnonia North to Argyll was sporadically settled by the Irish in the fifth century, central Ireland specifically invaded northern Wales.[19] More importantly, the Irish still had a foothold as late as the mid-sixth century. It has also been seen that the Gwynedd kings are a featured element of *Historia Brittonum*.[20] Thus either Cadwallon Lawhir, Maelgwn, or Rhun were most likely his patron because they have the most extensive extant saga materials surrounding him.

If Cian was a bard in Gwynedd, this would also help to narrow his floruit. Gwynedd's access to central Irish culture would have been greatly weakened by the second third of the sixth century when Anglesey was again firmly under British rule.[21] This would limit Cian's potential floruit to between the mid–fifth century and about 550.

This constitutes the only historical knowledge that is extant pertaining to the five bards named in Chapter 62 of the *Historia Brittonum*. However, several generalizations can be made from what is known which can guide one to a better understanding of the bards who are not remembered of the period. First, it must be noted that the two bards whose patrons are known were attached to the most prominent kings of important kingdoms, and therefore the other three quite probably were as well.[22] Second, they do all belong to *Y Hen Ogled*. This, as Bromwich pointed out long ago, was probably the main region that produced heroic age heroes.[23] Third, in the case of Talhaearn and Cian it has been seen that they could have lived well before 550. Neirin and Taliesin may have been active at mid–century, but there is no firm evidence that the former two floruits were specifically in the mid–sixth century. This confirms my initial conjecture; the poets were not all active in the narrow span of time suggested by their appearance in *Historia Brittonum*.

Of the five poets this source names, precious little may be learned. Fortunately, the Ninnian compendium is not the only source for the names of British Heroic Age poets. The triads of the Welsh offer eight additional persons—Cadegr, Argad,[24] Disgyfdawd,[25] Tristfardd, Dygynnelw, Auan Verdic,[26] Arouan, and Golydan.[27] Four more poets can be found in scrounging through materials pertaining to the era. One poem in elegy of Cynddylan gives Meigant, two semi-dubious sources name Heinin, one text names a Gwron son of Cynfarch, and a poem by Gwilym Ddu of Arfon claims a final bard for the period, one Kywryt.

Like so much of Medieval Welsh literature, the Welsh Triads are poorly understood. It has been assumed that the triads served as mnemonic devices and aided bards by helping them to learn and later remember the vast stores of knowledge they needed access to in order to create the depth and cultured ambience of their entertainments.[28] They would therefore have some value as traditional sources of information. However, little else is known about them. What is generally acknowledged may be summarized as follows. All of the known triads are to be found scattered in twelve manuscripts of varying ages and scholarly value. Those of Peniarth 16, triads 1 to 46 in Dr. Bromwich's edition, represent the oldest stratum of the triadic structure.[29] The poets named in that earliest group are Cadegr, Argad, Disgyfdawd, Tristfardd, Dygynnelw, Auan Verdic, Arouan, and Golydan.

Cadegr and Argad are to be found in triad no. 7, where they are listed as fathers of two Bull-chieftains.[30] Both individuals are otherwise anonymous and unlocatable.[31] Golydan of triad no. 34 is equally absent from any other records. Nothing may be learned from any of them.

In triad no. 10, Disgyfdawd is named as the father of three chiefs of Deur and Brennych. This suggests that he was from the Northumbrian region as well. Traditionally, Deur first became separated from Brennych in the mid–fifth century under Soemil, and Brennych was under an English king by 548. Contact with the free British states can be assumed to have ended within a generation, and practical British rule on a local level may have ended sooner. If this rough chronology and broad sequence of events can be used, then Disgyfdawd's sons probably ruled no later than the mid–sixth century. They likely would not have come to power in an area traditionally dominated by the Romans until the Germanic peoples had revolted somewhere in the middle of the fifth century. This would place Disgyfdawd between the early fifth and early sixth centuries.[32]

The four poets of triad no. 10 are perhaps the simplest to place. They are Tristfardd, Dygynnelw, Auan Verdic, and the *White Book* alternative Arouan, which the triad assigns to Urien, Owain son of Urien, Cadwallon son of Cadfan, and Selyf son of Cynan Garwyn, respectively. This locates the first two in the mid- and late sixth century. The bards of Cadwallon and Selyf would have flourished in the first third of the seventh century. The first two would have been located in Reged, the third in Gwynedd, and the fourth in Powys.

Meigant is the traditional author of "Marwnad Cynddylan," an early seventh century poem that praises the life of the fallen Powysian king Cynddylan.

This Cynddylan's territory was specifically centered north of Shrewsbury, and thus it may be conjectured that Meigant was active in that area as well. If this is true, then he was active during the early seventh century and in a territory north of Shrewsbury.

Heinin is known from *Hanes Taliesin* and the *Mabinogion* as Maelgwn Gwynedd's chief bard. This would place his years of service in the early to mid–sixth century, during the reign of his king.

The final known poet of the age is Kywryt, alleged bard of an unspecified Dunawt according to a poem written by Gwilym ddu o Arfon in a fairly late manuscript.[33] If the information Gwilym gives there is accurate, then the Dunawt in question is most probably the son of Pabo. If Kywryt was in the service of this king, he lived south of Reged around the mid–sixth century.[34]

This group of men represents the entire body of known British bards for the decades before 700. In many cases, their patrons and locations are unknown, but much can be deduced from the facts at hand. First, all the people who are locatable pertain to the British Old North[35] and seem to belong roughly to the period 450 to 655, the British Heroic Age. It should be noted that these dates approximate those which had been conjectured in Chapter 2. Of the bards listed above, the majority and most knowable of them are within a couple of decades of 550, and none were certainly active before 480.

DISTRIBUTION OF THE BARDS

Late fifth century	2	Gwynedd	4
Early sixth century	3	Reged	4
Mid sixth century	4	Powys	3
Late sixth century	3	Gododdin	1
Early seventh century	3	Brennych	1
Unknown	5	Unknown	5

These facts are of high significance for several reasons. First, it might safely be concluded that this large menagerie of poets represents most of the greatest literary contributors to the British renaissance in poetry. By understanding them and their motivations better it should be possible to accurately interpret the literary and legendary information about the fifth and sixth century that has come down to the present.

Second, it has been noted that five of the earliest poets are connected with no patron or region.[36] This implies two things. First, that the society in which they lived was fluid; many kingdoms and lineages that existed during their lifetimes were quite possibly forgotten within one hundred years of their deaths. This supports the theory about the presumed anarchic political climate in the last half of the fifth century as laid out in Chapter 4. Second, the fact that their names are remembered at all implies that, like the better known poets, they were associated with a king who at one point was of major importance.[37]

Third, it seems quite probable that the decades around 500 mark the reemergence of British poetry. This is the time of the earliest known bards as was laid out in Chapter 2. Their presence also explains the large number of chieftains from this period that are to be found in the extant literary and oral sources, while the specific details of chieftains before this period is negligible.[38] Data about these early kings must originally have derived from the poetry of the bards explored above and others like them.

Finally, the existence of these earliest poets and their timely placement in the last decades of the fifth century may help explain the massive body of legendary material regarding Arthur. In the decades before 500, when the bardic form of entertainment was reawakening, Arthur was by all accounts the most successful and beloved chieftain of the Britons. Thus the political, economic, and cultural upheaval caused by Rome's absence provided the necessary setting for these first bards, and as Arthur was the most prominent king of his generation he would have naturally provided the most popular topic. There may be little historical evidence to prove Arthur's existence, but he does sit on top of an overwhelming amount of legendary material. This is because his would have been the name on every bard's lip when they were reestablishing their craft. Because of the timing of Arthur's career, it would seem that Arthur was adopted as the regal standard of excellence.

As has been shown above, a historical Arthur would have been a heroic age figure. The extant material shows Arthur as a clearly military hero whose greatest assets were his fighting ability and his generosity, two basic and essential qualities for any heroic age ruler. It is only natural to conjecture that he, as a figure of a heroic age which was dominated by northern kings and chieftains, most likely came from the north as well. This suspicion will be fortified throughout the second section of this volume.[39]

CHAPTER 8

Conclusion:
The Historicity of Arthur

Arthur did exist as a major war-chief in the last decades of the fifth century. He was not as well-documented from a historical perspective as other heroes of Welsh lore. There were a rather large number of reasons for this. The earliest sources for the post–Roman centuries dated no further back than the ninth century, several centuries after Arthur and plenty of time for his accomplishments to be forgotten, superimposed over, or simply lost as the Germanic peoples took over all of England.

It has been demonstrated that only those men who had politically prominent descendants at the time of the oldest histories have been consistently recorded anyway. There is no question that Gwrtheyrn, Urien, and Cadwallon son of Cadfan were all historical figures; a variety of different sources and viewpoints attest to that. Gwrtheyrn was the most famed ancestor of Gwynedd's chief ninth-century ally, Powys, and would be vilified by Dyfed. The other two figures were from Gwynedd, and the dynasty there in the ninth century was attempting to legitimize its position and the traditional prominence of Gwynedd in Welsh politics through the *Historia Brittonum*.

Arthur's historical existence did not benefit Gwynedd and Powys, or Dyfed's opposing claims, hence the comparative disinterest that can be seen in his activities in *Historia Brittonum* and most other historical and pseudo-historical sources which were retrieved and rewritten at the time. Arthur was able to leave no familial legacy, and so ninth- and tenth-century historians had no incentive for recording him. This is the most important reason why historical records which mention Arthur are so few.

A third cause why so little information would have been available was forthcoming in a brief study of the early post–Roman period.[1] It was already known that *Y Hen Ogled*, both Romanized and non–Romanized, went through a period in which heroic age society dominated. However, it had not been determined exactly how this society had come about and what its time frame might have been. These were approximated with the help of Professor Chadwick's work in the cross-disciplinary studies of several heroic age societies. It was found that heroic age society in Roman Britain could have been functional as early as the time of the Germanic revolt in the middle of the fifth century. It was also reasoned that kingships, that is the development of governments with power over more than local areas, most likely began no earlier than that date. Probably, the first proto-kingships emerged up to thirty years later. In reevaluating Gildas' historical prelude, it was determined that Arthur may have been the *superbus tyrannus*, whose period of importance has been recently dated to approximately 480. Thus Arthur would have been an early dominant figure in the British Heroic Age.

A study of the bards who lived during the British heroic age provided some clues as to why there is no poetry on the earliest British heroes and Arthur in particular. It was found that no bards are known certainly before the last quarter of the fifth century, though three may have lived as early as the mid–fifth century. It may thus be assumed that before around 440 there were little or no oral records recording most of the early chiefs. The glamorization of chiefs by bards was a result of heroic age society, and therefore we may conclude that such a society was not fully matured until the very late fifth century.

One may also conclude from the above speculation that there is maybe a fifty year window of gray history which may well be irrecoverable. The period including the third quarter of the fifth century and the first quarter of the sixth century had poets and was, from what little evidence there is, an early form of a heroic age society. However, many of the poets' names and all their works have not survived.[2] Unfortunately, this the very period in which most scholars and the above essays have generally placed Arthur's career. That means that he would have had bards at his hall who sang his praises but not the good fortune to have those verses survive intact.[3]

Another reason why the bards' works could not have survived was detailed in Chapter 1. As Arthur lived before the massive political and social changes that occurred as Britain made its transition from Roman to British, so he preceded the accompanying linguistic changes as well. We have no poetry of any person before these dates. As has been seen, this is not because there was none. The severe linguistic changes that caused the development of Middle Welsh, Cumbric, Cornish, and Breton, and the political conquest of the Old North combined to eliminate any chance of the same rhyme schemes that worked in 500 from being functional even a generation later. The linguistic changes rendered the lore itself entirely incomprehensible by the ninth century, and the people of Germanic culture no doubt suppressed all native oral literature once they had conquered those regions. This left only the little folklore that had already been diffused to Wales to survive. Because of this happenstance, Arthur is not the subject of any of the earliest poems either.

The works of poetry connected with Arthur therefore would have lost their contextual and artistic integrity very early on. And yet despite that setback the stories of him survived and eventually thrived. His memory was kept alive in popular tales. His experiences with religious persons surfaced in politically altered *vitae* during the eleventh and twelfth centuries. The common man created tales about his life's accomplishments, and these adventures were passed down from generation to generation for centuries. They survived orally and without the benefits of strict meter or rhyme. Because there were no rules governing how the stories were told, they would become progressively less coherent. As with many popular heroes of the oral genre throughout the world, Arthur's tales were slowly exaggerated with each retelling and in each succeeding generation. As a result, his accomplishments, possessions, and abilities began to take on superhuman qualities.[4] The correlation of less traditional and more fantastic would eventually lead to him being seen as a mythical figure.

It was only a small step from the fantastic to assign the qualities of a demigod to him and his *teulu*, and Geoffrey of Monmouth and the Welsh of the later Middle Ages were happy to complete the transition. But it was beginning even three hundred years before that. The first known occurrence of this phenomenon appears three times in *Historia Brittonum*.[5] By about 1136, Geoffrey had Arthur defeating the emperor of the Romans.[6] In *Culhwch ac Olwen*, he is said to possess a ship, mantle, sword, spear, shield, and dagger, all of which have magical qualities. In the *Welsh Triads*, Arthur has become such a feared raider that any earth he walks upon is unable to grow grass for years.[7]

With the absence of solid historical evidence for Arthur thereby explained, I moved toward more positive explanations of Arthur's existence. A reexamination of Gildas' historical prelude to his treatise provided the first documentation. Specifically, a look at Gildas' *superbus tyrannus* without the benefit of later pseudo-historical works proved most useful. Gildas does not actually say that his *superbus tyrannus* is Gwrtheyrn. This is a correlation first recorded with Bede, and Bede's source for this connection is either unknown or a result of his direct translation of the phrase. Either way it is dubious. Pointing this fact out created a void in Gildas' narrative that allowed for the introduction of an equally plausible alternative, that Arthur was the man

Gildas was scorning. Supporting evidence was found in the tradition of Arthur's hostility with Gildas' family, and an alternate and negative tradition of Arthur focused on the *vitae* but to be found in other early and traditional sources. Arthur may well have been the person Gildas meant. If this is so, then there is a contemporary historical source that implies Arthur's existence, and it places Arthur in the same historical context as later pseudo-history and romance would.

This overhauled version of the fifth century, however, leaves two unanswered questions. First, if the *Annales Cambriae* entry for Camlann is to be considered accurate and Arthur met his end in either 537 or 539, there is a discrepancy of approximately sixty years between the latest theory on the *superbus tyrannus'* floruit and his death. An active life this long is highly unlikely in the rough and unpredictable society that has been outlined above. More likely such a reign, even of a powerful man, would not extend much beyond twenty years.

However, such an argument must not be pushed too far, nor should either of these two points in Arthur's rule be considered any more than very rough approximations.[8] The first is based on the very loose and unstable chronology of *De Excidio Britanniae*, while the second rests entirely on the *Annales Cambriae* dating of Camlann. As was noted above, the dates before 573 in this document and the *Historia Brittonum* are often simply guesses based on tradition. There have been several cases of numerology guiding the exact years both sources used.[9]

The second question is why Arthur could have been such a popular hero among the British if any of what Gildas had to say was true? He probably was not the leader at Badon, and any connections between himself and the rise of the Germanic people should have villainized him in the public consciousness. Perhaps Gildas exaggerated a point? Maybe he was speaking of a time so distant that by the time of his writing he could count on no person knowing any better. Certainly even more important was that, he probably possessed several traits that the people of the heroic age would have found irresistible. He was indisputably a highly successful chief. He was a raider, and quite probably a warrior, of such repute that his fame traveled widely. He was also generous. By all accounts he gave healthy portions of the loot to his men, and bountiful gifts to any bard with complimentary poems. These characteristics, more than political power, would have been praised by the bards of the heroic age and because of that remembered in the public consciousness.

These traits were later seen differently. In medieval France, his fame as a warrior took a back seat to his bounty. Chrétien and later writers used this aspect of his personality to justify their descriptions of a massive court with objects and clothing of beauty beyond the comprehension of mortals. They would soon term this, Arthur's capital, Camelot. They would also use the theme of his bounty to explain a new development. His generosity justified the increasing number of traditional and non-traditional persons who immediately began to appear at the court in search of their inclusion. It was the addition of the former that has made locating him so difficult.

PART TWO: GEOGRAPHY

CHAPTER 9

Introduction to a Study of Arthur's Geography

The preceding chapters have provided strong and consistent evidence that Arthur did exist. The next logical question regarding him is where precisely he conducted his career. As has been mentioned in the primary introduction, the wealth of Arthurian stories and references are rarely shy in providing his location.

Unfortunately, Arthur is never consistently located. In fact, he is put in every major area throughout the British world in the pseudo-historical and literary sources that mention him. Settlements and naturally occurring places in Wales, Cornwall, Lothian, Brittany, and several other territories are specifically named by a number of semi-reliable or totally unbelievable sources. This inconsistency presents a colossal difficulty for any modern scholar wishing to locate the historical Arthur.

As has been seen, though, there are a small number of pre-twelfth-century sources that both name and locate Arthur. Although they are mutually contradictory, it is necessary to use them as a point of departure for any study on Arthur's location. Therefore, a brief summary of the sources that contain these instances will be the objective of this chapter. This will be followed by a synthesis of the collected information. The sources listed below have been grouped by region for ease of reference. The dates in parentheses are the approximate year in which they were recorded.

CORNWALL
- A group of French canons were shown Arthur's Oven and Seat (1113).

SOMERSET

• The Lives of Cadoc, Carannog, and Gildas place him in the general Somerset area (1100–1130s).

• "Dialogue of Arthur and Gwenhwyfar" locates Arthur's court at Dyfneint (pre–1150).

• "Stanzas of the Graves" locate Erec's death at Llongborth (presumably Longport, Somerset) (pre–1150).

WALES

• *Historia Brittonum*: "Mirabilia"; a Carn Caball is placed in Herefordshire, Wales, the burial place of Arthur's son Amr (829–30).[1]

• *Culhwch ac Olwen* places four of Arthur's adventures in modern Wales (1080s).

• William of Malmesbury claims Walwen's grave is on a Welsh shore (1120s).

• Gwalchmei and Bedwyr are presumably located in Wales in *Englynion y Beddau* (probably pre–Galfridic and therefore pre–1136).

BORDERS/SCOTLAND

• One reference to Arthur's battle ferocity in *Y Gododdin* (ninth century).[2]

• *Pa gur?* places Arthur's men in Tribruit and Din Eidyn (Edinburgh) (ninth century).

• *Historia Brittonum*; the battles of Tribruit and Celidon Wood are probably Scottish,[3] if the battles themselves were Arthurian (829–30).[4]

• *Annales Cambriae*; the 537–39 entry notes that Arthur fell at Camblann. The site has been generally associated with Camboglanna on Hadrian's Wall, though after fifty years it remains a tentative solution (tenth century).[5]

• *Tri Thlws ar Ddeg Ynys Prydain* or *The Thirteen Treasures of Britain*; this list was traditionally believed to be one of the North, though numbers six and seven are doubtful, ten and eleven are otherwise unknown, and thirteen (Arthur's Mantle) is located specifically in Cornwall.[6]

• Five and possibly seven of Arthur's *Culhwch ac Olwen* adventures are located here (1080s).[7]

BRITTANY

• *Vita Goeznau*; Arthur stumbles across the saint in his adventures (1019).

• *Vita Euflami*; Arthur happens upon the saint (+1135).

Add to this a great many place-names spread throughout all the previously attested areas. In the main, these are place-names that have no history till well after Geoffrey's reintroduction of Arthur in the mid–twelfth century. They are therefore not of value for this study.

Nor is the sudden appearance of the name Arthur in the latter years of the sixth century. Dr. Bromwich once suggested that since all the names that make their appearance at that time come from houses which are Irish or were derived from Irish descendants, the personal name Arthur could be somehow derived from the common Irish name Art.[8] Regardless of the reasons, it seems unlikely that Arthur's career was the reason for the generation of Arthurs. Decades later, Higham pointed out that Cadwallon seems to have been an extremely important figure in Welsh history, and he never spawned a generation of namesakes. Similarly, the name Edwin did not become prominent until the middle of the eleventh century.[9]

Of the remaining references, the weight of instances seems fairly evenly spread throughout the British-speaking countries, with a slight numerical superiority for *Y Hen Ogled* but without the preponderance or even the materials which would warrant any particular reason for favoring the North. This becomes evident as the reader scrutinizes each reference in turn.

Both of the pseudo-historical sources, *Historia Brittonum* and *Annales Cambriae*, testify to Arthur's activities in northern England and southern Scotland. This region was possessed by the Germanic speakers by the time these sources are first known to have existed, in the eighth century. However, it has been established above that *Historia Brittonum* was patronized by Gwynedd's royal house. It has been demonstrated that this house claimed descent from the North, and inserted an inordinately large percentage of material from that region into the history they patronized. For that reason, the disproportionate number of references pointing to the North may be dismissed for the moment.

As the reader continues through the list, he finds that the quality of the remaining sources is generally questionable as well. *Y Gododdin* may have derived from the sixth century, but there is no certainty that the reference to Arthur does.[10] The Camboglanna reference to a Hadrian's Wall fort is only a possibility. The tale *Culhwch ac Olwen* is such a multi-layered composition that any simple reference to one scene taking place in one area means nothing without further analysis.

Having taken all the information into account, the standard pseudo-historical and literary material that precedes the twelfth century indicates no obvious favorite for the region in which Arthur was most likely active. A traditional study of the pre-twelfth-century literature is therefore a labor of futility. The results are suspect for their lack of one discernible and overwhelmingly favorite location, and the sources themselves are of questionable and varying value. The nature of the study ensures that it cannot be an efficient one because it does not account for each site where Arthur is located in the varying sources.

This is the conclusion most of the pro–Arthur scholars have come to over the last century. There is no way to distinguish one area as more of a favorite than any other by traditional means; therefore, there is no place that is clearly the most likely point of origin for Arthur.[11]

However, with firm evidence it is possible to determine a point of origin for the historical. The necessary missing component is to understand the context of all the sources listed above, and any others whose sources are demonstrably pre–Galfridic. To do this effectively, all the pertinent references to Arthur will be divided by the various motivational groups and types of writing under which they fall. For the most part, this will consist of the *vitae*, *Culhwch ac Olwen*, and the romances. Whatever does not fit easily here will be put together into an etcetera chapter. Several of Arthur's men appear in the earliest materials; these characters and their geographical associations will be divided as well. In all cases, the nature and purpose of each source will be discussed while keeping in mind the overall framework of its group. Individually, this will help us to better understand the broad context under which it was written. More broadly, this will be done to help us understand the limitations of each literary form, and the biases one must be aware of in studying references in that genre.

In addition to the studies on the references and the types of sources from which they are drawn it will be necessary to understand the direction and weight of the influence imposed by the *Historia Regum Britanniae* and Glastonbury Abbey on all of Arthurian geography. It will be seen that these two influences have channeled our understanding of that key feature much more than has been realized before. In generating international interest in Arthur, Geoffrey of Monmouth made the former nearly standard reading throughout Europe. And Glastonbury made full use of Geoffrey's fortuitous placement of many Arthurian events in the southwest. Its abbots would launch a literary campaign that focused Arthur and his court in the Glastonbury region and ultimately would cause writers such as Sir Thomas Mallory to locate Arthur in Winchester or London.

CHAPTER 10

The Geographical Influence
of Geoffrey of Monmouth

A study of Geoffrey of Monmouth's role in the development of the Arthurian legend is fundamental to an understanding of Arthurian studies in general and his geography in particular. Geoffrey stands as a bridge between the British heroic legends that had evolved around Arthur by the ninth century[1] and the romances of the Welsh, French, Germans and English that would emerge in the century following his book. In *Historia Regum Britanniae*, Geoffrey took legends, genealogies, and historical materials derived from the British Heroic Age and arranged them into a coherent, semi-believable life of a famous Briton named Arthur. In doing so, he helped make possible the transformation of Arthur from heroic age hero to romantic figure. His is the world that Chrétien de Troyes and those who followed him would build upon and from which they would pull their characters. In time, it would be his work from which the great writers of the High Middle Ages would create new knights for Arthur's world. Pertaining to Arthurian studies, *Historia Regum Britanniae* is the most important work in existence.

Historia Regum Britanniae was completed between 1 December 1135 and December 1138.[2] It is a pseudohistorical account of the British people from their mythical settlements in the generation following the Trojan War to perhaps 600 A.D. Its historical value is marginal in the best sections. It served more as historical fiction, and in that it was extremely successful, being one of the most-often copied books of the Middle Ages. The work was written by Geoffrey of Monmouth.

Of Geoffrey's life little is known. It is an unfortunately common problem in literary studies that here one must rely solely on the author's own book and scattered references to him in books and charters to gather any significant knowledge about the man. He calls himself Galfridus Monumentis, or Geoffrey of Monmouth. His cognomen implies that Geoffrey had a strong tie to Monmouth in Wales, whether by birth or otherwise. In a broader sense, this means that he was probably Welsh or a Welsh-born Breton.[3] Professor Tatlock assumed that Geoffrey was Breton because of his favoritism toward the Bretons and his contempt toward the Welsh.[4] However, Dr. Roberts has suggested he may have been Welsh and his unkind attitude to his countrymen was due to the political undercurrents of the English people during the time.[5] Regardless of the reasons for his feelings towards the Welsh, his ancestry would have given him access to a great many more and more traditional Welsh materials than an Englishman could have made use of.

One may also safely assume his place in society based on the records. Between the years 1129 and 1151,[6] Geoffrey is known to have signed six documents in the academic center of Oxford. This indicates that he was a person of modest standing. Further, he twice gives himself the title *magister* or teacher in these documents. Possibly he was a canon at Oxford, or an instructor there. Without a doubt, being active in that area would have brought him into contact with the most influential intellectual and cultural minds of his time. It may well have been this environment that helped him to form a good beginning for writing a history of his own.

Geoffrey's time in Oxford would also have put him near some of the most powerful men in England. That this is so, and that he made use of his exposure, is evident throughout *Historia Regum Britanniae*. His efforts are most clearly seen in the acknowledgments he gives at the opening of his book, his geographical predilections, and his several dedications. Geoffrey praises several powerful people through these means, and with the manipulation and subtle insertion of certain current events into the text of his work. In doing so he also implies a keen sense of political awareness. His several dedications indicate his ability to alter or change his loyalties as the political situation changed. This is a key point to which I will return.

The book is not, however, merely a collage of current events interpreted and molded together by Geoffrey. He also made use of several known sources of the ancient British. The text makes evident that he had accessed several traditional Welsh genealogies. For instance his pre–Roman king list is based on a collection similar to that found in the *Historia Brittonum*.[7] The five kings who in turn succeed Arthur in Geoffrey's work are the same five contemporary rulers whom Gildas upbraids in *De Excidio Britanniae*, and are listed in the exact same order.[8]

In this book, the floruit of Arthur is given by far the most attention and, because of this, a large number of sites are associated with him throughout the island. Many of them are first found in *Historia Regum Britanniae* and were later associated with Arthur in local lore and continental romance.[9] This is so much so that the places he names dominate all the Arthurian literature that followed. Because of his central place in Arthurian geography, a review of all Geoffrey's Arthurian sites and the reasons behind their inclusion in the volume is of primary interest if the post–Galfridic Arthurian geography is to be unraveled and its original form to be even glimpsed at.[10] What follows have been grouped by the sources he made use of.

Of the twelve battles that commence his reign, the conflicts near Dubglas River,[11] in Caledon Wood,[12] and at Urbs Legionum are from the *Historia Brittonum*, as is the description of Loch Lomond where he and Hoel go sightseeing. The *rutupi portus* where Arthur lands when he learns of Modred's treason is the same port where Ninnius listed Caesar's disembarkment. It is possible that Salisbury is Geoffrey's guess for Caer Caradoc.[13] Two earls of the Arthurian period are based there.

In addition, Geoffrey must have used at least two more sources for his geography, *Annales Cambriae* and *Historia Ecclesiatica*. *Annales Cambriae* would have given him Arthur's last battle at Camblan, which he probably equated to the Camblannus river.[14] *Historia Ecclesiatica* was clearly mined for the names of several Saxons who appear throughout the volume.

Along with these known sources, it is possible that Geoffrey was familiar with other, now-lost historical, pseudo-historical literary or even oral sources. In Book 5, he documents a British massacre of Roman troops around the year 300. He also gives a location for the event—he writes that the Welsh called it *nantgallon*, while the Saxons named it *galabroc*. This is modern Walbrook, near London. According to Geoffrey's story, the Romans were defeated and then decapitated, their heads thrown into a nearby stream by the victorious British chieftain. Such an episode is unknown in the native legend and Roman records.

However, it has found some support with archaeological evidence. In the 1860s, General Pitt-Rivers discovered a large number of skulls in the stream near Walbrook, with few complementary bodies.[15] The excavation was roughly approximated to the century that Geoffrey located his battle. This find may well be coincidence and luck on the part of Geoffrey, and the silence of more recent authors seems to indicate this conclusion. It is, however, also possible that Geoffrey accessed a now lost source here.

The story of how Stonehenge was built with Irish stones from Mount Killaurus seems also to hold some kernel of truth. Apart from the obvious error of locating the stone's origins in Ireland, this tale strongly resembles the current historical theory held by archaeologists and geologists that the structure was built of bluestones carried over the Bristol Sea and from an original site in the Prescelly mountains.[16] Such a story, so near the facts, could only have been the result of Geoffrey's access to an oral source of great antiquity. Geoffrey would then have molded this source to fit his own artistic needs, as was his habit. It would seem that Geoffrey's only misstep was in placing the story in the time of Merlin. He can be seen to have done so for several non-historical but one politically astute reason. In Welsh lore Merlin was the only person whose résumé could accommodate the performance of the transport. Merlin was also one of his favorite subjects. Finally, the timing of the feat seems to be very important. By putting the feat in the post–Roman era, and assigning the task to Merlin after he had established his subject's intense Christianity, he was attempting to make Stonehenge look vaguely Christian. More importantly, if the monument was formed by a Christian, that meant that credit for the accomplishment did not belong to the non–Christians.[17]

Other similarly intriguing pieces of knowledge appear dotting the epic as well, adding to the mystery about the materials Geoffrey may have used. Arthur's coronation takes place on Whitsuntide, a religious holiday in Geoffrey's time but not in the fifth century.[18] Tintagel was not used as a fortress for four hundred years prior to his book,[19] yet it is the chief stronghold of Gorlois the Duke of Cornwall and the home of Arthur's mother. Tintagel is well-known now as the chief archaeological source for pottery of Late and post–Roman Britain and must have been a prominent political site during this period.[20] However, given the information generally available ca. 1130, no person should have been aware of that without access to some accurate and ancient historical or pseudo-historical source material. On the other hand, Gorlois is unknown outside of Geoffrey and those sources directly dependent upon him. Likely he was not a historical figure. Again, it would appear that he took historical facts and added color as he saw fit. He knew that Tintagel had been active back then and needed to locate the story of Arthur's conception.

As the above evidence demonstrates, Geoffrey had access to many known sources, and possibly to others of which we may now only guess. He gives the reader enough information that can be verified to at least hint he had access to more. For this reason he presents a tempting history of fifth-century Britain. In the past, his work quickly gained some sanctity among those who wrote about the Arthurian world because of his tantalizing manner of presentation. However, as has been seen, Geoffrey's ethics concerning the truthfulness of his narrative were very flexible. If a local legend could be bent to his own personal taste, he did so with no apology or hesitation. His adaptability and ruthlessness as a storyteller make him a dangerous source for fifth- and sixth-century British history.

Geoffrey used historical and pseudo-historical source material such as the *Historia Brittonum* and *De Excidio Britanniae*, and possibly one or more much older sources in order to ingratiate himself with the more politically influential of his acquaintances. However, he also wrote for ecclesiastical advancement. Indeed, Geoffrey is known to have been promoted to the station of bishop of St. Asaph only a few years after he completed his most famous manuscript.

This motivation shows through in additional and more contemporary influences on the geography of Galfridic Britain. There are two themes in particular that recur throughout the Arthurian narrative, and indeed throughout the work. First, it is clear that Geoffrey attempted to curry royal and noble favor. He rewrote his preface several times in the face of changing political climates to adjust his stance. In all of them he thanked Walter, archdeacon of Oxford, for his source. He then gave three separate dedications: to Robert of Gloucester, to Robert again and also Walerin de Beaumont, and finally to King Stephen and Robert. Other details in the manuscripts indicate that these were written at different times and, again, as the political climate at court altered.

In addition, his attempts to flatter potential allies in the court may be found in the body of the manuscript, with somewhat more subtlety. Gloucester is named on several occasions and was the property of his chief patron, Robert.[21] Leicester is inserted as *Legecestria*, and was the property of the father and brother of Walerin of Beaumont, another patron.[22] Geoffrey had stayed in Oxford, *Oxenfordie*, during much of his research. This was a royal Beaumont palace after 1130.[23] *Caer Guerec* stands for Warwick, the earldom of Roger de Newburgh, whose father was a close friend of Henry I and therefore a potential confidant.[24] His central geographical site is Winchester, home of Arthur's court. The bishop there from 1129 to 1171 was Henry of Blois, nephew to Henry I.

A second very clear theme that emerges is that of his religious stance, and his knowledge of the state of the church in England. As was mentioned above, Geoffrey would eventually be granted a bishopric, and this book is likely to have been the key reason why he was given the position. To begin with, he several times mentions the archbishopric of *Durobernia*, Canterbury. Yet he never calls it a religious see. The omission was intended to be an insult. During the period in which Geoffrey wrote, William de Corbeuil was the man in charge of this bishopric. He was a weak and altogether inferior holy man who did much to weaken the prestige his bishopric had been building since its founding. Juxtaposed against his antagonism, Geoffrey flattered the bishoprics of two rising religious men, Alexander of Lincoln and Henry of Winchester, brother of King Stephen. The cities in which they were based are named in prominent roles in Geoffrey's version of Arthur's rule.[25] The contrast of Canterbury's impotence with their significance was intended to make his flattery even more effective.

In addition, Geoffrey seems to have chosen sites solely because they were in the news, so to speak, in church affairs. Bath,[26] Moray,[27] and the Orkneys[28] were all recently made bishoprics when Geoffrey was writing. They are all mentioned several times in the narrative.

Geoffrey's geography for Arthur's rule demonstrates a strong awareness of the political and religio-political environment of twelfth-century Britain. As Britain's twelfth-century interests occupied the whole of the island, so Arthur's activities are made to encompass all of Britain. For this reason, Arthur's battles, allies, and enemies are roughly but haphazardly spread throughout most of Britain. He fights battles in Glasgow, Yorkshire, and Somerset and has allies from Wales and Brittany. This is because the political and religious geography of the early twelfth century in Britain focused on these regions, and Geoffrey had a keen eye for inserting political sites into his story. This was likely an easier task than might be expected, since all evidence would indicate that pre–Galfridic geography was vague and extremely malleable to local conditions.

Geoffrey's choice of locations reveals the political web he was in and the chief purpose for his decision to write *Historia Regum Britanniae*. Geoffrey's primary motivation was ecclesiastical gain through the royal house. His method of currying the necessary favor was to put his patrons' and potential patrons' activities into the life of Britain's most famous hero. *Historia Regum Britanniae was* largely intended as a literary and artistic interpretation of Britain in the early years of the twelfth century. This was made evident in Dr. Tatlock's detailed study of Geoffrey's geography.

There are no verifiable facts that prove Geoffrey definitely had access to knowledge of Arthur's region of activity, and there is much to argue against it. Again, Geoffrey's special knack was in taking knowledge and altering it to fit the particular needs of a passage or chapter and the interests of a particular individual or group. *Historia Regum Britanniae* is a wondrous culmination of this talent. Because of the task he had set himself and the means with which he accomplished it, Geoffrey had no need for the correct historical information on his subjects. All Geoffrey wanted was old British and English personal and place-names and enough pseudo-historical information to make his story look accurate.

This said, and it being established that the manner in which Geoffrey associates Arthur to locations is quite random, one may take a more educated look at his geography. It is interesting that Geoffrey's Arthur does seem to have a faint predilection with southeastern Cornwall and Somerset. Several of his main subject's life experiences occur in these regions; he is born here and dies near the river Camblam-Camel. He wins his most important victory at Badon-Bath. As was stated at the outset, in these cases Geoffrey is simply making educated guesses, while Tintagel must remain a mysterious connection.[29] However, chance has located them all in a fairly small area.

CHAPTER 11

Arthur, the *Vitae* and Glastonbury Abbey

As influential as Geoffrey was, he was not the only significant factor to Arthurian geography. In 1066, William the Conqueror won the Battle of Hastings and began his consolidation of England. This act set in motion a series of events that would not only change the political foundations of England, but also would threaten to reshape the religious hierarchy in the British regions of what is now Great Britain. In response to this movement, the next century would see many religious houses throughout England and Wales begin to collate local legends involving the most famous holy men associated with their monasteries. They then hired professional biographers to write *vitae*, or lives of those saints.[1] The rewriting of their houses' history was designed to show that the most important people of each monastery had received God's special favor. By extension, this implied that the favor of the saints had been passed on to the houses they had been a part of.

The *vitae* allowed the religious house to reestablish and in some cases to extend any religious prestige it may have previously enjoyed and which was now threatened by the Norman conquerors. In addition, the abbots of these institutions hoped that they might gain greater power, prestige, and land in this period of instability and uncertainty. One might make a comparison to a classroom that has just learned that its substitute teacher will be in charge of the class from that point on. The class tries to convince the teacher that the rules of the classroom were slightly less stringent than they actually were. A good story might not be convincing, but nothing is to be lost in the attempt. If it is able to find some complementary evidence or create a believable facsimile all the better. Many monasteries took part in this movement, and a *vita* was made for most major Welsh and Cornish saints between 1067 and Geoffrey's publication of *Historia Regum Britanniae* in the 1130s. With the saints' lives as well as the legal documents that were attached to them, they were able to reestablish their place under the new Norman rule almost immediately.

A *vita* was simple enough to write. First, its chief saint or saints was shown to be superior to all contemporary secular and ecclesiastical powers. This was often done by putting him in situations where he was confronted by but managed to outwit the local king or be given some sign of his unique worth to God. Together, episodes such as these would serve to establish the saint's superiority over other religious leaders. Greater holiness then gave that saint's monastery a higher level of religious importance in the readers' eyes and made the bones of the saint more holy. The monastery could then cash in on the additional pilgrims who would come to see the bones and witness the monastery. These pilgrims would make more contributions which would also serve to raise both the economic and religious status of the monastery.

After establishing how important the monastery was through its most famous individuals, it needed to give evidence that all land it had a questionable claim over had been given to one of its saints by a ruler who had been his contemporary. This was rationalized by having their saint defeat or otherwise outwit him first (above). The gift then became an apology for whatever transgression he might have attempted and a means of averting any further miracles that might be undertaken by the saint at his expense.

Back in the twelfth century, the religious house associated with the saint would then claim they allegedly donated land by right of royal donation in the sixth century.[2] In such a way not only was a religious house able to maintain the control it had already accumulated throughout the transition from English to Norman rulers, but in some cases it was able to gain prestige and additional territories.[3]

This, then, is the bias of the *vitae*. One may not generally trust the personalities that are portrayed therein because the manner in which they are presented was designed for a specific purpose. Nor may one be certain of interactions, chronologies,[4] or events. There were many common and obvious reasons for a hagiographer to manipulate them to put the saint in a better light, or to put him in opposition to a particularly powerful king. On the other hand, to make these stories' details believable they were nearly always based on an oral tradition. It has been thoroughly established that the *vitae* do represent traditional oral material and therefore that it may be possible to cull historical material from them. This is only true, however, when the material does not directly conflict with the purpose of the *vitae*.[5]

Arthur is present in eight *vitae*, and is in all cases employed for the above listed reasons. His presence in the various stories allows the saints to claim prestige, and his gifts would have given the eleventh- and twelfth-century monasteries involved the land that they had claimed. However, as the *vitae* are based on traditional material they may also be used to help determine Arthur's whereabouts. In the examples below I will attempt to determine Arthurian geography through the use of the *vitae*. The *vitae* in which Arthur participates have been arranged in chronological order, with approximate year of publication, location of the episode, and land donated.

Vita Goeznau (c. 1019)

The saint is born in Brittany during the time when Arthur ruled Britain (c. 500).

Lifris' *Vita Cadoci* (1081–1104)

Arthur is seen twice here. The first occasion is in the prologue, and the hero is yet unborn. Gwynlliw, king of Glywising, has abducted Gwladus, daughter of Brychan, and is carrying her past a hill where Arthur, Cei, and Bedwyr are playing draughts. The three notice Gwynlliw and Gwladus with Brychan in pursuit. Arthur suggests they beat off both parties and take Gwladus themselves. Curiously, his out of character proposal is chastised by his companions. Instead, the three arrange a settlement between Gwynlliw, Gwladus, and Brychan.

In the second instance, Cadoc is full-grown and resides at a monastery in Glywising. Here a man who has killed three of Arthur's soldiers takes sanctuary. Eventually Arthur finds him and coyly accepts the request made by the saint for the right to give asylum. In return he demands one hundred cows, with the unusual stipulation that they be red in front and white in back. If he is truly a holy man, Arthur reasons, this will not prove a difficulty and he will be forced to keep his word. When the saint is unable to comply, however, he will have an excuse to violate sanctuary. Arthur is made to look the fool when his demand is met, and then later the cows turn to bundles of fern. Intimidated, Arthur grants that any refugee who might find his way to Cadoc's monastery will be given permanent refuge there.

Vita Carantoci (1093–1135)

Here Arthur is attempting to locate and defeat a serpent that has been plaguing the countryside. He runs into the saint and begs that he pray for God's assistance. Meanwhile, St. Carantoc had been directed by God to throw an altar into the Severn River and build a church wherever it beaches. Carantoc banishes the serpent for Arthur in return for the land surrounding the place the altar ends up. Thereupon he is again instructed by God to throw the altar into the Severn, and when Arthur finds it he again grants him the land around which it is found.

Caradoc's *Vita Cadoci* (1120s–1130s)

Cadoc's only scene involving Arthur is an episode where a soldier who has killed three of his soldiers is seeking asylum and Arthur demands one hundred cows in recompense. He suffers the same fate as in Lifris' version. However, Caradoc adds that, along with the tricks of the saint himself, an angel in a dream convinces Arthur to give up any thoughts of taking vengeance on Cadoc.

Caradoc's *Vita Gildae* (1120s–1130s)

Arthur here appears in two tales. In the first episode, Hueil is raiding from a Scottish base when Arthur kills him. Gildas absolves him of the crime. The second instance of Arthur's appearance is a British version of the famous story *Le Chevalier de la Charrette*, here placed in Glastonbury. Melvas has abducted the queen and taken her to Somerset. Arthur searched all of Britain for her, has found them both, and now threatens war unless his queen is restored to him. Gildas acts as an arbitrator between Arthur and Melvas. He manages to return the queen and protect Melvas from Arthur's wrath. In return, both kings agree to give Glastonbury a vague but large amount of lands.

Vita Illtuti (1120s–1130s)

While a soldier, Illtud goes to Arthur's court and gains fame. Both location and time spent here are vague.

Vita Paterni (1120s–1130s)

While residing in Ceredigion, the saint is visited by Arthur. The king admires and then requests the saint's tunic and is willing to pay handsomely for it. However, Paternus has no wish to part with it. Displeased at his rejection, Arthur returns to force the saint to hand over his tunic. At a word from Paternus, the Earth opens up and swallows Arthur. The king is then made to beg the saint's pardon and takes Paternus as his eternal patron.

Vita Euflami (+1135)

In this episode, taking place in Brittany, Arthur is fighting a monster and breaks off combat at dusk. Accidentally crossing the saint's path, he requests water of him. Through a miracle he is given it, and the next morning the saint himself defeats the monster. The land surrounding the area of the miracle is granted to the saint.

Arthur is mentioned in eight *vitae* and ten episodes, which makes him a uniquely popular king in Celtic hagiography.[6] In them, he is made to be associated with Cumberland, Brittany, Glamorgan, Somerset,[7] and Ceredigion (see figure below). This widespread location for Arthur is quite similar to the earliest literary evidence from other sources. Again, there is much evidence to show that Arthur quickly became a figure of the entire British people.

REGION OF ACTIVITY

Lifris' *Vita Cadoci*	Glamorgan
Caradoc's *Vita Cadoci*	Glamorgan
Caradoc's *Vita Gildae*	Cumberland and Glastonbury
Vita Illtuti	Not Given
Vita Paterni	Ceredigion
Vita Carantoci	Somerset
Vita Euflami	Brittany
Vita Goeznau	Britain

In addition, it should be noted again that the religious literary movement between the Battle of Hastings and the completion of *Historia Regum Britanniae* affected only Wales, England, and Brittany.[8] To my knowledge there are only three *vitae* for the Scottish saints and none for those of northern England. This indicates a distinct underrepresentation for these regions, and a clear and undebatable reason why the northern regions are not noted with the same degree of regularity as those areas more commonly associated with Arthur. For the current study, this negative evidence from northern England and Scotland also insinuates that the *vitae* are not a useful tool in the search for Arthur's location.[9] As the *vitae* were a product of Norman-controlled Wales, England, and Brittany, naturally those *vitae* that mention Arthur will locate him in these places. There would have been no reason for those areas that had long been Norman or which continued to be independent of the Normans to have written the saints' lives at this time. Further, there would have been little material to work with in any territory that had been under English control for so long that its oral memories had disappeared as it forgot the British language and became English speaking.

The *vitae* are late enough that another factor becomes possible: that Arthur had already become a fully developed pan–British figure. Because he was not confined to any one area, a monastery could plausibly bring him into its history. There was and remains no historical source which explicitly places him in any one area of Britain, and likely the situation was just as vague by the twelfth century.

This assumption was certainly accurate with regards to Glastonbury. The region surrounding it had been British until perhaps two centuries before it hired Caradoc of Llancarfan to write its *Vita Gildae* mentioning Gildas. Of all the ecclesiastic centers that would add Arthur into their traditions, this monastery was by far the most influential. To do so, it would put much more of its resources into creating literature that associated it with being the earliest English Christian site and having attracted some of the most prominent churchmen. A great deal of time and effort would be allotted to make it look as though Arthur had spent his career in the vicinity, much more than any other monastery of the period would manage. The result would be that the abbots here would promulgate an Arthurian legend of such strength and substance that it continues to hold many scholars' interest to this day.

The realities are much different. Glastonbury's origins are mysterious. There is archaeological evidence that Glastonbury Tor was inhabited in the fifth or sixth centuries. The occupation of the settlers, though, is of an ambiguous nature; the settlement may have been anything from a small secular group to a precursor of the modern abbey.[10] The textual remains are no more helpful. They allow only for a religious site beginning in the mid– to late-seventh century,[11] so that any claim that the remains in the Tor are those of monks must remain, at best, unproven.[12]

To be optimistic, the monastery's records for the next few hundred years are sketchy. They include visits from a number of unlikely personalities that are otherwise unsubstantiated. The materials become clear again in the ninth century. It is known that Wessex kings were regular contributors up to around 860,[13] that Mercian kings also made donations between 716 and 821,[14] and that between 860 and 939 there was a single grant of land.[15] In the reign of Edmund, Glastonbury quickly gained favor with the rise of a Wulfric in royal esteem. This Wulfric was brother to the Glastonbury abbot, Dunstan, and helped influence the king into again supporting the monastery. The royal favor continued with the next few kings, and ended abruptly with Edmund Ironside and Cnut. At this point the monastery stagnated and began to sink into oblivion.

This history, of fortunes and reversals entirely outside of its control, is quite common when dealing with religious houses; they may rise or fall with changing political climates or even with the personalities of different abbots. However, something of interest happened between the years following 939 and the time of the Domesday Book, when Glastonbury's holdings were second only to Canterbury. A little over a two centuries after that, in 1300, this religious nothing had been transformed into the most powerful monastery in all of Britain. Glastonbury's medieval renovation is nothing less than a meteoric improvement in prestige. Needless to say that it was highly unusual. Certainly the *vita* craze alone cannot account for Glastonbury's changed state, so some other explanation must be found. Understanding why will be the focus of the remainder of this chapter. The answers to be found will explain several aspects of Arthur's geography and its strong literary predilection for the southwest. The investigation will begin with a brief history of Glastonbury's activities during this period, and a documentation of its long habit of forging documents to give it greater antiquity and therefore more enhanced religious prestige.

Several instances lead the observer to hypothesize a potential connection between Glastonbury Abbey and the reason why Arthurian geography tends to focus on the southwest. Sometime after 1120, Glastonbury claimed that St. Patrick was the abbey's first leader, though Patrick's writings would attest to the contrary. In his *Confessio*, the Irish patron saint made clear that he never returned to Britain after spending his childhood in northern Britain, being kidnapped, escaping and being educated as a religious man, and returning to Ireland. Already established as the nominal leader of Christianity in Ireland, he directly states that he had never served as an abbot anywhere in Britain.

Caradoc of Llancarfan (c. 1130) placed Gildas in Glastonbury as a recluse in his version of the *Vita Gildae*, but no independent record or tradition of his presence there exists.[16] In fact, if the other details that Caradoc supplies are true, it seems highly unlikely. Gildas' birth in Strathclyde and his relationship with two Pictish kings are but two examples of many that demonstrate the *vita*'s liberal and at times radical interpretations of history.

Glastonbury was exceptional in its creativity, and was in no way bound by the facts in that regard. It would use a British hero to increase its prestige. In about 1130, it dared to declare it had once been visited by the great British hero Arthur.[17] Through this, the seed was planted and the basic tradition soon adopted that Arthur had established his capital and spent most of his career in that region. The connection was fortified when Geoffrey of Monmouth published his *Historia Regum Britanniae* in the late 1130s, and Geoffrey happened to locate many of Arthur's life occurrences in the area.[18] Within a century of Geoffrey's work, the historical record becomes inundated with a large number of Arthurian sites in the Somerset area.

This process was only accentuated by Glastonbury itself and its economic needs. When a severe fire brought the abbey into financial straits around 1191, the next step was taken. The tomb of Arthur and Guinevere was soon "discovered." King Henry II funded the project and helped verify the royal couple's remains by sending several respected members of the royal court to visit and observe the exhumation. They stood as witnesses while the ancient tomb was opened and the supposed bodies of Arthur and Guinevere rapidly crumbled to dust in the atmosphere.

In this project the monks of Glastonbury were again the happy recipients of good fortune, and perhaps even the willing accessory of a king. Under normal circumstances, an English king would have had no interest in disinterring a British king. However, the situation in this period was an unusual one. King

Henry II had been fighting the Welsh for some time by the 1190s, without much success. It is quite probable that he knew something of the legend surrounding Arthur.[19] What is more important, he had probably been made to understand that the legend of Arthur's return in the time of the Welsh's greatest need was a widely held belief among the Welsh. He would have known that many Welshmen were clinging to this legend as they fought the English. It served as a source of hope to them. To prove that Arthur was dead would have ended those beliefs made his enemies less entrenched. For Henry, the exhumation of the long-awaited Welsh savior was designed to lower British resistance and hasten his conquest of Wales. He was most happy to support a project to uncover this sleeping king and to reward the monks who did him this service. It is possible though in no way provable that he sent believable people to the site as observers to give the exhumation as much authenticity as was possible.

Henry's successors were also pleased to authenticate the event of the opening of the tomb. It served much the same purpose for them and against the troublesome Welsh as it had for Henry. Thus the fragile and manufactured connection of Glastonbury to Arthur was one that was given support by both a religious establishment and the royal family. This dual agreement and active persistence is the reason why the tie of Arthur to the southwest survived in the face of Welsh and northern claims. This is the reason the post–Galfridic Arthur has been so consistently associated with Cornwall and Somerset in an unusually large amount of the literature.

With the tradition established, it began to grow. At least some of the *Perlesvaus* material was taken from Glastonbury, and it places Arthur in the Somerset region. Soon, the evidence indicates that local folklore began to emerge to rival Wales, among them South Cadbury's insistence that it held what had once been Camelot. An overwhelming number of sites in southwestern England have Arthurian traditions, though of course it is rare that any of these connections emerge until centuries after *Historia Regum Britanniae*'s publication.[20] The coincidence between Glastonbury, Geoffrey, and this phenomenon is too striking to be chalked up to chance.[21] One can only assume that once Glastonbury had established itself as an Arthurian site, legends were drawn toward the area.[22] The extant information agrees with this conclusion; Somerset has no legitimate pre–Galfridic legends that can be distinguished from this influence, and Cornwall's place-name evidence is equally unconvincing.[23] In fact, there is no record in the Ninnius compilation, Gildas, or any of the meager pre-tenth century literature that locates Arthur in the south of Britain.

Despite its relative chronology, the southwest certainly has a large number of place-name evidence and local legends. However, Scotland, Wales, and

Brittany have their share of sites as well. The reasons that the southwest became the more popular choice for Arthur's region of activity were Geoffrey of Monmouth and Glastonbury's claims. Geoffrey gave specific locations to a popular British hero who had before then been given only vague geographical connotations. As a result, he gave the British people something physical to cling to, and they embraced it. His reputation only strengthened the validity of his associations for the medieval mind.

Glastonbury made full use of the fortuitous southwest connections to be found in *Historia Regum Britanniae.* In the face of overwhelmingly contradictory evidence, the monastery at Glastonbury has insisted it contains Arthur's remains throughout the centuries. And, because of a political landscape that occurred in a reign over eight hundred years ago, Glastonbury obtained the seal of authenticity from the royal house of England that Arthur was from the southwest.

Geoffrey, Glastonbury, and the resulting local legends have somehow melded together so that it has seemed somehow authentic for the modern scholar; the fact is that it is not. As will be seen, many of the Arthurian romances may be otherwise shown to have been heavily influenced by Glastonbury. If a piece of literature locates Arthur specifically in Somerset or Cornwall, it is simply a clue that this source may have been influenced by Glastonbury. Most probably, it is not evidence that Arthur was from the area.

CHAPTER 12

Arthur's Geography in the Pre-Galfridic Tradition

The previous chapters have demonstrated that *Historia Regum Britanniae* marks a turning point in the perception of the geography of Arthur's Britain. After this landmark book of British history and under Glastonbury's careful and steady influence, a good portion of the literature pertaining to Arthur began to place him in the southwest. Although other places in Britain and Brittany would be named as his capital or the location of one of his more important accomplishments, after Geoffrey he became a figure more and more associated with Cornwall and Somerset.

And these alternative sites would often not stem from any traditional sources. Much of what is extant was determined according to the individual or political motivations of the authors or patrons who treated the subject of King Arthur. The works that were composed before Geoffrey, Glastonbury, and the involvement of English-Welsh politics in the literature of Arthur are therefore the more reliable in determining Arthur's geographical location.[1] Because of their superior credibility, they will compose the primary point of reference throughout the second part of the volume. Specifically, the next four chapters will consist of a thorough survey of Arthur and his earliest companions in the pre–Galfridic sources.

The most important element in this endeavor will be the definition of a pre–Galfridic source and the procedure for defining a member of this group. The most obvious tool is the date of an individual Welsh work, but where determining whether or not a poem or story preceded Geoffrey of Monmouth it is unhelpful. Modern Welsh scholarship has been able to date most of the Arthurian British literature only to "before 1150,"[2] while Geoffrey published in the 1130s. This leaves a dispiriting twenty-year window in which almost all

Welsh Arthurian literature may fall. Few Welsh works can be safely called pre–Galfridic purely on the basis of date of publication.

A second method is more productive, but highly tedious and may often be misleading. This is the process of finding Geoffrey's influences in the content in question. His inspiration might include place-names, Latinized Welsh, or any direct knowledge of the unique plot or nontraditional characters to be found in *Historia Regum Britanniae*. That evidence may be supplemented by a work's method of presentation; something that claims to be the work of Taliesin has a good chance of being rich in Welsh tradition, while anything with elements of the French romances has most likely been influenced by Geoffrey and his romantic and historical successors. This painstaking process is not always that accurate even if carefully done. The human psyche is intriguing in that it is unsatisfied with incomplete knowledge on a topic of interest. It will happily accept and stubbornly cling to any knowledge that completes its understanding of a subject, even if that knowledge can be proven to be incorrect. The results of any study along these lines, therefore, cannot be objective by their very nature. That said, this method is the more accurate of the two, and it is likely to give a fairly strong indication of any geographical preferences in the literature.

In the next few pages, each of the pre–Galfridic Welsh sources will be presented separately but within the categories of ninth-century materials, pre–Galfridic works immediately preceding the history, and *Trioedd Ynys Prydein*. In each case, the locations which that source associates with Arthur will be identified and examined for nontraditional influences. This procedure will be employed with all literature labeled pre–1150 and before. However, *Culhwch ac Olwen* and the *vitae* will not be evaluated here, as the forms of literature they represent pose unique difficulties. They are dealt with in Chapters 10 and 13, respectively.

Probably the first extant work that mentions Arthur is *Y Gododdin*. Tradition has it that this poem or collection of poems was originally composed around 600 or earlier by a poet named Neirin. It was written to commemorate the deaths of many warriors of a Lothian *teulu*, as well as mercenaries from around Britain who had died at the Battle of Catraeth.[3] Because of its context and the viewpoint of the stanzas, it was probably first created in Lothian. Within the poem there is a stanza that commemorates the Strathclydian participants in the Battle of Strathcarron. The stanza, by its orthography and context composed later than the main poem, indicates that *Y Gododdin* was transferred to Strathclyde at some time after it was formed. The level of decay to be found especially in B1 and A78 indicate that the entire composition was in oral form for an extended period. The manuscript history of the extant copies as well as several internal indicators demonstrate that the poem was brought south to Gwynedd at a later time in two forms, orally (B), and in written form (A).[4]

In the elegies, Arthur is mentioned in Stanza B38. He is made the standard of martial excellence by which the warrior Gorður is compared. The Arthur in question could be none other than the British hero, so the nature of this excerpt is of prime importance for Arthurian studies. Unfortunately, this stanza's age has traditionally been viewed with skepticism. Most recently, Professor Koch has reviewed its orthography in his edition, translation, and historical recreation of the British classic *Y Gododdin*, and has determined that it was probably written before 638.[5] If Professor Koch is correct, this means that Arthur was a legendary warrior among the Lothians. Even if his dating is inaccurate and the Arthur elegy belongs with the Strathcarron material or slightly later, it suggests that Arthur was a renowned and long-dead northern hero before by the seventh century.

Next in order of age is the *Historia Brittonum*, which contains a northern section. Among the many references to northern persons, Arthur himself is mentioned. It is frustrating that he is named in only one place—Chapter 56 is devoted entirely to him. The pseudo-historical chapter consists mainly of a list of battles Arthur is said to have won against the Saxons. Many of them have proven to be unlocatable to even the best linguists, Kenneth Jackson especially. However, several have been widely agreed upon. Linnuis, where the second, third, and fourth battles were fought, could possibly be located in Lincolnshire.[6] The seventh battle, Cat Coit Celidon, translates to the "Forest of Caledonia," or Scotland. The ninth battle, at the City of the Legion, has been traditionally placed in York or Caerleon. Tribruit, battle number ten, has been tentatively sited in the north.[7] The eleventh battle, Mount Agned, is possibly in Edinburgh.

It has often been suggested, with good reason, that many or all of these battles were not originally fought by Arthur.[8] In light of the oral nature of fifth century history and his already proven ability to gravitate important people to his cycle of stories, attracting famous events as well seems more than plausible. However, it is of note that most of the locatable battles belong to *Y Hen Ogled*.[9] And, since the nature of drawing people to an orbit inevitably brings those which were closest in time and geography first, it stands to reason that the north was Arthur's area of political influence during his lifetime.

Additionally, the *Mirabilia* which are appended to *Historia Brittonum* also contains one reference to his son and one to his dog. These latter two passages do not concern the reader here, however, because they refer to the developing literary figure of Arthur. Here his character is already being associated with the supernatural.

Following *Historia Brittonum* chronologically are the collection of dates

THE BIAS OF *HISTORIA BRITTONUM*. The areas of interest for the *Historia Brittonum*, shown in black, illustrate the regions where post–Roman segments are known to have been formed or stored. It shows that Gwynedd and England to its west and north up to the Scottish border were of interest.

and events known as *Annales Cambriae*. The *Welsh Annals* were formed from a ninth-century *Northern Chronicle* which would have been taken from a *Northern Memorandum* of the eighth century (or earlier),[10] which itself would have been first put in written form well after the events of the fifth and sixth centuries which the annals record. However, *Annales Cambriae* was only written down sometime in the tenth century, which is why it is listed after the *Historia Brittonum*. The source names Arthur twice, in 516 and again in 537 or 539. In the first instance, the event associated with Arthur is the Battle of Badon. The site of this battle has proven difficult to locate, though guesses have focused on the southwest based on its mention by an assumed southern Gildas and the place-name itself.[11]

The second battle, Camlann, is more easily locatable. The final battle of Arthur has tentatively though routinely been linked to the Roman fort Camboglanna (Birdoswald) over the last half-century. The Camlann entry is the last historical or pseudohistorical record of Arthur.

Below is a table of all the above discussed sources, with a list of all sites in these sources and their geographical location. The level of probability that these locations are the correct ones and that the sites do belong to a historical Arthur have been quantified into the subjective categories of probable, possible, and uncertain.

Source	Site	*Y Hen Ogled*	Wales	England	Cornwall
Y Gododdin	Lothian/Strathclyde	Probable			
Historia Brittonum	Linnuis			Uncertain	
	Cat Coit Celidon	Probable			
	Urbes Legionis		Possible	Possible	
	Tribruit		Possible		
	Mount Agned	Probable			
Annales Cambriae	Mount Badon			Uncertain	
	Camlann	Probable			

This is the extent of the historical and pseudo-historical materials which name Arthur. In addition, there are several pieces from the same rough period. These other sources also possess a heroic age philosophy, though these materials are in a literary form. The first to be discussed here is *Pa Gur?*, the literary work with the most heroic age features. *Pa Gur?* will be followed by the Arthurian poems in the *Book of Taliesin*, "Gereint Filius Erbin," "Ymddiddan Gwenhwyfar ac Arthur," and finally *Trioedd Ynys Prydein*.

Pa Gur? is named for the first two words in its first line, which translates to "What man?" The piece is to be found in the *Black Book of Carmarthen*. It has no obvious Galfridic influences; there is no sign of chivalry in the words nor is Arthur looked upon as a great king. The place-names are entirely foreign. *Pa Gur?*'s date of origin is unknown but has usually been placed in the category before 1150. Internal evidence makes it likely the work is at least two centuries older than this.[12] The piece begins as a dialogue; Arthur is trying to gain entry to another king's hill-fort for himself and his *teulu*. The lord's porter, Glewlwyd, denies them, insisting that Arthur tell of his own worthiness and the fame of his band in order to earn the privilege. Arthur obliges him, assigning stories and abilities to the members of his group. As he continues, the piece quickly becomes an antiquarian catalogue of various events and individuals. It is here where three Arthurian place-names are given—Afarnach's home, Disethach, and Eidyn. Of these, only Eidyn may be safely located, in Edinburgh.[13] Afarnach may be a Welsh figure based on his inclusion in *Culhwch ac Olwen*, and Disethach is entirely unknown.[14] *Pa gur?* was composed by an antiquarian; it contains lists of British names that probably no longer had any geographical reality by the time the piece was put to parchment.

The next Arthurian works, the poems found in the *Book of Taliesin*, have an entirely different history. These poems all claim to have been written by the sixth-century poet Taliesin. During his career, this well-traveled bard was patronized in turn by Cynan Garwyn, Urien of Rheged, and at one point Gwallog of Elmet. Twelve of his poems are still extant. If they were written by Taliesin, and several generations of scholars have found no reason to dispute that finding,[15] then there lies within them a knowledge and understanding of the period which well exceeds that to be found in any other source. From what has been learned in studying them, Taliesin likely lived within three generations from Arthur, making him that much more tantalizing as a source of information. It is unfortunate that none of these poems make any mention of Arthur or his *teulu* by way of praise or allusion. Along with these probably original Taliesin works, however, several more pseudo–Taliesin poems also exist in the same collection, among them the Arthurian work *Preiddeu Annwn*. This, as was discovered in *Origins of Arthurian Romances*, is a piece with a great deal of traditional knowledge.[16]

Taliesin is a unique figure in British culture. For some reason that is not made clear in the extant literature or historical records, by the ninth century he had been singled out as exemplifying all those mystical powers associated with bards. As a result, he was assigned the abilities of travel through time and space, a superhuman familiarity with nature, the *awen*, and the otherworld. Because of his extraordinary qualities, no subject and no time period was considered beyond the body of his knowledge. In the extant pseudo–Taliesin poems, he speaks as though he has been to the most distant times and places with a familiarity and knowledge of detail that is convincing.

The internal evidence suggests that these poems were composed by later bards, however. Most probably, the individuals responsible for these extant writings were using what may have been traditional knowledge and employing Taliesin's voice in order to raise the prestige of their weakening profession. As the *vitae* had done for monasteries, taking one of their number and making him appear to have supernatural abilities may have been designed to give all bards more esteem in the public eye.

The evidence for this conclusion is quite simple to interpret, and again comes directly from the poems themselves. In *Preiddeu Annwn*, the poet spends the entire final stanza belittling the clergy and daring them to retaliate with their supposedly superior powers. The Taliesin persona claims to have greater mystical and historical knowledge than any ecclesiastic, and he is daring them to prove otherwise. This is a consistent theme in the pseudo–Taliesin poems. As Dr. Haycock has pointed out, the poems may have been formed by court poets intent on stabilizing the bard's position in society in the face of the rising stature of the church orders.[17] Taliesin was simply their vehicle, a famous poet who had already been associated with the supernatural in traditions.

If the materials in the pseudo–Taliesin poems were from court poets of the eleventh or twelfth centuries, much of the material in the poems would have been based on traditional knowledge and educated speculation designed to create the image of an omniscient Taliesin. It is perhaps fortunate that the one poem that does name Arthur provides no geographical associations for Arthur.[18]

The poem "Gereint Filius Erbin" is by an anonymous clergyman and is to be found in the *Black Book of Carmarthen* and the *White Book of Rhydderch*. It is to be dated to before 1150, probably before 1100 and therefore anterior to Geoffrey. The chief figure in the poem is Gereint son of Erbin, who is possibly a composite figure.[19] He is named as fighting alongside Arthur. The poem has only two locations directly associated with it—Llongborth and Dyfneint. Llongborth could be a Cambrization of Longport, Somerset, as Professor Sims-Williams has argued.[20] Alternatively, it could be the rare word seaport, in which case Llongborth could indicate any port in Britain. However, if Gereint is a composite figure of several Cornish and Somerset figures, Llongborth most likely belongs there as well. The other place-name, Dyfneint, is the rough equivalent of modern Devon or Somerset. It seems to confirm a southwestern orientation.

Next in order of probable age is the misnamed *Ymddiddan Gwenhwyfar ac Arthur*, or *Dialogue between Gwenhwyfar and Arthur*. The piece exists in two manuscripts, one from the sixteenth and the other from the seventeenth century. Based on internal evidence, the common original dates to before 1150.[21]

Ymddiddan mainly involves a conversation between Gwenhwyfar and Melwas, though either Cei or Arthur also takes part. The dialogue centers around Melwas' attempts to convince Gwenhwyfar that he is a worthy lover. She refutes him by making comparison to Arthur's men and Cei in particular. The third character (likely Cei) is present in the traditional testing role of the gatekeeper.[22]

Beyond this *Ymddiddan* is unclear in its nature; the two extant versions to be are obviously very different at several key points. This only adds to the difficulty of finding a coherent theme or even an original intent for the passage. The author's previous book discussed the longstanding assumption that it may have something to do with Gwenhwyfar's abduction in the British tradition, or that the piece might have been a precursor to the story as found on the continent. The similarities in the characters involved (apart from the absence of Chrétien's probable addition, Lancelot) does support a superficial connection and suggests a deeper one. The large variance in content between it and later continental versions could be due to a garbled oral tradition or an innovative transmission from a common original manuscript. However, both versions have consistent characters, are directly related to Arthur, and possess the same one locatable place-name and personal name, Dyfneint and Geraint, respectively. The former may be equated with Somerset, while the latter belongs to either Somerset or Cornwall. If this version has been altered from an original that could have inspired the continental romances, it would have been at some point well before both manuscripts' common original.

There are three more significant Welsh documents that have been dated to before 1150: the genealogies and regnal lists, *Ymddiddan Arthur a'r Eryr* and *Englynion y Beddau*. By a general consensus these have all probably been influenced by Geoffrey. In each case, the arguments are straightforward and compelling and the author sees no need to go over them here; the works in question do not contain any relevant indications of geography, and so the point is moot anyway. This leaves the first three pieces of literature as useful for the targeted study. All the geographical locations that have been found in them are listed below.

Source	Site	*Y Hen Ogled*	Wales	Cornwall	England
Pa Gur?	Afarnach's home		Possible		
	Disethach				Uncertain
	Eidyn	Possible			
"Gereint ..."	Llongborth			Possible	
	Gereint				Probable
"Ymddiddan ..."	Dyfneint			Probable	

This second group is much less consistent than the first. The one site that may be associated with the Old North is so well-recognized as not to be trustworthy, and the presence of the Cornish sites may be due entirely to the association of the character Gereint with Arthur. This association is not one that is supported by other early sources. As has been suggested by the evidence, it seems reasonable that the legend of Arthur quickly spread to encompass all of Britain. As this happened, each region claimed him, including Cornwall.

Combined, the evidence presented here makes even the most tentative conclusion difficult.

The most substantial body of folkloric material surrounding the figure of Arthur is to be found in *Trioedd Ynys Prydein*. This work is composed of several collections of triads relating the abilities, achievements, and fabulous objects of many of the heroes and kings of the British people. The triads were first written in the eleventh or twelfth centuries.[23] However, certain details indicate the triads were a mnemonic device for bards[24] and therefore that they were significantly older than this. The early triads often name otherwise unknown figures of post–Roman British history,[25] suggesting ancient sources, or access to sources now lost.

Arthur is mentioned in the *Welsh Triads* with regularity. He is found in Triads 2, 12, 20, 26, 37(R), 51, 52, 53 (Peniarth 50), 54, 56, 57, 59, and 93, while a formula involving aspects of his court may be seen in Triads 9, 18 (VYR), 65, 73, 74, 85, 86, 87, and 88. Arthur himself is all that interests us here, so I will confine myself to the first list. The geographical associations are listed below by triad number.

Triad no.	Site	*Y Hen Ogled*	Wales	Cornwall	England
2	not given				
12	not given				
20	not given				
26	not given				
37(R)	London		Certain		
51	King of Britain				
52	Caer Oeth ac Anoeth	?	?	?	?
53	Camlann	Possible			
54	Celliwig		Certain		
56	not given				
57	not given				
59	Camlann	Possible			
93	not given				

It becomes clear that Arthur's location is not generally given a specific designation in *Trioedd Ynys Prydein*; apart from a unique instance involving the single most important port on the island he is not placed anywhere in the traditional materials to be found in triads 1–46. This reticence could mean one of three things. First, Arthur's region of activity may have been forgotten by medieval bards. In turn, this suggests he may have lived in an area that had been conquered early on by the Germanic culture group. Northumbria was gone by the early seventh century, while Lothian and Reged were conquered by people of Germanic culture in the seventh and eighth centuries. As was seen above, the British-named geographical locations of all these regions would have disappeared early on as the conquered people learned the language of their conquerors. Once the home of Arthur had forgotten its place-names as well as its culture and history, bards and imaginative peasants may well have reestablished him in more familiar areas closer to home.

Second, Arthur's location may have been so well known that his court had no need to be named or located. If this were so, his location may simply have been forgotten over the centuries and then widely reclaimed later on a popular level after the Galfridic explosion. The third option is that those Triads that place him and are extant, being much later than the first forty-six, were influenced by Geoffrey and have retained their inspiration's ideal of Arthur as a pan–British hero without any regionality.[26] In this case, his court could have been nonspecific in Welsh legend by the time Geoffrey wrote.[27] None of these suggestions are mutually exclusive to the other options.

This concludes the list of significant pre–Galfridic Welsh sources that have any allusions to Arthur's geography. Of the material, no clear favorite emerges as to where Arthur belongs. He is too evenly spread out over the island to even make a suggestion. Arthur is clearly a pan–British hero, which is the same conclusion that has been commonly deduced by any scholar who has gone beyond his historicity.

That said, the evidence shows that there is a slight majority of opinion that places him in the north. This realization is noteworthy. As the keepers of British knowledge were in Wales, Cornwall, and Brittany throughout the Middle Ages, it does seem strange that any northern tradition should have survived about Arthur. Its strength would have run contrary to the interests of these kingdoms. The fact that his connection to the north thrived in spite of very clear political interests to the contrary suggests there may be some truth in the convention. The chapters below will provide more reasons for understanding why this northern tradition, unassuming as it may be in the pre–Galfridic material, was able to persist through Arthur's many different incarnations through varying political and cultural atmospheres.

CHAPTER 13

Arthur's Men in the
Early Welsh Sources

The previous two chapters have shown that the material pertaining directly to Arthur possibly locates him in *Y Hen Ogled*, though the simplest solution is that he was a British hero shared by the entire culture group. This chapter will pursue the same objective of using the pre–Galfridic materials to determine his location. However, the method here will be different and less direct. The characters earliest and most closely associated with Arthur will be examined to better understand their geography.[1] This, in turn, should provide a wider perspective for the problems involved in Arthurian geography.

The study of the people with whom Arthur was earliest associated may seem at first glance to be a roundabout way of getting the same information that can be found through a direct examination of Arthur, but it is not. Whereas Arthur might have been intentionally put all over Britain, there would have been much less reason to do so with less popular heroes.

A careful examination of the Arthurian materials could have an additional advantage as well. The nature of the development of heroic age literature can potentially be used to trace Arthur's origins by tracing its progress in reverse. In a heroic age, one individual or *teulu* is often made the beneficiary of praise poetry by one or more professional entertainers. As the heroes of the stories and the entertainers who tell them die, much of it is lost. However, the surviving literature tends to go to another phase of development.

In time and under a precise set of circumstances, the poetry of praise and the memory of deeds done begin to coalesce into longer narratives in which the subject remains the centerpiece. As the literature continues to mature (or degrade depending on perspective) other heroes, from outside the original *teulu*, will be added to the story as secondary characters. It is the expansion of the cast of characters that is of interest here.

These heroes will enter into the orbit of the stories by a consistent pattern. Initially, characters from the same area and approximate era will be drawn in. With time, these heroes will come from an ever widening area and from an ever broader chronological era.[2] Such is most probably the case with Arthur and the literary personalities that had become a part of his court by the time Chrétien and the romance writers of the continent began to explore the Arthurian world.

The key, however, is the measurable growth of Arthur's orbit. Those heroes who were earliest and most consistently associated with Arthur are the most likely to have been from the same general region as Arthur.

This approach has certain benefits over a direct study of Arthur's associations. By the ninth century, Arthur himself was a pan–British hero. Geoffrey's pseudo-history would simply put that reality on paper. For the British people, that meant that legends and place-names throughout Britain were already associated with him by then. As has been seen, his wide-ranging popularity and the lengths that the local populations would go to in order to bring some piece of Arthur to them makes locating Arthur's original region of activity through a direct examination highly problematic. The only progress made after centuries of confusion has been to realize that no progress has been made.

Those heroes present in the earliest Arthurian sources, however, should not have suffered the same geographical dislocation as Arthur did. Hypothetically, their general point of origin should have remained reasonably static in the oldest sources even as they were absorbed into Arthur's orbit.[3] Because of their retention, it is feasible that their adventures were generally allowed to remain in the same geographic context as well. This would be particularly so when a hero's story was not directly associated with Arthur, as will be seen.

One might also object that there is no means of gathering a reasonably large number of characters who were attached to the literary Arthur at a very early date. To this I must agree and will simply apologize that the results of this study cannot be certain because of the small sampling. That said, the individuals earliest associated with Arthur are Cei, Bedwyr son of Bedrawc, Drust son of Tallwch, Hueil son of Caw, Drutwas son of Tryffin, Gildas son of Caw, Medrawt, Anwas, Llwch, Llacheu, Belatacudros, and Mabon son of Modron. Obviously these were not all the names of historical men. Mabon and Belatacudros, for instance, are known to have been euhemerizations of British gods. However, all of the heroes listed above were associated with Arthur by the ninth century,[4] and in every case they have been found in more than one pre–Galfridic tale associated with Arthur. In the pages below, each of these characters and all the sites with which they are associated have been listed.

Cei

Cei is the most popular and famed individual of this group, being present in nearly every work of literature where Arthur appears. Later legend made him Arthur's step-brother and an overbearing steward. However, in the earliest sources he is Arthur's ablest and most trusted man. Cei appears in *Trioedd Ynys Prydein*, and plays key roles in *Culhwch ac Olwen, Vitae Cadoci, Dialogue, and Pa gur?* Cei's participation at all times is that of a gatekeeper; he maintains a standard of behavior which he holds even Arthur to at all times.

The first pre–Galfridic source in which Cei is mentioned is *Pa gur?* In it, Arthur approaches a gate and is asked to tell the porter holding the entrance about himself and the men in his company. Arthur proceeds to speak of all their greatest accomplishments. In this, Cei is given preeminence. His doings in Celli (Wig),[5] Pen Palach,[6] Disethach,[7] Din Eidyn,[8] Emrys,[9] Ystafngwn,[10] and Môn[11] are spoken of in turn. Celli is in Cornwall, Din Eidyn is Edinburgh, Emrys and Ystafngwn probably refer to Welsh sites, and Môn is Anglesey. It is possible that Pen Palag refers to the Cat Palaug found in *Culhwch ac Olwen*, and therefore to a significant site on Môn as well.

In *Trioedd Ynys Prydein*, triad 26W in Dr. Bromwich's edition, Cei, along with Arthur and Bedwyr, is said to have attempted to steal Drystan's swine over the course of a year. Drystan is said to have been in Glyn Cvch ym Emlyn, the Cuch River on the border between Carmarthenshire and Pembrokeshire. He is also listed in triad 21, along with Bedwyr, as one of the four battle-diademed men of the Isle of Britain.

In *Culhwch ac Olwen*, Cei is Arthur's best and most respected warrior. It is he who first offers to find Olwen for Culhwch and he alone who confronts Yspaddadden.[12] He and Bedwyr steal Gwrnach's sword[13] and take Dillus' beard. The only place name he is associated with in the story is Caer Lloyw, Gloucester, where he leads the attack to free Mabon son of Modron.

Cei appears twice in the *Vitae Cadoci*. In the first scene he, Bedwyr, and Arthur are playing dice when they see Gwladus daughter of Brychan is being abducted by Gwynllyw. He in turn is being pursued by Brychan. Arthur suggests to his companions that they should kidnap the damsel for himself, but Cei and Bedwyr restrain Arthur by reminding him that theirs is the path of nobility. They leave their game and end the pursuit; serving as negotiators between kidnapper and father, they help Brychan and Gwynllyw reach a settlement.

In the second episode, Arthur has found that a fugitive from his law has taken refuge with a now fully matured Cadoc. Arthur confronts him, demanding that the criminal be handed over to him. Cadoc is unable to do that, and so he and Arthur come to a settlement. Arthur will accept one hundred cows of a specific color in return for the guilty man's freedom. Cadoc miraculously transforms the cattle into the required color and sends them across the river Usk to Arthur. Cei and Bedwyr are sent to collect them. Once they are across, the cattle turn into tumbleweed in front of their eyes. The river where this takes place is in Glywising.

The fifth source in which Cei is named is *Dialogue*. In it Cei acts as Gwenhwyfar's protector from Melwas, who is by the context a lesser member of Arthur's court. The scene seems to take place in Dyfneint, modern Devon. This is the extant to which Cei is named in the pre–Galfridic Welsh sources.

Bedwyr

Probably the second most commonly known early Arthurian figure is Bedwyr, a seemingly quieter man than Cei who possesses only one arm.[14] In Cei's company, he appears in *Trioedd Ynys Prydein, Vitae Cadoci,* and *Culhwch ac Olwen*. However, he is given a separate billing in *Pa gur?* There he is said to have been the hero at the Battle of Tryfrwyd.[15] This site has, unfortunately, remained unidentified though it is probably a part of the Old North.

Drust son of Tallwch

Drust ap Tallwch appears in *Trioedd Ynys Prydein and Culhwch ac Olwen* as well as several independent native tales. In addition, the figure Culfanawyt, the father of his traditional lover, is consistently associated with him. This character is to be found in *Trioedd Ynys Prydein and Culhwch ac Olwen*. Drust is listed eight times in the former, although he is only given a geographic location in 26W. Here he is located in Glyn Cuch in Wales. In *Culhwch ac Olwen* Drust, here "Iron fist,"[16] is simply listed among Arthur's *teulu*.

However, Drust is almost definitely a northern figure, as Dr. Bromwich has observed,[17] and more recent work has confirmed.[18] This is for several reasons. The name is found most frequently among the Picts who in post–Roman times were confined to the Highlands of Scotland. His father is named as Tallwch which, as Dr. Padel has noted, is linguistically similar to the Talorcan who is father to another Drust in the Pictish king lists.[19] Finally, it has been documented that the name listed as that of Iseut's father, Culvanawyt Prydein, is a traditional character of the Old North. Vanawyt has been seen as a variant of the place-name Manaw.[20] This was a smaller region within Lothian. As secondary support, the name of Drust's kingdom in the continental romances is exclusively Loenois or Loonois, which translates to modern Lothian in the Edinburgh area.

Hueil son of Caw

The figure who is next most commonly mentioned in conjunction with Arthur in the oldest Welsh sources is Hueil son of Caw. He is consistently named as an enemy of Arthur, and a vague figure of the north. His dealings with Arthur are touched upon in *Culhwch ac Olwen*,[21] the second *Vita Gildae*,[22] and one other and much more corrupted source, *Chwedl Huail ap Caw ac Arthur*. In all of these instances he has come down for a raid on Arthur and died in the attempt.

Drutwas son of Tryffin

Drutwas ap Tryffin is named in *Culhwch ac Olwen* and several independent sources as one of Arthur's men (see Chapter 8 above). He is consistently named as the son of a Dyfed king who was likely active during the fifth century. However, Drutwas is never placed there, and is geographically unlocated.

Gildas son of Caw

Gildas son of Caw is also associated with Arthur. He is listed as a member of Arthur's court in *Culhwch ac Olwen*[23] and as a member of a clan hostile to Arthur in Caradoc of Llancarfan's *Vita Gildae*.[24] It seems that Gildas is a figure of the north for several reasons. First, his father, Caw of Prydein, is said to have lived beyond (from the reference point of Wales) Bannawc, a mountain range just north of Antonine's Wall.[25] This would make Caw a Pict. Also, Gildas' traditional brother was Hueil. As was demonstrated above, he is a figure unanimously linked to the north. Gildas himself has been tied to Strathclyde in the literature.[26] There can be little doubt as to Gildas' northern origins.

Medrawt

Medrawt is also most probably a northern figure. He is named in *Annales Cambriae* as fighting at Camlann. According to Dr. Bromwich and a long list of other scholars, the site was probably Birdoswald on Hadrian's Wall.[27] Local legend claims that he kidnapped Guinevere and took her to his fortress at Barry Hill in Scotland. Both the chronicler John of Fordun (c. 1385) and the historian John Major (1527) also located him in the north,[28] regarding him as a hero.

Mabon son of Modron and Belatacudros

Mabon son of Modron was a Celtic god of the region around Hadrian's Wall[29] as well as France. He is listed in *Pa gur?* as a vulture at Elei[30] and in *Culhwch ac Olwen* as a prisoner at Gloucester.

In the form of *Beli*, Belatacudros is a part of the long list of Arthur's court in *Culhwch ac Olwen*. He appears there under the guise of Reidwn's father.[31] Historically, Belatacudros was a god worshipped particularly along Hadrian's Wall. There he was the center of a fertility religion[32] and possessed horns.[33] His presence is also implied in the pseudo–Taliesin poem *Preiddeu Annwn*, where the destruction of a coven of witches, their symbolic cauldron, and presumably the god that was being worshipped are the main goals of the expedition. Though ousted from his religious position with the coming of Christianity, Belatacudros would remain a prominent figure in British culture well into the Middle Ages. His popularity would be transferred to Wales, where he would be placed at the head of dozens of lineages. However, in Britain he was originally confined to the Borders area.

Llwch, Anwas, and Llacheu

The other characters are far less common, and a study of them considerably less informative. Llwch and Anwas appear together in *Pa gur?* Here they are said to have been the heroes of a battle in Din Eidyn, or Edinburgh.[34] They also appear in Arthur's court in *Culhwch ac Olwen* without any sort of geographical orientation. Additionally, Llwch appears in *Preiddeu Annwn*, though again he is not placed anywhere specifically. Llacheu is also named in *Pa gur?* as well as in *Culhwch ac Olwen*. He is listed with Cei as having fought at Ystafngwn.[35]

In a more digestible form, the sites listed in this study may be summed up as follows[36]:

Y Hen Ogled: 8	Wales: 8
Somerset and Cornwall: 2	Unknown: 2

One may note that there seems to be as many Welsh figures as any of the others, and from this it might be inferred that Wales in fact has a strong claim as Arthur's area of origin. However, there are very specific reasons why Wales is mentioned eight times. The two episodes in the *Vita Cadoci* take place in an adventure that involves Arthur, as does 26W of *Trioedd Ynys Prydein*. As was noted at the outset of this chapter, Arthur was a renowned figure, and therefore any episode that directly involves him has most probably been influenced by his widespread fame and pan–British quality.[37] The setting of 26W of *Trioedd Ynys Prydein* may be explained in a similar fashion; they may involve the characters in question, but Arthur is present here and that may well have influenced the location. The rescue of Mabon takes place in Wales, yet again Arthur participates. Modron is a god of the Hadrian's Wall region who has simply been relocated.[38] Similarly, Belatacudros was worshipped only near Hadrian's Wall, yet he appears in the Welsh genaeologies. This limits Wales to three instances. Further, *Dialogue* is also directly connected with Arthur and not Cei, who was simply there with him. This distinction eliminates one Cornish site from the list. With these things in mind, the results look as follows:

Unknown: 6   *Y Hen Ogled*: 10
Somerset and Cornwall: 1   Wales: 3

In looking at the adjusted disbursement of the place-names associated with these heroes, one is immediately cognizant of the second-largest category, Unknown. As has been discussed above, there have been massive social, linguistic, and cultural changes since the fifth century in Wales and Cornwall, so that this may be the location of several of the now unknown sites. However, the British language became extinct from Cumberland north sometime around 1100 and had been dying for several centuries before then. Most Cumbric place-names would have been forgotten shortly thereafter in oral legend[39] so that it is likely the category of Unknown denotes a northern site. In conjunction with this likelihood, it should be noted that the only non-northern sites that remain in the list above are to be found in *Pa gur?* Painfully little is known about this single source (see above). In contrast, the information that indicates *Y Hen Ogled* derives from four separate sources coming from various influences. They most probably have not developed from a common source and are therefore more credible.

Of the characters themselves, a more clear body of evidence for a northern theory may be seen:

Cei: Unknown   Bedwyr: Unknown
Medrawt: *Y Hen Ogled*   Mabon ap Modron: *Y Hen Ogled*
Hueil ap Caw: *Y Hen Ogled*   Belatacudros: *Y Hen Ogled*
Gildas: *Y Hen Ogled*   Llwch: Unknown
Drutwas ap Tryffin: Dyfed   Anwas Edeinauc: Unknown
Drust ap Tallwch: *Y Hen Ogled* Llacheu: Unknown

Here one will immediately see that there are six characters to be associated with *Y Hen Ogled*. In addition, there are five persons associated exclusively with now unknown place-names. There is only one individual on the list who is specifically not listed as coming from the Old North, Drutwas ap Tryffin. However, no extant legend exists that would connects him with any battle or site in Wales. As was discussed in Chapter 5, there is also no record that Drutwas was ever king of Dyfed, his native country. It is only his genealogy that places him in this region.[40] This implies that he did not necessarily spend his career in Dyfed, where the laws of primogeniture and the rules of Irish succession would have left an entire cousinhood with the same opportunities as he had for succession. Since Drutwas cannot be tied to this region, there is no evidence to place him anywhere in Britain. He, too, is therefore an Unknown figure and may very well have lived in the north with Arthur or any other British figure.

In contrast, the northern figures are consistently placed in northern sites in the literature. Here there is little debate. Drust and his father's name are both Pictish. Caw came from a region beyond Banawc and therefore in Pictland. This implies that his sons Hueil and Gildas came from the north as well, and evidence to be found in both *Vitae Gildae* and independent legends agree here. Medrawt's traditional location is the north, and the hypothesis that the Battle of Camlann took place at Camboglanna on Hadrian's Wall would seem to supplement that opinion. Mabon son of Modron and Belatacudros are listed as deities worshipped by the troops of Hadrian's Wall and nowhere else appear with such frequency until centuries later. It is highly likely that they are northern figures as well, added to Arthur's *teulu* after they had been transformed from Celtic gods into a pair of British heroes.

The author will not claim the above associations to places or persons as incontrovertible evidence that Arthur was a northern figure, but again the evidence does lend itself to that conclusion. With those locations with known biases out of the way, a majority of the remaining places are from that region. Where identifiable, all of the above persons are associated with the north.[41] The only exception to this result is Drutwas ap Tryffin of Dyfed, who is linked to Wales only by lineage. In itself this study stands as intriguing evidence that Arthur was a northern figure. In conjunction with the previous and following chapters, it adds substantial weight.

In addition, it should be pointed out that Mabon son of Modron and Belatacudros may provide an additional clue as to Arthur's location. Of all the early figures associated with Arthur, they are the only characters that may be located by archaeological means, which gives their location added significance. They are both also found in a limited area, which is not the case with any of the other early members of Arthur's *teulu* listed here. Both gods were, during the late Roman and sub–Roman periods, specifically worshipped in the region around Hadrian's Wall.[42] This fact suggests that Hadrian's Wall may have been the focus of Arthur's activity during his lifetime. Of course the nature of the heroic age and the above study based on it does not allow for such a refined result, but it can make such a suggestion. Chapter 16 will present a great deal more evidence to support this hypothesis.

CHAPTER 14

Culhwch ac Olwen and the Location of Arthur

The three previous chapters have thoroughly researched the geography of Arthur and his earliest warriors in the British sources, except for the fantasy tale *Culhwch ac Olwen*. The study of this literary work has been given a separate chapter because of the vast number of personal and place-names to be found throughout its many episodes. The intricacy with which the tale has matured is also unique, requiring special attention that is not required to make use of the smaller and simpler pieces studied above.

Culhwch ac Olwen is a version of the universal wonder tale known as "Six Go Through the World."[1] The story begins when Culhwch's step-mother tells him about the beauty of Olwen and gives him the *tyghet*, or personal taboo, that he may not marry anyone if it is not her. Olwen is the daughter of a giant, Yspaddaden, whose own *tyghet* is that he will die when his daughter is married. Having set the hero with a quest, she warns him of the hurdles he must face. She tells Culhwch that to avoid his fate, Yspaddaden makes himself difficult to find, so that even that task may prove too much without luck and aid. The tasks that Yspaddaden sets his daughter's suitors are nearly impossible. To counter this difficulty, Culhwch decides to go to his uncle Arthur's court to enlist the famous king's services. For his part, as soon as Arthur realizes the boy is his nephew he readily decides to help him, and the search begins. Despite difficulties, it is not long before Cei and five others find Yspaddaden. It is at this point that the giant assigns Culhwch forty tasks to accomplish before he will give Olwen away as a bride. Several additional labors that arise in working through the primary assignments, and a few unrelated undertakings occupy the remainder of the tale.[2] Their eventual accomplishment results in the death of the giant and the marriage of Culhwch to Olwen.

From a literary standpoint, the narrative is composed of at least three separate tales and some much later isolated additions that have been stratified and blended with one another over the course of several centuries. The first and original layer was purely mythological and possibly consisted of Culhwch, Olwen, a limited number of the tasks, and the basic plot.[3] The second one introduced historical characters from all across the Celtic world and superimposed Arthur's court on the construction of the tale. This stratum was added no later than the tenth century. The final major addition was to the peripheries of the general storyline, specifically the court list and the exact course of the Twrch Trwyth. These were likely the product of the late eleventh-century political climate.[4] Additional characters, placed there without any purpose or introduction, were also added up through the fourteenth century.[5] However, *Culhwch ac Olwen* was probably put into completed form some time after 1081.[6]

The divisions numerated above are naturally not precise. For instance the mythological base was likely added to and remodeled dozens of times before it developed into something even resembling the extant version. The Arthurian layer itself may well have been influenced by local legends throughout the island from various time periods. However, even briefly explaining the basic and main divisions of the story does make the reader aware of a chief problem with the text, that of its composite character.[7]

Despite this obstruction, *Culhwch ac Olwen* is potentially a valuable source of information on Arthur. Dozens of little-known adventures are directly associated with him, as are several obscure characters of British legend. In addition, *Culhwch ac Olwen* offers some strong evidence of Arthur's origins once the non–Arthurian material and the obvious regional and chronological biases of the various contributors to this tale have been taken into account. Working through the mass of materials to see this will be the objective of the chapter.

In the following pages all the personal names, place-names, and tasks listed in *Culhwch ac Olwen* will be catalogued (for specific names listed, see Appendix C). Various resources will be employed to determine a probable locality for as many of the listed subjects as possible. The results of this survey should reveal a large amount of mythological and post–1000 material. Unfortunately, though what remains should include Arthurian material, it will also contain legendary and folktale materials from throughout Britain that were added either before or after Arthur's inclusion and which will likely remain camouflaged.

If the theory concerning the development of heroic age literature holds, however, *Culhwch ac Olwen* will have much more poignant and useful information to offer the topographically oriented scholar. Above, it has been shown that Arthur was a historical figure who lived in a heroic age. Professor Chadwick demonstrated that such powerful figures often became the center of a literary cycle.[8] If the body of materials that were inserted into *Culhwch ac*

Olwen with Arthur were a part of this Arthurian cycle, then it may contain some evidence of where he was active. Therefore, the most obvious non–Arthurian elements will be filtered out immediately. This will be followed by an attempt to identify the material that was added to the tale along with Arthur at some time before the tenth century. To accomplish this goal, the findings of the initial survey will be progressively screened. It is hoped that this process will provide more clues about Arthurian geography.

The results of this exercise will be complex. Arthur and the characters and adventures who were earliest associated with him should remain. However, a large portion of the characters and place-names who have survived this chapter's screening process will also be those elements in *Culhwch ac Olwen* that were added from throughout the Celtic world along with Arthur but not necessarily as a part of his cycle of tales. For this reason, there will be characters who are not subject to the laws of Arthur's heroic age literary development. Indeed, it is very probable that many of the remaining elements will not have been added along with Arthur, but were added at any point between the original addition of the mythological elements and the tenth century. These may be elements which are now indistinguishable from the Arthurian body. It would be difficult and perhaps impossible to isolate all of these non–Arthurian elements effectively and accurately, and a minimal effort will be made in this regard. The results of the experiment conducted here will not be absolute. However, with all known influences accounted for, there should be a distinct majority of names that belong to one region. It is this region in which Arthur most likely was active.

Each stage in the elimination of names will be directed at one particular layer of development. The first screening will be an obvious one; all objects, literary devices, and persons which clearly belong to the years following 1000 will be identified and eliminated. Second, all names and places that are in any way mythical in nature will be addressed. This will leave a majority of the names in the Arthurian court list and a small number of *anoethau*, or tasks. In the third filter, the court list and all adventures not directly associated with Arthur will be deleted. The court list will be cut out because it is the easiest place to add names to. It is also known that the list was added to the story in the eleventh century.[9] Those sections not associated with Arthur directly are the most likely episodes to have been added separately from Arthur.[10] Finally, it will be seen that most of the remaining Welsh material centers around the area where the story was created, Dyfed, and the course of the Twrch Trwyth. These will accordingly be taken away from consideration on the grounds that the bias of the author or his patron likely contributed to the strength of Dyfed's presence in the story. It will also be seen that some of the Welsh entries that remain could also have been the result of this same eleventh-century influence. For this reason they will be taken out of the equation as well.

In the pages following, the personal and place-names as well as the tasks assigned by Yspaddaden have been divided into three lists. These have each been further differentiated by dividing the subjects included in each list by the category or categories to which they may best be assigned. Most of these categories are self-explanatory. However, several require a specific definition. "British" denotes a British locale or name that has no certain location but is a product of the British language, e.g., Scotland, Wales, British England, and Brittany. "Pan-Celtic" indicates a Celtic locale or nomenclature which has at any time been occupied by a Celtic speaking group, so that Ireland and France are included. "Post–1000" is an entry that was clearly brought into the story at a date later than 1000, usually as a result of literary influences. For instance, the two Esyllts are a result of the development of the Tristan legend. Cognates and emanations of other names have both been grouped under this heading as well.

Several entries below have belonged to two distinct categories; for instance, if the subject was a twelfth-century figure from Brittany he would be in the post–1000 and Brittany categories. In these cases I have listed both the geographical location and the chronological position of the subject. Each time this happens, both effected categories are accounted for in the chart that follows. The category of "Doubles" records the number of times this occurs, so that the reader might be aware of the number of instances as well.[11]

PERSONAL NAMES; TOTALS

Total: 439	Wales: 45	post–1000: 9	Title: 1
Uncertain: 82	Animals: 35	Objects: 8	Doubles: 34
British: 80	Myth: 29	Brittany: 6	
Literary: 78	Ireland: 16	France: 6	
Y Hen Ogled: 60	Dumnonia: 13	Pan-Celtic: 5	

PLACE-NAMES; TOTALS

Total: 77	Literary: 9	Ireland: 3	pan-Celtic: 1
Wales: 29	Cornwall: 4	France: 3	Myth: 1
British: 11	Europe: 4	Uncertain: 3	Doubles: 5
Y Hen Ogled: 10	Fabulous Places: 3	Brittany: 1	

TASKS; TOTALS

Total: 42	Animal: 6	Ireland: 3	Doubles: 5
Y Hen Ogled: 9	Universal: 4	pan-Celtic: 3	
Wales: 5	Myth: 5	British: 2	
Literary: 4	Uncertain: 5	France: 1	

An initial survey of the personal and place-names and task locations of *Culhwch ac Olwen* reveals a great deal of interpolation and nonsensical material. The Personal Names list of 439 persons clearly has a preponderance of persons from *Y Hen Ogled* over anywhere else. However, it is not the dominant group. There are only 60 characters who may be located there, while 82 belong to the category of Uncertain and another 80 to the broad category of British. The numbers in these latter two groups create a rather large potential margin of error. On the other hand, it seems somewhat likely that many of these geographically undetermined characters were originally from *Y Hen Ogled*. As was mentioned above, northern figures would have been lost or forgotten at a much higher rate when the language of Cumbric was forgotten around the eleventh century, and they would have been lost at a growing rate as the north came under progressive English influence in the centuries up to then. By 1100, that is by the time Arthur had been superimposed on *Culhwch ac Olwen*, many of the oral tales of the region would have been forgotten.[12] In Wales and most other British areas, no similar event is known that would have obscured a large number of the known persons in these regions prior to that time.[13]

The large number of subjects in the British and Unknown categories may be a sign of how undisturbed and therefore how valid the list is as a literary source for the fifth and sixth centuries. It is well known that a number of northern heroes of the British Heroic Age were, from a literary standpoint, transplanted to Wales in the centuries following the political demise of the northern British states. The small number of northern figures who are known to have been relocated have occasionally been used to forward the hypothesis that these individuals represent a rather larger unknown pool of figures that were similarly transferred.[14] That this phenomenon has occurred in *Culhwch ac Olwen* as well may be tentatively confirmed by the fact that several known northern figures are artificially connected to Wales, e.g., Mabon, whose worship as has been seen above was focused on Hadrian's Wall, and Gildas, whose father was likely a Pict. It seems a plausible suggestion that many, if not most of those figures in the British and Unknown categories were in similar transition from the north to Wales when the story was put into final form. That hypothesis would explain the vagueness of their geography.

The 77 place-names seem predominantly of Welsh origin, with a noticeably smaller complement of names from *Y Hen Ogled*, Cornwall, Brittany, and Ireland. However, this list is highly suspect. The categories of British and Uncertain are extremely small in comparison to those found in the Personal Names and *anoethau* lists. As pointed out in the paragraph above, it is well known that some of the northern heroes of oral literature were transplanted to Wales. It has also been seen that the tale *Culhwch ac Olwen* contains further evidence of this trend in the personal names, with the suggestion of more in the large numbers of British and Uncertain subjects. One should expect to find a larger number of these sites than any other as well. The fact that one does not suggests that many of the places that may originally have been of northern origin had, by the time this story was written, been successfully transplanted to Welsh sites. Historically, this would have been a simpler and therefore quicker process than with the figures. Once the regions of *Y Hen Ogled* had been occupied by the Germanic peoples and easy communications with the old British states had broken down, it would only have been a matter of time before the out-of-sight cities were forgotten.

The list of 42 tasks, though predominantly revealing a northern affinity, is undeniably mythological in origin. The plot itself belongs in that venue and, though historical elements and characters have been added, the basic nature of the story and many of the episodes clearly belong in the realm of mythology. A good portion of the adventures which are not immediately apparent as such may well have been associated with Arthur or the other Celtic figures that were integrated into the story at some time before the tenth century.[15]

Taking the above notes and conclusions in mind when reading through the revised lists helps to pick out a good deal of extraneous materials. When one deletes all clearly nonessential items, characters, and episodes, the lists are reduced accordingly:

PERSONAL NAMES

Total: 344	Wales: 41	Dumnonia: 13	pan-Celtic: 5
Uncertain: 82	Animals: 29	Objects: 8	Doubles: 27
British: 81	Myth: 29	Brittany: 4	
Y Hen Ogled: 59	Ireland: 16	France: 4	

PLACE-NAMES

Total: 40	*Y Hen Ogled*: 8	Ireland: 3	Brittany: 1
Wales: 8	Cornwall: 4	France: 2	pan-Celtic: 1
British: 9	Europe: 4	Uncertain: 3	Doubles: 3

THE TASKS: LOCATIONS

Total: 36	Animal: 6	Ireland: 3	Doubles: 2
Y Hen Ogled: 7	Universal: 1	pan-Celtic: 3	
Wales: 4	Myth: 5	British: 2	
Literary: 4	Uncertain: 5	France: 1	

The numbers are reduced by nearly one-quarter by deleting obvious post–1000 additions. It should also be pointed out that the majority of the names that have been eliminated here appear only in the court list. As was noted at the outset, this would be the simplest and most obvious place to add a name. At that point, one more person or place would not affect the plot but could be placed with Arthur without too much effort. Because of this, inserting them would leave little or no evidence that they had been put in later.

The second stage will involve deleting all material that is clearly of mythological origin or precedes the year 400. As Arthur was not a mythological figure and most probably lived in the fifth or sixth century, this procedure is intended simply to tighten the chronology of the items here under observation.

PERSONAL NAMES

Total: 309	Wales: 38	Objects: 8	Doubles: 20
Uncertain: 82	Animals: 27	Brittany: 4	
British: 79	Ireland: 12	France: 4	
Y Hen Ogled: 57	Dumnonia: 13	pan-Celtic: 5	

PLACE-NAMES

Total: 35	*Y Hen Ogled*: 8	Ireland: 3	Brittany: 1
Wales: 7	Cornwall: 4	France: 2	Doubles: 3
British: 6	Europe: 4	Uncertain: 3	

THE TASKS: LOCATIONS

Total: 26	Animal: 5	Ireland: 1	France: 1
Y Hen Ogled: 6	Universal: 1	Pan-Celtic: 2	Doubles: 1
Wales: 4	Uncertain: 4	British: 2	

In the Personal Names, only the categories of *Y Hen Ogled*, Wales, Ireland, and Animals are affected. In turn, this would suggest that the mythological material derived mainly from the same three main regions. It is reassuring that two of these areas are British, indicating that the initial tale was likely British as well. Of the excised names, only Mabon mab Modron is lost within the *Y Hen Ogled* group. As has been seen in an older source, *Pa Gur?*, this character was associated with Arthur independent of *Culhwch ac Olwen*. The three excised Welsh entries may make no such claim. The difference between the two groups implies that most of the pre–400 material in *Culhwch ac Olwen* belonged to Wales and that whatever materials Mabon represents were being added to the Arthurian cycle at around the time Arthur was introduced into the wonder tale.

As occurred in the elimination of materials dating to after 1000, those elements of the *Y Hen Ogled* category remain nearly unaffected. The place-names list yields similar results. Here, only the categories of Wales and British were affected. The material from the north was clearly of limited chronological scope; it was composed primarily of historical and legendary figures who lived between 400 and 1000, particularly the latter fifth century to the eighth centuries. The most logical focus of that body would have been the British Heroic Age, which extends roughly from the late fifth century to the middle of the seventh century.

One more filtration of *Culhwch ac Olwen* has been conducted below. Here the court list has been removed. In eliminating that bulky, unuseful hiding spot for all manner of individuals, it is my hope that a significant number of unknown literary additions and later historical figures will also be eliminated. This is done with the full knowledge that some of the characters listed only in the court list are traditional and may well have been contemporary to Arthur. It is hoped that in potentially taking away characters that were traditionally associated with Arthur but were not connected with him here a great many more individuals who were never in any way associated with him will be shorn away. The results are as follows:

PERSONAL NAMES

Total: 94	*Y Hen Ogled*: 15	Ireland: 2	Brittany: 2
Uncertain: 20	Wales: 14	Dumnonia: 2	pan-Celtic: 2
British: 22	Animals: 18	Objects: 4	Doubles: 7

PLACE-NAMES

Total: 13	*Y Hen Ogled*: 2	France: 1
Wales: 5	Cornwall: 2	Brittany: 1
British: 1	Ireland: 2	Doubles: 1

This evaluation is, obviously, one of significant reductions. The average margin of decrease is over two-thirds. The losses in most categories reflect this overall trend. The categories of British, Uncertain, *Y Hen Ogled*, Wales, and Objects are approximately equally reduced. The category of Animals is not nearly so affected, but its remaining contingents often fall into one of the other categories. Animals has no geographic designation in any event.

The main significance of this reduction is that it successfully eliminates several categories from serious discussion. Ireland, Dumnonia, and Brittany now contain only two or fewer selections in both the personal and place-names list.[16] This is an insignificant number, especially when one considers that characters and place-names from across the Celtic world were added to the tale along with Arthur and his band.

With all the above considerations in mind, there remain only two serious potential points of origin for the Arthurian element of *Culhwch ac Olwen*, Wales and *Y Hen Ogled*. However, as was noted at the beginning of this chapter Wales, and particularly Dyfed, is the location at which the story was put in finalized form. This should, reasonably, give a distinct numerical advantage to Wales even after the obvious signs of tampering have been eliminated. After all, if an individual were to write in medieval Wales one would find it a more immediate and real influence than that of any other region. It would undoubtedly be more influential than an area that was at that point under the control of the hated English. There is also the strong likelihood that the story ruminated in Wales for some time before being written, no doubt accruing place-names and local heroes as it went. To determine just how much influence the location of its final revision had, all the Welsh sites in *Culhwch ac Olwen* have been categorized below by their specific early medieval kingdom.[17]

PERSONAL NAMES

| Total: 43 | Dyfed: 13 | Gwynedd: 4 | Powys: 3 |
| Wales: 8 | Glywising: 10 | Dubonnia: 4 | Gwlad: 2 |

PLACE-NAMES

Total: 30	Gwynedd: 4	Doubles: 1
Dyfed: 15	Dubonnia: 4	
Glywising: 6	Gwlad: 2	

The list of Welsh personal and place-names reveals an already assumed pattern. Despite having already removed the obvious Dyfed influences, a distinct majority of the Welsh characters and geography may still be placed in that region, while the other kingdom of any significance seems to be Glywising, its neighbor. It is obvious that the folklore and culture of Wales and particularly Dyfed had a heavy impact on *Culhwch ac Olwen*. It may also have had a quite late influence. While there is no direct evidence that Dyfed influenced the geography of the locations and individuals in the tale, it is very possible that the chase of the Twrch Trwyth is just one example of this phenomenon (see map below).[18]

It is known that Wales had a serious impact on the last redactions of *Culhwch ac Olwen*. On the other hand, *Y Hen Ogled*'s can only have weakened with time. It was politically nonexistent when the tale was written and could not have had any real influence on the story's development after the ninth century.

In addition, it may be assumed that the Welsh material that is known is a fair indicator of the Welsh material that is not known. It may further be

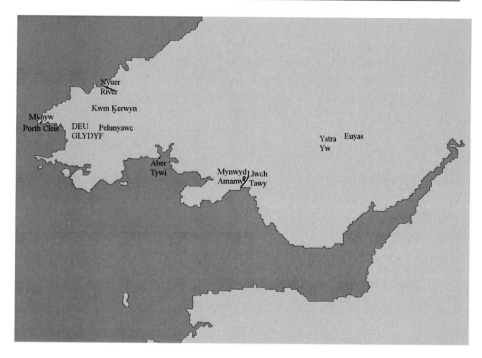

THE ROUTE OF THE TWRCH TRWYTH. The approximate route of the Twrch Trwyth, showing that the story of *Culhwch ac Olwen* was meant to be a Welsh story and that its focus was on Dyfed.

assumed that only a very small amount of the Welsh personal and place-names listed in the story belong to the period 400 to 1000. These conclusions seriously weaken the argument for Wales as Arthur's original home and only strengthen the theory that has been emerging over the past few chapters, that Arthur is primarily a northern hero.

Finally, it has been noted above that the body of oral knowledge containing Arthur was added to the story during the tenth century or before. This chapter revealed that the northern figures were predominantly added during this period, making it likely that the people associated with Arthur are the same persons as these northern figures. When one has made the appropriate reductions with all of the above in mind, the following results bear this out[19]:

FINAL RESULTS
PERSONAL NAMES

Total: 51	*Y Hen Ogled*: 12	Ireland: 2	Brittany: 1
Uncertain: 4	Wales: 8	Dumnonia: 2	pan-Celtic: 1
British: 11	Animals: 9	Objects: 4	Doubles: 3

PLACE-NAMES

Total: 13	*Y Hen Ogled*: 2	France: 1
Wales: 6	Cornwall: 2	Brittany: 1
British: 1	Ireland: 2	Doubles: 1

Looking over the numbers, it seems impossible to resist the following conclusions. First, that the author or authors who finally put the story in a finished form inserted a great many Welsh personal and place-names randomly from local legends, and rationally, as in the case of St. David's. Second, that they also had access to a body of tales about Arthur and the men who were already associated with him. These individuals likely introduced him and made Arthur the centerpiece of the tale.

This Arthurian body of information most likely came from the North. It is this region from which a majority of the *Culhwch ac Olwen* figures of the fifth through the ninth centuries derive. It is also known that Arthur was a part of a heroic age. As was mentioned before, the literature that derives from a heroic age generally adds figures from roughly the same era and geographical location as the central character of the literature.[20] Since it is known that Arthur existed, that he lived in the late fifth or early sixth centuries, and that those figures that are most commonly associated with Arthur do come from the North, it is only reasonable to conclude that Arthur, too, came from this region.[21]

CHAPTER 15

Arthur in the Romances[1]

The sources that have been employed above have tied the figure Arthur loosely to *Y Hen Ogled*, though there are several locations and persons in the earliest sources that are clearly not from the British North. These anomalies, and patron or author-motivated materials with like geographies, have often been employed to label Arthur a pan–British figure from the outset of his existence. The specific examinations conducted above have shown that this is not the case. I hope that the previous chapters have also provided an alternative explanation for these inconsistencies; they are probably the result of the development of heroic age literature. The British tales about Arthur were associated with ever broadening geographical and temporal boundaries in Britain as the name of Arthur spread and the literature surrounding him developed. The further into the Middle Ages his name was carried, the more place-names and British persons were attracted to the Arthurian orbit and the larger the area and chronological range from which these were drawn. By the ninth century, that is by the time some extant materials were first written, the corpus in question included a range of persons and place-names from Cornwall, Wales, Brittany, and Ireland and from throughout all of post–Roman British history. Despite all the additional materials, however, it would seem that the majority of these were still of northern origin.

On the continent, matters were slightly different.[2] Certainly Arthur became internationally known, but an association with his war-band did not hold the prestige there that it did with the Welsh. There was also the simple matter that France and the surrounding regions were not in the midst of their own heroic age when Arthur was transferred there. Because of this, the continentals did not generally add new faces from their own history as they adopted him. One does not find Charlemagne or Clovis as a member of

Arthur's court. Nor were continental authors generally concerned to include local sites in the Arthurian world, either. Only Brittany seems to have been added in with any regularity, and only there likely because the area shared a common heritage with the British. For this reason, the literature that made its way there often preserved only the regional biases of whatever area had possessed the information before it was transferred.[3] Because of this often one-layered influence on continental romances, these highly refined versions of the original stories may be more reliable than their insular counterparts in this respect.[4] They are, therefore, worth analyzing in an attempt to better understand Arthur's geography.

However, before scrutinizing the romances, one must be aware of two potential biases which they may have and that have not been confronted before. First, one must keep in mind that each useful author must have used a source, and this source must have been ultimately of British origin. Because of this, one must be aware of the unintentional geographical biases a writer may have passed along in his literature from that source. If, for instance, a continental writer used a source that was taken from Wales, but which was ultimately of Cornish origins, he would be faced with a story that contained locations from both regions, and would most probably be oblivious to this fact because he would not recognize the place-names. This problem is compounded by the fact that any region of British denomination in the fifth century may have served as the ultimate source for any one of the romances.[5] However, the most likely region from which to have gained direct access to knowledge of Arthur during the twelfth century was southern Wales. This is because it was the only area in all of Britain where English and Welsh-speaking peoples were on friendly grounds and could interact informally. This was especially true of the Norman-allied Bretons and the Welsh.

Because of this state of affairs, it has been said that southern Wales served as a receptacle for the Arthurian material that made its way to the continent.[6] For this reason, one must be especially cautious of any poet or writer who places Arthur there. If there is any evidence of placement in another region, one may give the latter association some superior mark of reliability.

The second problem to be aware of is that, since the continental authors were not directly culturally involved with their subject, Arthur's geographical location was of no immediate concern to them. For this reason, an author might take a contemporary site and make it Arthur's capital for nearly any reason. If, for instance, a poet's patron was intimately associated with a specific section of England, or Brittany, the poet might be inclined to name a site in that area so that he could ingratiate his patron. If he himself had had direct contact or knowledge of a British region, he might use that area because he could describe it better than whatever area his source used. On occasion,

Breton authors moved Arthur to their homeland to please their patron or to enhance their monastery.[7]

Among the extant continental written literature, the first author is Marie de France. Unfortunately, little is known of her, but what is generally acknowledged may be summarized as follows: She wrote in the final decades of the twelfth century, probably in England and certainly for an English audience. The Henry whom she praises in her general prologue was either Henry II or his son Henri au Cort Mantel. The former individual was the one-time husband of Eleanor of Aquitaine, who likely introduced him to the Arthurian genre. He would also marry Maud, as has been seen,

It is of note that Marie only wrote one romance directly pertaining to Arthur's court, *Lanval*. This poem places Arthur exactly in Carlisle.[8] Aside from perhaps an interest in the late Normanesque Scottish king David (1124–1156) or his then former wife Maud, there would be no obvious reason to have located the hero in this area.[9] On the contrary, it seems odd that Henry's patron would have placed Arthur there. Henry himself was associated with southern England and Normandy throughout his reign.

Chrétien de Troyes, the next recorded romance writer, is much better known. His access to British sources through Marie de Champagne and Philip of Flanders has been well documented, as have his direct influences from them as well as a large body of classical and contemporary literature.[10] As modern studies have demonstrated, he was a man with a unique ability to fuse the knowledge to be gathered from a wide variety of sources and create a romantic poem of the highest caliber.

In his poems, Chrétien often and variously locates Arthur. He uses the place names *Cardoel*[11] and *Carduel* in Wales[12] and *Cestre*,[13] *Carlïon*, or *Cama(a)lot*,[14] *Winchester*[15] and *Quaradigan*[16] to place him. This indicates confusion, or at best widely varying traditions. Cardoel is Carlisle, while Carduel is an unknown city. Carlïon or Cama(a)lot, are usually translated as Caerleon, Cestre may be seen as a French version of Latin *Castrum*, Welsh *Caestre*, fortress. The "Car" of Carlïon is most likely a modernized version of Welsh *Caer*, a fortress. It is no longer a matter of debate that Chrétien did have access to ancient British sources, and as neither Marie nor Philip had any known political or personal interests in Britain, it is at least likely that the sites Chrétien names were those he found in his various British sources.

After Chrétien there are a number of romance poets and authors who appear over the next sixty years and write for a varying selection of patrons with vastly different tastes and values.[17] Two of the earliest authors in this group associate Arthur with Glastonbury, and one other with the Somerset region. As has been seen above, Glastonbury's motives were as simple as attempting to locate Arthur's life and death near its monastery to increase its prestige, power, and wealth. So, when an author states that one of Arthur's chief residences was in this area, one may pass over the testimony without putting much belief in it. Caradoc's *Vita Gildae* says that Arthur came down to Somerset to find Melvas.[18] The *Perlesvaus* author connects Arthur to Titiague (Tintagel).[19] Robert de Boron links the grail with Avalon.[20] Given what has been learned these are inherently unlikely testimonies. Further, they can be shown to be products of Glastonbury. In the case of the former two pieces, both works admit to being written by a Glastonbury literary mercenary or having gained information from the monastery. In the latter book, the author's mention of the Vales of Avalon has been thought to imply his reliance on a Glastonbury source as well.[21] As has been or will be seen, each of these sources also provides an alternate and more consistent location for Arthur.

Actually, the vast majority of those significant works based on traditional sources lists the same site for Arthur's home, Carlisle. The composite known as *Didot Perceval* names it as a chief residence,[22] as do most of *Perlesvaus*'s references,[23] *Le Chevalier Á l'Épée*,[24] *La Mule Sanz Frein*,[25] a vast number of Robert de Boron's mentions of the capital,[26] *Meraugis de Portlesguez*,[27] *La Vengeance Raguidel*,[28] *Fergus*,[29] *Gliglois*,[30] *L'Atre Périlleux*,[31] Béroul's *Tristan*,[32] *The Vulgate Version of the Arthurian Romance*, *La Folie Lancelot*, *Hunbaut*,[33] *Yder*,[34] and all the Continuations of Chrétien's *Perceval*.[35] In addition, Thomas and the extant work of Gottfried von Strassburg name "Caerleon" in both their respective *Tristan* versions, even though they place the site in England. A brief summary of these works' sources should show the validity and quality of all the above romances as potential reservoirs of traditional knowledge.

The Didot Perceval was written between 1190 and 1212. It is also known that several elements of his piece derive from no known sources. However, it appears to contain traditional materials and therefore the sources for *Didot Perceval* probably included British elements.[36] *Perlesvaus* is likewise a haven of traditional material, even though it clearly has been influenced by Glastonbury.[37] It was finished between 1191 and 1212 or 1220 and 1225.

Le Chevalier Á L'epée and *La Mule Sanz Frein* were most probably written by the same author, a "Paien de Maisières," in the years around 1190. The name is undoubtedly a parody of Chrétien, as are the two Gauvain romances a parody of that Arthurian hero. Both belittle the anti-hero Gauvain, who is in serious quest of two ridiculous items while events of great importance go on around him. The author may or may not have had access to traditional material; his focus on the parody does not allow any particular evidence for a conclusion either way. For this reason these two romances are not reliable sources.

The *First* and *Second Continuation* of Chrétien de Troyes were composed in the decade 1190 to 1200. The first is noteworthy for its use of Gauvain as the main hero, as opposed to his role as a contrast to Perceval in *Le Conte*.

The evidence of the text and from Chrétien would indicate that his role here is a traditional one. However, Peredur is a traditional Welsh hero and Gauvain is not, leaving the situation not fully explained.[38] Still, the traditional matter associated with both heroes indicates legitimately British materials.

The Second Continuation is probably by Gauchier, a professional hagiographer. Because of his craft, he likely had access to oral materials from the period. He otherwise proves himself uncreative; his account of the adventure of the Stag's head is taken directly from *Peredur*. Because of these facts, Gauchier likely accessed materials from a British source.

Robert de Boron most probably wrote after 1191, the year of the so-called discovery of Arthur's body by the Glastonbury monks. The reason for this is that he otherwise makes it clear that he was aware of the event. Robert was not an inventive man; he seems to have been rather a collator of information. Thus, in conjunction with the knowledge that his work is of relatively early date, it is safe to say that his writing is potentially fairly close to the traditional materials from which his stories derived. His only flaw as a source of information is that he was likely persuaded to introduce some Glastonbury elements into his creation. Unfortunately, only a small and inconsequential portion of his work has survived.

Gottfried von Strassburg's *Tristan* was written in the first decade of the thirteenth century, while his source, Thomas, wrote his own version around 1170. The works are both well-versed in courtly romance and it has been suggested and well-reasoned that Eleanor of Aquitaine or someone at her court was Thomas' patroness.[39] If this was true, there would have been no purpose in writing Arthur into Carlisle, though that might have been the source of his information.[40] As has been seen in my earlier work, many facts come together to show that Thomas did have access to traditional material[41]; the dragon, the tongue, Tristan's originally Pictish name and its connection to the oldest version of the Celtic dragon story in *Tochmarc Étaín*. Gottfried and Thomas are most definitely reliable sources. More importantly, they clearly place every aspect of their tales in Scotland and northern England.

Béroul's *Tristan*, written in the late-twelfth century, is generally thought to represent a more primitive version of the Tristan legend because of his general absence of the romantic elements that characterize more developed Arthurian romances. However, as was demonstrated in *Origins of Arthurian Romances*, though he is at times using older information than Thomas he has followed his predecessor in the broad outline of the plot and character developments. His Cornish place-names may be either the product of an older source or his own artistic additions.

Meraugis de Portlesguez and *La Vengeance Raguidel* were probably both written by a Raoul de Houdenc, a native of Hodenc-en-Bray, in the first quarter of the thirteenth century. The works themselves seem to be rather later versions of the romance movement; they parody romance. In the former, Gauvain is given the ridiculous task of obtaining a "Sword of Strange Hangings," while the hero himself is at one point forced to dress like a woman. This shows a comedy dependent on a strong tradition of Arthurian literature, and the author's literary courage and creativity. In addition, no features in the romance strike this author as traditional or original to the romance movement. This is not a reliable source.

In the latter, the burlesque often takes center stage. Again, the author only makes use of stock motifs and adventures instead of adding details and stories to the body of Arthurian literature. There is no reason for believing that this work has made direct use of any British source either.

The Third Continuation of Chrétien, by Manassier, was composed between 1214 and 1227. It continues many of the motifs begun by Chrétien, where they reach a conclusion. However, no new motifs or details of Celtic provenance emerge. In addition, the author adds a number of new characters, none of whom are British. Whatever source Manassier was drawing on was either the same one as Chrétien, or was not a Celtic source at all. It is impossible to determine which option is the correct one because of his lack of departure from his predecessor. For this reason it would be irrational to use Mannassier's work here.

Fergus was written by Guillaume le Clerc between 1200 and 1233, probably to celebrate Alan of Galloway's marriage in 1209. The story itself is probably named after a Scot who was a son-in-law of Henry I of England. The plot has clearly been drawn from all of Chrétien's romances, though the setting has been placed only in Scotland. The author need not have drawn directly from any traditional material. In addition, since the locations were integrated into the tale for the express purpose of paying homage to the patron and his subject, the locations it gives are hardly worth mentioning.

The Vulgate Cycle was composed anonymously between 1215 and 1235. It is based on Robert de Boron's work but also incorporates other elements. It is an attempt to historicize the newly created cycle of romances pertaining to Arthur's court by fitting many of the now-standard elements of the Arthurian world into a coherent chronology. The cycle is therefore a composite of many known sources thrown together without any better pattern than fluidity. If the author names Carlisle, he has probably used no original source, instead relying on someone like Chrétien. *La Folie Lancelot* (c. 1230) is based on this version of the Arthurian romances and the equally conglomerative book *Prose Tristan*.

The Fourth, or *Gerbert Continuation*, was written from 1226 to 1230. As with the Mannassier continuation, Gerbert shows no hint of independent use of Chrétien's source. It is, therefore, difficult to decide whether he had any such source or was merely creating his conclusion artistically.

The romance *Yder* was composed in the second quarter of the thirteenth century. The hero is a traditional one, the French equivalent of the Welsh Edern mab Nudd. One may, therefore, have some hope for the romance as based on older sources. In addition, it contains a traditional theme of Yder's romantic liaisons with Guinevere and his killing of a bear for her. Because of these connections it may be considered a fairly reliable source.

The anonymous romance *Gliglois* was composed in the first half of the thirteenth century. It contains little or no traditional material. In addition, the author has made use of no traditional storyline. It is a moralistic tale. It contrasts Gauvain's traditional attractiveness to women and his lack of constancy to Gliglois, a squire who is only after one woman. This work is also quite useless in determining traditional locations.

Hunbaut is also a moralistic Gauvain romance of the first half of the thirteenth century. In it Gauvain is contrasted with Hunbaut consistently and unfavorably. Additionally, the romance contains no original or Celtic material, instead focusing on the theme of courtly attitudes and stock motifs. It is anonymous.

L'Âtre Périlleux is another anonymous work of the mid–thirteenth century. The story is based on nothing previously known, is not a moralistic tale, and does not contain motifs or details that might be considered unique to the Arthurian genre. Nor is there any hint that the author has used any other unknown sources. Most probably, the author simply had his own story and wished to place it in the *Arthuriana* world.

This summary of the various Arthurian literary sources of the continent reveals that many of the sources which name Carlisle as Arthur's chief city are derived from sources with reasonably strong British elements. They also tend to have traditional plots. Of the twenty-seven sources listed here, eleven seem to be reliable and ten of these name Carlisle. It is an intriguing fact that many of these sources also tend to have traditional heroes: Perceval (5), Tristan (2), Yvain (1), and Yder (1).[42] These heroes also seem to be traditionally northern,[43] indicating no geographical vagueness. This seems an extraordinary set of circumstances and cumulatively indicates that the north, and specifically Carlisle, was Arthur's area of activity (see below).

Title	Source	Region	Influences	Hero[44]
Lanval	Traditional	Carlisle	English king	Lanval*
La Charrette	Traditional	Caerleon	Marie	Lancelot*
Le Conte du Graal	Traditional	Carlisle	Philip	Peredur
Yvain	Traditional	Carlisle	Unknown	Owain

Title	Source	Region	Influences	Hero
Didot Perceval	Traditional	Carlisle	Unknown	Peredur
Perlesvaus	Traditional	Tintagel	Glastonbury	Peredur
Perlesvaus	Traditional	Carlisle	Glastonbury	Peredur
Le Chevalier À L'Épée	Nontraditional	Carlisle	Unknown	Gauvain*
La Mule Sanz Frein	Nontraditional	Carlisle	Unknown	Gauvain*
Robert de Boron	Nontraditional	Somerset	Glastonbury	Gauvain*
Robert de Boron	Nontraditional	Carlisle	Glastonbury	Gauvain*
Thomas' Tristan	Traditional	Carlisle	Unknown	Drust
Gottfried's Tristan	Thomas	Carlisle	Unknown	Drust
Meragis	Nontraditional	Carlisle	Unknown	Meraugis*
La Vengeance	Nontraditional	Carlisle	Unknown	Gauvain*
Fergus	Nontraditional	Carlisle	Alan	Fergus*
Gliglois	Nontraditional	Carlisle	Unknown	Gliglois*
L'Âtre Périlleux	Nontraditional	Carlisle	Unknown	Gauvain*
Béroul's Tristan	Possibly	Carlisle	Unknown	Drust
The Vulgate	Nontraditional	Carlisle	Unknown	Gauvain*
La Folie Lancelot	Nontraditional	Carlisle	Unknown	Lancelot*
Hunbaut	Nontraditional	Carlisle	Unknown	Hunbaut*
Yder	Traditional	Carlisle	Unknown	Edern
First Continuation	Possibly	Carlisle	Unknown	Gauvain*
Second Continuation	Traditional	Carlisle	Unknown	Peredur
Third Continuation	Possibly	Carlisle	Unknown	Peredur
Fourth Continuation	Possibly	Carlisle	Unknown	Peredur

In addition to the continental Arthurian romances, attention should be called to the fact that some oral traditions pertaining to Arthur did survive in the north despite the extinction of Cumbric and all material northern British culture. Three stories were eventually recorded beginning around 1400: *Sir Gawain and the Green Knight* (c. 1400), *Syre Gawene and the Carle of Carlyle* (c. 1400), and *The Turke and Gowin* (c. 1500). The first very clearly places the adventure in the northwestern midlands,[45] while the second focuses on the Carlisle area. The third poem is not specifically located. It seems strange that any oral literature regarding Arthur or any other traditional British heroes should have survived in regions that had been under Germanic rule for many centuries. That they did indicates how strong the traditions of Arthur were in those regions.

The second most common synonym for Camelot—Caerleon[46]—has no authority as a historical alternative. The site is known not to have been occupied in the sub–Roman period. This, and the probability that southern Wales served as a receptacle for all insular British materials as it passed onto the continent, makes it likely that Caerleon is yet another example of the transference of a northern British hero to Wales. It is probable that Caerleon was either the British site chosen by the southern Welsh to relocate Arthur,[47] or it was a site whose name was linguistically similar to Arthur's historical home and was somehow confused with his true original home.

Place-name evidence supports the latter conclusion, and gives a likely northern equivalent. During the eleventh and twelfth centuries Carlisle was given several equally proper pronunciations, *Cardeol*,[48] *Karlioli*,[49] and *Caerleoil*,[50] in various documents.

This fact could have easily produced honest confusion among the native Welsh. Alternatively, it could have aided in the intentional and outright dislocation of the original site to Wales. Regardless of motives it would appear that the second-most common Arthurian capital in the literature leads right back to Carlisle.

That Carlisle and not Caerleon-Caerlion is the older and more traditional of the two sites may be shown with a brief survey of all the sources which name Caerleon. Professor West's indices of French literature show four works which list Caerleon as Arthur's home. Robert de Boron, the pseudo–Robert volumes, and the Vulgate Cycle have all been shown to be unreliable as sources for traditional materials (see above). A fourth, *Le Lai du Cor*,[51] also contains the name. A brief summary of its components will point out the romance's lack of traditional British elements, and therefore its unreliability here.

Robert Biket created the poem *Le Lai du Cor* in the last half of the twelfth century. It is, therefore, one of the earliest known Arthurian romances, and most likely has some British elements. However, it centers on the medieval theme of the chastity test. The author's focus on a medieval theme and away from a traditional story and characters make me hesitant to accept its reliability or basis in traditional sources.

In addition, the Welsh romances *Owain: Chwedl Iarlles y Ffynnon, Historia Peredur ab Efrawg, and Chwedl Geraint ab Erbin* also name Caerleon as Arthur's chief residence. These are the youngest of the Welsh Arthurian tales, and they have often been accused of being strongly influenced by Chrétien. While this may not be entirely true, it is fairly clear that Caerleon does not appear in any of the older Arthurian tales. In addition, Owain and Peredur are obviously northern figures, while Geraint is most probably of Cornish origin. The geography of all these tales has been fabricated as part of the transference to Wales. The fact that they were most likely put in completed form in southern Wales would seem to settle the matter.

Arthur has often been located in London as well, though of course this is a historical impossibility. A theory why London is so heavily featured may be easily predicated if one takes in mind the political atmosphere of the twelfth and thirteenth centuries. First, it should be noted that, though London was not the capital of England during this period, it was fast becoming the most important city in the country. Its location on the Thames made it ideal for trading, while its southern location made it useful as a city from which English kings could control their French possessions. Any writer in the employ of an English king or even vaguely aware of English geography would have made this connection.

Another reason for this correlation may well have been the tradition of England as being fully under the control of the British. The theme of loss and recovery of sovereignty is also Celtic and particularly British. It is apparent in the Welsh tales *Geraint, Peredur*, and *Owain*.[52] Before Chrétien's period, the theme was in nearly every extant British tale. Gildas, *Historia Brittonum, and Armes Prydein* all mourn the loss of Britain and imply the return of sovereignty to the British people. Tales of the twelfth century still speak of London as the main seat of Celtic Britain. Even *Historia Regum Britanniae*, a document of pseudo-history and invention, contains this theme.[53] The sovereignty component continued in the continental literature. It is clearly in *Erec et Enide, Le Conte du Graal, and Yvain*.

It has been seen here that the romances not only agree with the native material in making Arthur a northern hero, they also place him in a very specific place with remarkable consistency, Carlisle. As will be seen in the next chapter, this would have been an ideal area to live in the context of the fifth- and sixth-century military and political scene.

In addition, the Carlisle-Caerlion-Caerleon confusion has been discussed; it is why there are a sizable number of romances that locate Arthur there. Finally, London has been associated with Arthur for one of two reasons. It could have been the medieval sovereignty theme, which consistently made London a site of pan–British kingship. Alternatively, it is likely that the affairs and associations of the Norman kings with London in the twelfth and thirteenth centuries somehow biased continental writers. This influence may have been in the form of direct imitation of contemporary events, or a reflection on their patron's relationships.

CHAPTER 16

Carlisle-Camelot: A New Option[1]

The past few chapters have attempted to lay out all the information about Arthur in the most digestable and fully informed manner possible. With the same data at hand, other scholars have come to quite different conclusions. Professor Jackson used as his basis the Arthurian battles listed in the *Historia Brittonum* and Arthur's presence in *Y Gododdin*. Using the very few battles he was able to locate,[2] and with the full knowledge that many of them may not have been originally associated with Arthur, Jackson conjectured that Strathclyde was likely Arthur's region of activity. Additionally, he argued that the Arthur comparison that is made in *Y Gododdin* (B.38) had been superimposed on the original version of the stanza when the poem was transferred to Strathclyde in the early seventh century.[3] This was in agreement with Professor Koch's more recent linguistic findings on that particular stanza.[4] However, Arthur may also have been a Lothian hero, or simply a northern hero of such renown that he found his way into a rather large poem on northern heroes. Any of these possibilities would be consistent with the development of heroic age literature.

Dr. Bromwich focused on the limited pseudo-historical evidence of *Historia Brittonum* and Gildas, and what is known of the political scene of sixth-century Britain.[5] She preferred Yorkshire because this is the area from which Germanic Northumbria was created in the decades following Arthur's traditional death (537 or 539?).[6] The conquest implies that there was a conflict in Northumbria during Arthur's lifetime. Further, it implies a region in need of heroes.[7] Both of these suppositions were sound when she made them. However, now a Yorkshire theory has several potential flaws as Arthur's power base.

First, Dr. Bromwich makes one very accepted but entirely uncertain assumption, that all British chiefs occupied themselves by attacking German-speaking peoples. This is not the case. The fifth-century British were in the midst of a heroic age. Here the martial prowess of an individual was of primary note. Who one was fighting is inconsequential in that cultural philosophy, only how one fights and how worthy his adversaries are. For a king to add to his prestige, he attacked neighboring tribes and demonstrated his abilities. This could be done if the best opponents were or were not a member of his ethnic group.[8] A British warrior would win praise if he killed a Germanic speaker every day or a Briton.[9] Arthur would have been a famed chief if he had fought only people of Germanic culture throughout his career (as has been assumed), or defeated only his fellow Britons. It is very clear that leaders who followed Arthur in the sixth century did both or either. Several Taliesin poems indicate that Urien had fought British chiefs in the beginning of his career. Cadwallon allied himself with the Mercian Penda against the Northumbrian Edwin. As powerful as Maelgwn was, he does not seem to have fought anyone of Germanic culture throughout his career, though there is a great deal of evidence to suggest that he attacked his fellow Britons. Arthur need not have been near the Germanic settlements to have been where the most conflict was. Conflict would have been all around him during his career.[10]

Second, the natural capital for a Yorkshire kingdom is York, and this site would have been a strategic liability to any kingdom facing south. York itself was created by the Romans as a central location to provide reinforcements and supplies for the entire line of Hadrian's Wall, and as such was situated with access to the sea. It was placed far enough south to be relatively safe from a northern Pictish land invasion, yet far enough north to give military support and supplies to the entire wall. It served effectively as a command center when the enemy was northern. As a chief fortress to a southern enemy, York would have been entirely ill-equipped. It was in proximity to no known defensive structures in that era, nor was the structure itself defended at any period.[11] If one is to assume the Yorkshire kingdom was facing a southern enemy, York would have been strategically isolated. All this makes even less sense when one realizes that York was on the edge of that area we understand to have been the Anglo-Saxon frontier in the late fifth and early sixth centuries.[12]

This scenario falls apart entirely when one adds in what has been learned of northern Britain over the last decade.[13] Recent evidence has found that Hadrian's Wall and many of the sites of the old *dux brittanum* command were either reoccupied or refortified in the fifth or sixth century.[14] This, apparently, was where authority was centered in northern England. With the roads inevitably falling into disrepair, York would have been a long trip from there in sub–Roman Britain, giving that site little strategic value to the men along

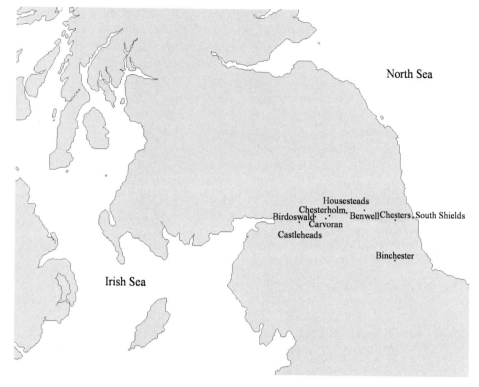

North Sea

Housesteads
Chesterholm.
Birdoswald   Benwell Chesters, South Shields
Carvoran
Castleheads

Irish Sea   Binchester

REFORTIFIED SITES OF NORTHERN BRITAIN AROUND 500. This map showing the refortified Roman military installations of northern Britain illustrates the pattern of the areas under study here. It seems unlikely that these settlements would have been randomly reoccupied and refortified at roughly the same time while the rest of what had been Roman British military sites were in the main abandoned.

Hadrian's Wall. Rome was no longer sending its troops, money, or military equipment to Britain either, so that even this function was now obsolete. For these reasons, York and therefore Yorkshire are no longer tenable as regions of activity for Arthur.

The forts that were in use, however, may provide some clues. They covered a large area: Benwell, Birdoswald, Castleheads, Carvoran, Chesterholm, Chesters, Homesteads, and South Shields.[15] In addition, other Roman forts below Hadrian's Wall were occupied and have evidence of a military presence during the sub–Roman period—Carlisle,[16] Corbridge,[17] York,[18] Aldborough,[19] and Malton.[20] All these fortifications had also been of the string of strongholds held by the office of the *dux brittonum* during the Late Roman period.[21]

That many of the forts under the jurisdiction of this office seem to have inexplicably come into use around 500 is notable, but much more so than at first glance. They are an anomaly in post–Roman Britain. Nearly all forts used in the Roman period were left unoccupied after 400 in Scotland, Wales, and England.[22] For the most part, they would never serve a practical military function again. Yet the *dux brittonum* sites became active amid the general disrepair. This oddity suggests that there was an unusually centralized power or cooperative powers in the borders area during the late fifth century. It is also possible that the individual or individuals responsible for their occupation reinvested the title of *dux brittonum*. If one were to argue that the men who commanded these structures were functioning as independent and nonaligned polities, one must explain why this area was refortified by several independent chiefs while no other region in Britain was.

That there was a powerful kingdom in this area is necessary given the evidence. Only a powerful kingdom, or several kingdoms acting in close concert,[23] would have had the ability to collect the money and organize the manpower necessary for such a widespread policy of reoccupation and renovation as may be seen in these twelve defensive structures.[24]

Other evidence comes from the unlikely source of religion. Both the regions of Cumberland and parts of Yorkshire show a remarkably high number of Christian artifacts during this period. They are greater than those to be found anywhere in Wales.[25] In fact, the *vitae* tradition evidences major conversions occurring throughout sixth-century Wales indicating a still-expanding Christian population. Along the *dux* forts, this indicates both the dominance of one ruler or group and their Christian orientation.[26]

Further evidence for both authority and money is evident in the remains of the Hadrian's Wall fortifications and nearby occupations. Six of the Hadrian's Wall sites have Germanic military artifacts from around 500 and a few only contain Germanic equipment.[27] This implies the structure was solely occupied by Germanic speakers. However, no historical or literary record even suggests a Germanic state this early and this far north. These facts imply that mercenaries were being employed along the wall.[28] A British king who had control over most or all the above-mentioned enclosures and could have employed people of Germanic culture effectively as mercenaries during this period must have had a great deal of power and prestige.

The archaeological remains thus indicate a powerful authority around Hadrian's Wall at the end of the fifth century. This person was almost definitely knowledgeable of Roman warfare; the very use of Roman forts indicates this. It is safe to assume that he would have been based along Hadrian's Wall, where the majority of the used defensive structures are located,[29] and where the island was best prepared to deal with raiders or invaders from any direction. It now remains to locate a likely center of activities for this person.[30]

Luguvalium was one of the forts refortified during the fifth century.

During the Roman period, it had been of special importance because of the natural port it was near on the western end of the Wall. After the departure of Rome, that same feature along with the difficult terrain surrounding it from the south would have made it the logical capital for any sub–Roman chieftain wishing to reinvest the title of *dux brittonum* or reuse the forts from that command. This is for several reasons.

From a military viewpoint, the region itself was defended on the north by Hadrian's Wall, on the west by the Irish Sea, and on the south and east by a rough terrain. The existing road system and tradition would have favored controlling the wall from this site as well.[31]

Unfortunately, there is no extant record of any powerful chieftain or chieftains in this region during the fifth century. In fact, there are no records of any Cumbric kings before the mid–sixth century, when Urien and his contemporaries begin to appear. This indicates that our anonymous chief was for some reason forgotten, or that his association with Hadrian's Wall was somehow lost. To match a chief with this region in this time, therefore, one must not only select a likely figure, but also explain why his connection to Hadrian's Wall was not remembered.

There are a number of known fifth- and sixth-century British kings who are not associated with any specific kingdom. However, of all the many kings of *Y Hen Ogled* who are unplaced, only Arthur seems to have been famed to the extent proposed.[32] As has been seen above, only Arthur is associated both with the year 500 and the Carlisle region in the literature and histories. In addition, it has been seen that a consistent number of scattered references to him in the pseudo-histories corroborate the theory that he might have held a position of unusual power and authority in his time.

Historia Brittonum says that Arthur fought with the kings of Britain. If he had held the office of *dux*, he would have done so without necessarily being a king. Nonetheless, his strategic importance and prestige would have made him the obvious selection as their leader.

Second, it has been said through the centuries that Arthur was based in a legionary fortress. Luguvalium did not keep a legion during the Roman period, but it had supreme importance in the Late Roman Empire. It controlled Hadrian's Wall, which in turn was responsible for keeping the Picts and northern British at bay. The prestige of this site could certainly have confused many contemporaries and later writers into thinking that it had housed a legion.[33]

Arthur's placement in Old Carlisle would also explain two unique and apparently quite ancient literary connections—with Mabon map Modron as well as Belatacudros and his derivatives.[34] Both these figures began their existence strictly as deities of the Hadrian's Wall area.[35] These two figures are

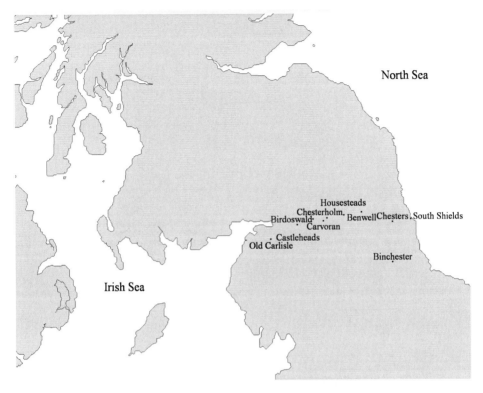

North Sea

Housesteads
Chesterholm.   .
Birdoswald· .· BenwellChesters.South Shields
·   Carvoran
· Castleheads
Old Carlisle

Binchester

Irish Sea

OLD CARLISLE AMONG THE REFORTIFIED SITES. The previous map of Roman installations reoccupied around 500 with the site of Old Carlisle overlaid. It demonstrates
how the proposed home of Arthur would have been a logical command site for the
other settlements.

Arthurian characters and were Celtic deities, yet they are almost unknown
outside of the Hadrian's Wall area.

It has been noted in passing that the religious objects found in the Old
Carlisle area surpassed that of any Welsh site in the same period. Further, it
was suggested that whichever leader was active there had a great deal of influence in not only converting his people, but also in making them believe in the
religion. In my previous book, I demonstrated that Arthur may well have led
a crusade against active practitioners of the fertility religion. This indicates
not only a religious king, but also one fully capable of bringing other people
to share the intensity of his beliefs.

If Arthur was in control of Hadrian's Wall, he could be assumed to have
died in or near it. This conjecture is supported by a legend and historical entry
of Arthur's final battle that is nearly as old as the legend of Arthur himself—
that he died at Camlann. Dr. Bromwich and many others have theorized that

this site may be associated with the Roman fort at Birdoswald (Camboglanna), on Hadrian's Wall. So, why was Arthur's connection forgotten? It was not. The name was altered or substituted, but the evidence always leads back to Carlisle.

It has been seen in this chapter that the onomastic evidence places Arthur south of Antonine's Wall, and in an area of at least mild Romanization. The previous chapters have cumulatively shown strong literary reasons why Arthur should be considered a figure who was active north and west of the Germanic settlements of Northumbria and Mercia. His ties to two Hadrian's Wall deities link him with that region. His probable death at Camboglanna fix him here as well, as does his fame, and the obvious power the man who controlled that area would have had. The mysterious Ninnian phrase referring to him fighting with the British kings and his traditional connection to a legionary fort would also best be explained if he was responsible for controlling the Hadrian's Wall region. If Arthur did control the defensive structures of the old *dux brittonum* command, then he may have been a man of some prestige without necessarily being a king. If he did make use of the *dux* fortifications and was based in Old Carlisle, then his capital could easily have been mistaken for a legionary fortress. Luguvalium's significance in the Late Roman Empire and the role that it played in relation to Hadrian's Wall would have made it seem to be a legionary fortress for any person not familiar with the organization of Rome here. If it is possible to determine Arthur's stronghold, Old Carlisle is the most likely place for him to have lived his life.

CHAPTER 17

The Location of Arthur

Looking over the evidence—negative, traditional, and non-traditional—there is a surprising amount of consistency. Geoffrey seems to have disqualified himself as a legitimate source by taking the political situation and social events of his own time and superimposing it onto the Arthurian world. The *vitae* as a body indiscriminately uprooted any figures their patronizing monasteries needed and placed those individuals near themselves. Arthur was no exception to this rule, and Glastonbury took more liberties than most with him.

The pre–Galfridic items to be found in the Twelve Battles of *Historia Brittonum*, *Pa Gur?*, and the triads seem to place him all over Britain. However, he is more often to be found in the Old North than anywhere else. That is odd considering that northern England had been conquered by the Germanic peoples and Scotland had come under the rule of the Scots by the time all of those items were written down.

A study of Arthur's men in the earliest literature accomplished much the same task, again with individuals located all over the island but with a focus on northern England and southern Scotland. A euhemerized god, localized exclusively to Hadrian's Wall, was even among their number. *Culhwch ac Olwen* proved to be even more of a challenge, but eliminating all of those elements known to be mythological or to have been added after Geoffrey of Monmouth revealed a continuing theme.

The romances were more specific. Elsewhere, I had already enumerated the potential pitfalls in using the materials. However, my prior work had proven the benefits of the attempt and in the process had provided the methodology with which to responsibly critique and obtain potentially accurate information from them. Careful examination of each individual tale with a focus on each tale's reasons for being written as well as the time, place, and circumstances they were written in tended to weed out a great majority of those written. Listing the placement of Arthur's home among those remaining revealed a nearly unanimous selection; they pointed undeniably to Carlisle.

Archaeology conducted over the last few decades seemed to support the working hypothesis that Carlisle might have been Arthur's one-time capital. Carlisle, or rather now Old Carlisle, has in recent years been excavated as a Late Roman and probably a sub–Roman site. Work on Hadrian's Wall has suggested that the site may have been the wall's western anchor during the late stages of the Roman occupation. Old Carlisle has been suggested as the site of the elusive Luguvalium, which was the legionary fortress for the wall.

More broadly, it was seen that the entire wall appears to have undergone some sort of a refit in the late fifth and early sixth centuries. It is a possibility, especially given the unusually Roman nature of the sites, that one individual was responsible for the reinhabitation and refortification of the entire system. That figure would have been unusually powerful for the year 500, and may also have been responsible for holding back the Pictish raids that had been periodic during the Late Roman period, and of whom Gildas complained so heavily.

If Arthur was holding court in Old Carlisle, he may very well have been responsible for the refortification of the wall. His control of at least part of Hadrian's Wall would have put him in constant conflict with the Picts. That would give some credence to the legend regarding Hueil's raid on him. More than likely, any nearby chieftain wishing to make a name for himself would have targeted Arthur as well.

What exactly does a geographical context for Arthur mean to our under-standing of Arthur? Potentially, a great deal. It can give us an idea of the extent of his power and the threats he may have dealt with in his career.

His placement far away from the regions settled by the first Germanic settlers suggests that his primary opponents were Celtic. It is very possible that he spent the majority of his career raiding and being raided by Irish, Pict, and other Briton leaders. If this is the correct assessment, his treatment by the British historians is easier to understand. As *Historia Brittonum* was written with the main theme of showing the strength of a united British people, Arthur would have been employed there for the purpose of establishing him as a great leader against the Germanic peoples and a precursor to the Gwynedd dynasty's ancestor, which explains why the list of his battles there spreads him through-out the island. Gildas' lack of interest in Arthur can be explained as a matter of the chieftain not fitting into the historian's black and white view of British history; he was successful in battles and a good king, but was neither moral nor focused solely on fighting the invaders.

With luck and a good deal more investigation, being able to locate him may even provide insights into the culture and mindset of the man himself. If Arthur was able to call upon the resources necessary to repair some or all of the Hadrian's Wall fortifications, then he was in control of a great deal of territory, wealth, and manpower. Could he have been an over-king? A successor to Vortigern? Is it possible there were several larger British kingdoms in play during his lifetime and his name was the only one fortunate enough to survive?

Locating the site of his hall could prove equally useful. The idea of trying to repair and reuse the wall instead of basing himself in the hill-forts of the pre–Roman kings suggests that he was continuing to think like a Roman. This might suggest he had a Roman ancestor or a Latin education. As will be seen in the next section, it is a certainty that his Roman affinity gives some idea of the time-frame in which he was active.

PART THREE: FLORUIT

CHAPTER 18

The Chronological Tradition

Arthur can then be placed in a historical context located in northern Britain, probably at the western end of Hadrian's Wall in the legionary fortress that was known in the Middle Ages as Carlisle. In coming to both conclusions, the assumption has occasionally been made that Arthur's floruit fell into the post–Roman period at around 500. I am of the opinion that he was active in the first century after the Hadrianic Rescript. However, I also believe that the manner in which such a supposition is generally come to is deeply flawed. For the sake of clarity, that manner is laid out below.

The chronological tradition of Arthur begins with Gildas, who doesn't even mention the man. He says that the Picts attacked the Britons from nearly the moment the Romans left. He then informs his readers that an Agitius was appealed to for help against the Picts, explaining that he had so much influence among the Romans that he had been elected three times to the office of consul. When Agitius refused to send aid, the Picts continued their attacks, and the Irish began to make a nuisance of themselves as well. The Britons were apparently unable to resist the attacks of either group.

To counter the threat posed by the two foreign cultures, a single over-king and his council decided that a third party, the Anglo-Saxons, would be better prepared to deal with the northern threat, while it is implied that he would confront the Irish. It was this over-king who invited a small group of the first Germanic settlers onto the island and settled them along the eastern coastline. Once they had proven their worth as mercenaries, this same king allowed for more of them to be settled in Britain, likely along the northern frontier so that they would be at hand to defeat any new offensive by the Picts, but possibly along the eastern coast in the Saxon Shore forts where there would have been an already established housing and supply system in place.[1]

The mercenary leaders demanded more provisions, and when these were not forthcoming they and their men revolted. Much of the island was devastated during the ensuing attacks. It was only when Ambrosius began counterattacking with his guerrillas that the war became a two-way struggle. In time it would come to a head at Badon, where the Britons won a decisive and likely pitched victory that paused the war for at least forty-three years.

It has often been repeated that Gildas was forced to guess at many of the events that took place before his birth, and that the name of Agitius is our first indication that he had access to living memory in his historical account[2]; that he must have spelled it phonetically, and with flaws, is a good indicator that the event was at the very extent of his real knowledge. It is at this point where the modern use of his denunciation begins in earnest.

Agitius is normally taken as a convoluted form of Aetius, a Germanic Roman serving as a general in 446 and active in and around Gaul. It seems unlikely that Gildas would have made up a name, especially as he is generally so loath to give them at all. It seems even less likely that he could have invented one that in any way resembles that of a prominent Roman leader at any time during the fifth century. That he names someone who was powerful during the same mid–fifth century that he appears to be speaking of is even more unlikely if he created the name. Unless we are to start playing extremely long odds, Aetius was what Gildas meant.

Gildas then goes into a diatribe about how kings were chosen all over the island on the basis of their unchristian virtues during the period of peace that followed Badon. However, he had already mentioned a single king of the island, the one who had been solely responsible for inviting the Germanic peoples into Britain. If there had been only one king, then his one kingdom should have fought off the Germanic peoples, and as the kingdom that did so it should have maintained control over the Britons after the war was ended. That sequence of events certainly seems more feasible than the idea of a kingdom crumbling while its villages were still mainly in British hands, then a large group of leaderless but still British villages finding a leader before they were conquered, followed by that leader then quietly giving way to multiple kingships after the general peace that followed Badon.

What seems to be happening is that Gildas knows the contemporary island is ruled by petty kings, but he is not able to envision a post–Roman Britain that is or that might be ruled by some precursor of it. So, though he makes comments about the state of kingship and earlier had said that *civitates* and not kings were writing to Hadrian and Aetius, he can only see the Germanic peoples coming into Britain with the permission of an island-wide government. Clues of such an agreement may have been a part of the cultural history during his time. Indeed, modern scholarship has come to see that Germanic mercenaries were taking up defensive posts all along the eastern and southern coast of England on the Saxon Shore mentioned above. However, it would appear that here again Gildas' relative chronology was off; Germanic warriors had been stationed in Britain for at least a century before the Roman withdrawal and under Roman authority.[3]

With it shown that the first group of Germanic peoples were not first brought over at some time after 446, there is not only no need for any over-king but also no evidence that there was one. Gildas' invention was named Vortigern, which translates into English as "proud tyrant" anyway.[4]

The next leader to appear in Gildas' history is Ambrosius, who is not present in any of the extant British genealogies and therefore may have been little more than a local leader. His war ends with Badon, which places him at Gildas' birth and forty-three years before Gildas wrote.

The ensuing period seems not to have concerned Gildas apart from his allegation that people had forgotten the horrors of the Germanic attacks and had set themselves to internal fighting. Beginning to come to his point, he notes that his people had begun to elect the least moralistic among them to be their leaders.

Gildas' flaws as a firsthand witness were not grasped by later historians, and Gildas was the only Briton that was known by medieval historians to have written any sort of a history of the British fifth century. Because of his unique position as the only witness for the entire period, he was latched upon as the one true source of information for the years between the departure of Rome and roughly the year 600. Later historians would accept everything he wrote as factual, only altering his words to interpret or add details to what he had written.

Bede would follow Gildas, and he would attempt to set the historical events of his predecessor into a chronologically sensible framework. He would repeat much of Gildas' early fifth-century events verbatim, but he would add dates wherever he felt he understood one of Gildas' passages well enough to clarify him. For instance, he was the first person to connect Agitius to Aetius and to date him securely to 446. However, he misread Gildas on two important points. First, he misunderstood Gildas in thinking the one length of time he did give—the interval between the Battle of Badon and the time of his writing—as forty-four years. Gildas wrote that the event had occurred forty-three years and one month before he wrote his letter. Second, Bede misunderstood Gildas' wording in where the space of time occurred. Bede believed that Badon took place forty-four years before it actually did. The difficulties in his history only compounded from that point. From a source which has not come down to us, he knew or calculated that Gildas was born in 493, which meant that Badon occurred in 493 as well. Subtracting forty-four years from that point gave him a precise date for the emigration of the Anglo-Saxons as 449. Coincidentally, that was three years after Aetius had been elected as consul for the third time. With an easily cross-checked date to prove that his calculations were correct, Bede would use his two derived dates to rationalize a year by year framework for the period. His reputation as a meticulous Latin scholar has expanded into a respect for his scholarship, and that has made the dates he arrived at as nearly beyond scrutiny.[5]

The Anglo-Saxon Chronicle would make use of Bede's 449, continuing his process of fleshing out the spread of the Germanic peoples in Britain using that date as a starting point and the living history contained in the various kingdoms' oral histories as foundations upon which to establish a string of tangible dates. There would be little point in going over the overlapping interests and multiple sources at work in determining each kingdom's relative chronology in the chronicle at this time. All that is relevant is that everything was built off of Bede's interpretation of Gildas' account. *The Anglo-Saxon Chronicle* was put in its final form by the tenth century and under the watchful eye of Alfred the Great.

Historia Brittonum left the date of Badon vague, never bothering to place it between a pair of events with sound dates.[6] Its omission of a tangible year for this key battle is significant because the history likely relies on information that precedes and in this era is more accurate than anything Bede might have been able to use. This, and the absence of any dates in the period before 600 in general suggests that the *Northern Memorandum, Historia Brittonum's* main source here, contained no years for any of the events in that general time frame.

This conclusion is supported by the fact that *Historia Brittonum* is the first extant source to directly associate Badon with Arthur. Despite the fact that it was written some three hundred years after the fact, the age of its source makes possible that this connection is a historical one and therefore if there is a year to be found or derived for Badon it would be there.

On the other hand, the difficulties in locating Badon chronologically may just be an indication of the source's limitations pertaining to the fifth century; as early as the *Northern Memorandum* in the late seventh century, Arthur's ahistorical participation at Badon may have been put into a history. There is no way of being certain if Arthur was present or not; we may only speculate as to the date and how our uncertainty here affects our understanding of Gildas.

The *Annales Cambriae*, composed largely of the same source materials as *Historia Brittonum*, also associates the battle with Arthur. However, it gives specific dates for all the events that it lists. *Annales Cambriae* ignores Bede's derived year of 493 and, again from a source which is not extant or through machinations that are no longer apparent, decided on the year 517 for the battle. Regardless, the date was first associated with the event in *Annales Cambriae*. Because we can be certain its common source with *Historia Brittonum* had no years for the events it recorded, we may safely conclude that 517 was an addition made by a contributor to the *Annales Cambriae*.

The *Annales Cambriae* date for Camlann is 537. This appears to be an entirely arbitrary year. It has no clear significance in the British records other than as the year when Arthur died. No significant individual comes to power in the years following. It is not associated with any event or campaign among the Germanic or Irish records, either. Because of this lack of materials, the author has no theories as to why that particular year was chosen.

Geoffrey of Monmouth was the great synthesizer of British history. As has been seen he put Arthur into the common consciousness of Medieval Europe as a historical figure. Geoffrey dominated thought about the geography of Arthur because he was able to put what had been isolated incidents in his personal life into the larger context of Arthur's reign and British history. The same was true with Arthurian chronology. He took Bede's now-standard 449 for the invasion of the Anglo-Saxons, presenting more dates and fully developing stories to his audience where there had been only references before regarding the key figures of the fifth century. And when he came to Arthur, he expanded his reign and fit it in tightly in line behind Vortigern, Ambrosius, and Arthur's father, Uther, and just before Maelgwn, whom he believed had died in 547 following that individual's obit in *Annales Cambriae*. Geoffrey had his chief character crowned in 490, fighting Badon in 500, and dying at Camlann in 542.

Geoffrey had no real concern for accurate dates. The over-kings he lists after Arthur are proof of that. They are the kings listed in Gildas, and they rule consecutively in the exact same order as they are presented by him in *De Excidio Britanniae*. As has been seen many times with him, he took the source material he had and molded it into whatever he needed. This was so with Gildas' conveniently given kings. It was also so with chronology as well as the historicity and geography of Arthur.

Not that Geoffrey could have derived the stable chronology he was after making use of the sources he had at his disposal. Even using the most careful scholarship and painstaking research that likely would have been beyond the abilities of any scholar at that time. Gildas was vague, and as has been seen those who derived dates from him were either misinterpreting him or simply guessing based on the materials he had given in his writing. Modern scholarship has no way of knowing where any of the other dates for Badon or Camlann came from, only that the sources at our disposal are later and seem to have used materials that date after Gildas. Because of the lack of accuracy in any of the extant sources on this point, when scholars cite any of the dates between 490 and 517 for the Battle of Mount Badon and 537 to 542 for Camlann, they are doing so without any credible historical sources. The reality is that there is no direct evidence for the dating of any single event or even for any arbitrary year in Arthur's career. The pages below will attempt to rectify that situation.

CHAPTER 19

The Romanitas of Arthur's Era

In 410 and after decades of insurrections and would-be emperors coming from the island, the Roman emperor is said to have declared that Britain would have to take care of itself for the time being. The Roman Empire never again returned to the island. As the decades passed, Britain eventually became less and less Roman in its culture. By the time Arthur became a part of the European consciousness, the native cultures had overwhelmed it entirely. This chapter will place Arthur's birth and floruit in some relative chronological context with this process of de–Romanization.

Arthur as a name is derived from Latin *Artorius*. The British hero has been called, in Latinized British, *Arcturus*, "the bear," by several later medieval writers, but this is not so in the earliest Welsh traditions, nor in Geoffrey of Monmouth's *Historia de Regum Britanniae* which brought the name to continental Europe. Arcturus may possibly represent a legitimate tradition associating the hero with brutality and strength, but it is not his original name[1]; Arthur is. For this reason, it is safe to conclude that Arthur must have been raised within a culture that was at the least nominally Roman.

It is not known how long Britain remained Roman in its outlook. However, we know that it survived for some time after 410. As has often been remarked, St. Germanus visited the island in 429 on a religious issue. During his stay there, he had no trouble speaking with the natives in Latin and without a translator. It is possible that he returned there in 437, 441, or 445.[2] If he did, he had no trouble communicating with them then, either. This despite the fact that the elite on the island seem to have been leaving for the continent from the late fourth century and had been taking with them the personal tutors that had been teaching proper Latin for generations. It should be remembered that even during Germanus' known visit the youngest people who could have learned Latin and been an adult under Roman rule would have been 37. The fifth century was a period where 55 was a maximum life-span for the average person.[3] If all Roman learning had ceased in 410, the people who could still speak to Germanus would only have been a small portion of the total population. If he did come later, then the portion of the community who could speak to him would have been even smaller. Latin must have been taught beyond 410.

Evidence for this can be seen elsewhere as well. In contacting Aetius at some time in the middle of the fifth century, the British people did so as citizens of the Roman Empire.

It is unknown when exactly the Britons ceased to think of themselves as Roman, but events on the continent would eventually force them to do so. In 476 what remained of the Western Roman Empire would be conquered by the Ostrogoths. Though contemporaries seem not to have understood that the world had changed with that event, they had certainly grasped it within the next generation.

The same must have been true of the Britons. By at latest 600, but possibly as early as 540, traditional British bards would be using ancient Celtic forms to sing the praises of kings wearing strictly Celtic jewelry, fighting Celtic battles, and living in very non–Roman halls.[4] Between a century and two after the last Roman legion left, all Latin cultural influence would be gone.

The question, then, is when exactly did *Romanitas* end in Britain? At the far extreme of this range we have Gildas. He has a rich understanding of the Roman legal system and writes in a Latin that only Golden Age writers could match.[5] It has been noted that his education is at odds with what is known of the Romano-British state of decay during the late fifth and early sixth centuries[6]; however, what is known may well be inaccurate. Gildas did address his most famous letter, *De Excidio Britanniae*, to lay people as well as to fellow ecclesiastics. This implies that well into his adulthood, the British kings or at least their clerks could be expected to understand Latin. Unfortunately, we have no other indications throughout the sixth century that a working knowledge of Latin persisted among the nonreligious community and therefore no way of limiting the date-range of *Romanitas* through this means.

On the other hand, we cannot look on Gildas as an isolated scholar existing in a cesspool of barbarianism any longer, either. Patrick, writing at some time before 493,[7] might not have had the brilliance in his writing that his later contemporary possessed, but he certainly was a more than competent writer of colloquial Latin.[8]

Personal names are also a good indicator of where the culture considered itself during this time. Padarn Peisrud, or "red tunic," of Gwynedd likely was known as Latin Paternus in his own time. Padarn seems to have no Celtic etymology,[9] and therefore no history before its post–Roman introduction. His epithet has been thought to refer to his Roman office.[10] Tradition and genealogical studies have shown that his active life was over by roughly 400. Cunedda of Gododdin, a Celticized form of Constantine, was similarly a person of the fourth century. Both men have been seen as *foederati*, or more broadly as the leaders of satellite states that were either formed or supported by Roman Britain to give her a shock absorber from any incursions.

However the Roman names continue well after the watershed of 410. Patrick and Ambrosius are both distinctly Roman names, and both of these men were likely born around the middle of the fifth century. Aircol Lawhir, or Agricola of Dyfed, was probably born around 500. Merchiaun, or Meirchion, of southern Wales was active at some point in the same era. The grandfather of Urien, a man of the same name, was likely active around 500. It is interesting to note that Latin and even Romanized names almost completely disappear in the generation born much after 500. After that time, Latin becomes rare and inconsistent among the laymen.[11]

The story is only slightly different among the ecclesiastics. Three prominent saints of the middle and late sixth century were called Paternus, and may have been born anywhere from the early fifth century to the middle of the sixth. Illtud's pupils Paul Aurelian, Samson, and Leonorus all have distinctly Latin or biblical names and were all active into the middle of the sixth century and later. Of all six individuals, Leonorus is known to have been born in 507 or 508, perhaps a decade after the secular names cease to be Latin. Likely the names of churchmen continued the Latin tradition longer because of the church's connection to the continent.[12]

Other indicators can be found in the large Roman towns and cities. Public works, by Roman custom the responsibility of the wealthy, began to fall into disrepair toward the end of the fifth century.[13] B- and D-ware amphorae, dating through the early fifth century and perhaps later, have been found all over the western coast. These indicate not only trade with the continent but a continuing respect for things Roman.[14]

Coins have been found dating to the last days of Roman Britain but in a state of heightened wear. This has often been taken to mean that the Roman economy persisted for decades after 407,[15] though this is a false indicator. While the money was certainly used for some time, the Roman economy in Britain had been dependent on a constant influx of new coins coming to the island via the soldiers and bureaucracy. At the point when there was neither an influx of soldiers, bureaucracy, or coins, the island would have slowly but inexorably turned to a barter system. This would have occurred regardless of the continuation of Roman culture, but it may have taken decades to complete. The result would have been the unusual wear found on the coins.

The very use of traditional Roman forts in the sub–Roman period implies a continuing knowledge of Roman strategy. As archaeology has earlier attested, hill-forts were the normal defensive and high-status sites among pre–Roman Britons, and they would regain their former importance by the time of Mael-gwn and the Battle of Catraeth—events of the mid–sixth century at the latest. And in fact, the physical remains indicate that many of the Roman sites were abandoned long before then. The only region in which the occupation of Roman forts was the rule rather than the exception appears to have been the area around Hadrian's Wall. In contrast to the rest of the island, the Roman forts there were being refortified as late as the early sixth century. If Britain gave up on the fortification system within a few decades, the north was decades behind and therefore would have carried on the Roman culture longer.

Based on the limited evidence to be found pertaining to Roman culture in post–Roman Britain, it would seem that the Britons as a whole considered themselves Roman till at least the middle of the fifth century—the time of their request to Aetius. This may well have continued for several decades after-ward. However, by roughly 470 or 480 prominent individuals were no longer being given Latin personal names. In the years surrounding 500, several Roman forts were refortified in the north and the final generation of religious indi-viduals with given Roman names were born. The generation born before 470 likely was not active into the second quarter of the sixth century, and as they died off the last connections to the Roman past were gracefully forgotten in favor of the new culture of kingships and warriors. The Britons may have still spoken Latin for a generation longer, but when Gildas wrote only a decade or two later it was likely only the ecclesiastics who still considered themselves to be Roman.

CHAPTER 20

Bardic Chronology

In Chapter 6, all of the known bards who were active between roughly 410 and the middle of the seventh century were listed. Wherever there was sufficient information, each of them was examined individually and as part of any group they were found associated with. Attempting both studies allowed for a contrast with each other that was often helpful in determining more accurate data. With that as a foundation, it was a relatively straightforward process to obtain the most accurate location and floruit possible in a majority of cases. The assumption was that, even if Arthur's bard was not known, knowing where the heaviest bardic activity was might give some indications of where the culture of the heroic age was centered. That, I assumed, was the most likely region in which the British Heroic Age's most popular figure would have been active.

It was also noted that all of the kings associated with the known bards of the period are among the most famous of British heroes. Arthur, as the most famous king, may well have employed one or more of the men on the list.

This chapter has a slightly different objective. The presence of bards in British society signals the reemergence of the native culture and with it the beginnings of a heroic age. Bardic poetry and storytelling skills praised the accomplishments of specific kings whose lives revolved around the hall and raiding, activities directly at odds with Roman culture. Kings such as Arthur probably were not around before the bards and certainly would not have been remembered at all without them.

We start again with the seventeen poets: Talhaearn Tat-Aguen, Neirin, Taliesin, Cian, Bluchbard, Cadegr, Argad, Disgyfdawd, Tristfardd, Dygynnelw, Auan Verdic, Arouan, Golydan, Meigant, Heinin, Gwron son of Cynfarch, and Kywryt.

Neirin, as Aneirin, is associated strictly with Gododdin. Because of his association with Catraeth and its date-range of 540 to around 570, it can be safely assumed that he was active in that period.

Taliesin wandered from Cynan of Powys to Urien of Reged with a short period at the court of Gwallog in Elmet. This would make him roughly contemporary to Aneirin, a product of the middle of the sixth century.

Tristfardd, Dygynnelw, Auan Verdic, and Arouan belonged to Urien, Owain son of Urien, Cadwallon son of Cadfan, and Selyf son of Cynan Garwyn, respectively. Their patron's careers would correspondingly place them in the middle of the sixth century, at the decades before 600, before 634, and the years before 600.

Meigant is associated exclusively with Cynddyllan in Cyndrwynyn and therefore was active at some point in the last quarter of the sixth century or the first quarter of the seventh. Heinin was Maelgwn's bard, and active around 530. Kywryt was with Dunawt of the Old North, a king who flourished at roughly the same time as Owain son of Urien around 600.

Given his prominence in *Historia Brittonum* and the history's purpose, Talhaearn belongs to Gwynedd, or less likely Powys. Because of the Irish origins of his name, Cian could only have been associated with Gwynedd. Neither of these individuals can be connected with either a king or even a rough time period.

Disgyfdawd was Northumbrian. Chronologically, it can only be certain that he was active before the entire region was conquered in about 605. He may have been one of the first new masters of the old art born in the middle of the fifth century, or he could have active into the seventh century.

The unassociated bards are Bluchbard, Cadegr, Argad, Golydan, and Gwron. Of these, Gwron son of Cynfarch is potentially dateable to the mid- to late-sixth century because of his patrilineage. If Cynfarch was an unusual name, which seems reasonable after consulting with Bartrum's book on medieval Welsh history and literature,[1] then it may well have been the same man as Urien's father. This would put him in Reged and with roughly the same floruit as another son of Cynfarch, the famed Urien. Reged, modern Cumberland, was an area that included Carlisle—Arthur's likely capital.

Bluchbard is of interest because of our lack of understanding about him. He is the only one of the five poets listed in the *Historia Brittonum* for whom something cannot be reasoned through directly. However, all the other men on the list belong to either *Y Hen Ogled* or Gwynedd. Considering the theme of that particular history, namely of connecting Gwynedd with the Old North's history and traditions, it is safe to say that Bluchbard was from one of those two areas as well. As only two of those bards can be roughly dated, and those to the middle of the sixth century, Bluchbard's floruit must remain a question mark.

The other three bards—Cadegr, Argad, and Golydan—are chronologically and geographically unknown, nor does there appear to be any means of making an educated guess as to where or when any of them belong. This means that if it is to be assumed that the name of Arthur's poet has survived it might be either Bluchbard or Gwron, but the possibility remains that it could have been one of these three individuals as well.

For our immediate needs, however, such a conclusion is unnecessary. To put the data in more digestable form, the raw data is as follows:

Region	no.	rough or relative dates for each bard
Gwynedd	4	?, ?, 632, 535
Gododdin	1	540–570
Reged	3⅓	540–570, 540–570, 570–600, 540–570
Powys	1⅓	540–570, Selyf son of Cynan
Elmet	⅓	540–570
Cynddyllan	1	c. 575–625
Northumbria	1	Before roughly 605
Old North	1	570–600

The statistic that emerges above is undeniable. Many of the bards wrote during the same era, perhaps the high point in the British warrior society. However, nowhere are the dateable bards to be found before 535. It is also interesting that Reged is the region in which the largest number of bards are known, and all those that are dateable were active during the sixth century. This is an unsuspected result given that Gwynedd was responsible for the survival of much of the information we have on the history of the period. Despite its centrality to our historical records of the period, the data we have is focused on a region that by the ninth century had been British for a couple of centuries.

What this means is that, as a gatherer and recorder of history during the ninth century, Gwynedd may well have added information about her bards to an already existing body of information, but that data was originally not focused on her, nor did the knowledge Gwynedd added do any more than supplement the original body. This conclusion is in agreement with what has already been determined about other historical materials Gwynedd produced in the ninth century.[2]

Two items may be drawn from the above exercise: that there are no bards that can be dated any earlier than 535 and that several bards can be located but not dated. A number of possibilities could explain these results. One could make the argument that the bards did not become active until roughly 535. In this hypothesis, the bards who are not dated were attached to patrons or kingdoms that were forgotten over time. The problem with this theory is that history seems to come into focus with Gildas at about this time, and the British kingdoms largely stabilized at about that juncture as well. From roughly 535 on, we can be fairly certain we know who was king in any fair-sized kingdom at any given time. Given what we do know, it seems unlikely that such a large portion of the bards whose names have come down to us would be able to so totally elude all study.

What seems more likely is that at least some of the bards listed above come from a time anterior to 535, a period before our knowledge of the British becomes comparatively strong and while the kingdoms were still in the process of development. Several details point to such an option.

As the "father of poetry," Talhaearn Tat-Aguen's epithet can have only three interpretations in my estimation. Talhaearn may have been the first prominent bard to appear in the post–Roman period, and it was he that all later bards sought to emulate. He may have inspired all later poetry well after the bardic class had been reinstated. Finally, Talhaearn's title may be nothing more than another example of Gwynedd propaganda whose title has no basis in reality. It has already been suggested that his implied accomplishments may be little more than propaganda. However, our understanding of the history seems to argue against that suggestion for several reasons. For one, it should be remembered that it was a part of *Historia Brittonum*'s mandate to promote intra–British relations, and because of this the accomplishments of other dynasties and kingdoms are occasionally included, though never exaggerated. This leaves open the possibility that Talhaearn was exactly what he is claimed to be, if he was from a kingdom not related to Gwynedd.

However, it has been seen that much of what has been put into the history was placed there, and its place especially worded, to promote Gwynedd or a closely tied kingdom as well as to include some accurate information. The developments of the past few decades have also determined that individuals were never reappropriated to Gwynedd's history so much as their place was occasionally exaggerated within it. Talhaearn is not specifically assigned to any individual, which suggests that he was active early on in post–Roman history.[3] For these reasons it seems safe to assume that Talhaearn may well have served Gwynedd, Powys, or Reged very early on in their respective histories. If this is the case, it is more likely that he was only the most famous bard of that particular kingdom.

Cian has also been noted as possessing a name whose point of origin was most likely Gwynedd. The reason for this was that a part of Anglesey was still in Irish hands into the sixth century, and the clan which held that kingdom was the Ciannachta or children of Cian. Any Irishman trained while the Ciannachta held part of Anglesey would have reached the end of his career by or before roughly 535. That bard would have been active for decades before that.

Finally, there is Disgyfdawd and his sons. The former individual was a Brennych bard who sired three kings. His children's vocation seems unusual; bards and kings were generally from different classes apart from the occasional ruler who happened to take up storytelling. However, what is noteworthy about this foursome is the region in which they were active—Northumbria. It is known that Æthelfrith had conquered the entire region by about 605, so that this can be considered a hard *ante quem* for the rule of Disgyfdawd's sons. After Æthelfrith had united Northumbria he seems to have had no internal concerns for the rest of his career.

The implications of the passage are far more intriguing.[4] As Disgyfdawd is neither listed as royal nor associated with any lineage, he is the same type of figure as Ambrosius and some of the other very early kings: a person who likely had no royalty in his family history before his sons began their own reigns. This would suggest a much earlier date than the early seventh century for the floruits of his sons. Kingship and the reestablishment of the bardic order, as has been seen, were already occurring in the late fifth century. That would be the more likely time frame for the father.

One may take this assumption a step further. Though Æthelfrith was from the same kingdom as the historian Bede would be, and though Bede would have taken some satisfaction in recording the defeat of the false Christian Britons at his hands (he did so with the Battle of Chester), none of Æthelfrith's battles with the British are mentioned within the borders of Northumbria, and so from the years 592 or 593 until roughly 605. This suggests that the conquest occurred prior to a time when Bede's sources were recording history. On less certain grounds, Taliesin and several isolated poems relating to Urien and his confederates name several enemies and allies but mention none of Disgyfdawd's sons anywhere. This may well take us back to before the middle of the sixth century and again before 535 for the floruit of Disgyfdawd's sons.

To reiterate, there are only a relatively small number of names for the bards of the British Heroic Age, and yet as has been seen there is evidence that three of them dated to before the middle of the sixth century. Several more are associated with no king and no region—an indicator that they were active before then as well and during a time when kingdoms and kingships were in flux. Though the inability to directly associate Arthur with a specific bard means that he cannot be tied directly to any time period, the suggestion of bardic activity before the middle of the sixth century and back to the late fifth century, coupled with the relative plethora of northern bards, does not preclude the date-range that has already been established.

CHAPTER 21

Caradoc of Llancarfan

Caradoc of Llancarfan was undoubtedly one of the most talented religious men to take up writing during the twelfth century, and might very well have been an equal to the greatest lay writers of his day if his life had been lived outside of a monastery. As things stand, all that remains of his writing prowess is to be found in his hagiographies. He has three surviving works in the genre. To some extent, they are typical of the style; they take whatever minimal native materials there were to be found and organize them into a coherent narrative in order to forward the agenda of the patronizing monastery and raise the prestige of the saint.

Caradoc not only managed the tasks set to him, he seems to have excelled at the work. It is known that he was referred to other monasteries twice; each of his extant saint's lives was written for different houses than his home. One key ingredient that appears in all of his work is his addition of northern characters taken from a northern context—suggesting that he made use of a pool of knowledge that none of his contemporary hagiographers were aware of. Three times in his *vitae* Caradoc implied that he had access to a body of knowledge from the north. In the *Vita Cadoci*, he placed the protagonist in a northerly area when he brought the Pictish giant Caw back to life. In the *Vita Gildae*, he tells the reader that Hueil was coming from the north, from Scotland, when he clashed with Arthur. Finally, the *vita's* opening lines locate the saint's place of birth in the north at Strathclyde. As it has been seen that Arthur was from the north as well, those episodes involving him may well have had some kernel of historical truth as well.

More important than Caradoc's northerly associations, however, are his and his patrons' biases. In the case of all three instances, the presence of the character in the north or from the north did nothing to further the designs of the patronizing monastery. No land grants are involved with Caw, Hueil, or Strathclyde, nor could they have been considering the Welsh location of Caradoc's patrons. One could argue that Caradoc has not made the most of his opportunities here; it certainly would have been possible for him to transplant Caw, Hueil, and Gildas into a Welsh or Cornish setting just as easily as Arthur had already been localized there. Moving these characters would in fact have been preferable, allowing Caradoc's employers to benefit from the additional fame of those widely known individuals. And yet he did not, and the (now established) northern origins of Arthur confirm that Caradoc's source or sources were giving him accurate historical information here. As was seen above, Hueil's raid on Arthur was deeply rooted and traditional, as was the belief that his kingdom was in Scotland. That Gildas and Caw, Hueil's father and brother, would similarly be located in that region, and are placed there in a separate section and a different book, respectively, can be used to argue nothing else.

It seems reasonable that, as a professional hagiographer, Caradoc had some access to traditional knowledge in addition to that offered to most of his fellow writers. In fact, having just such a cache of information on the local legends of the north might well have given him a significant advantage over other hagiographers of his day. Whether he had this access because he was a collector of the local lore and could not resist throwing unedited native segments into his *vita*, was an oral storyteller of some sort, or even if he was from the north and had heard stories involving the subjects he injects into his stories is unclear. Whatever the case may be, Caradoc's writings are unique to the *vitae* tradition and therefore of great value in any study of which they are a part.

Knowing this additional Caradoc source means that just as the locations he associates with Arthur, Caw, Gildas, and Hueil in his writings are a reasonably accurate reflection of the historical reality of the fifth and sixth centuries, so it is safe to work under the assumption that any information to be found in his hagiographies are equally correct from a chronological standpoint. Just as the originally Cumbrian hero Arthur slowly gathered characters that had been active in areas further and further away from his original region of activity, Arthur was broadly located around Cumbria in the *Vita Gildae*. Just as Arthur slowly attracted people that were more distant in time from him, those to be found in the four Arthurian Caradoc episodes likely include some of his contemporaries as well.

CHAPTER 22

Gildasian Chronology

In the introduction to the chronological portion of this book, Gildas' received chronology was reviewed as it passed to Bede and then *The Anglo-Saxon Chronicle*. It was noted that because Bede's Latin was so strong, he had a reputation in the Middle Ages for being an accomplished academician with a powerful and penetrating intellect. Because of his stature in this regard, his interpretation of the sequence and dating of events in early post–Roman history was never really questioned by the English scholars who followed him. As has been seen, this is a trend that continued with Geoffrey of Monmouth and lasted well into the modern era.

Fortunately, through the efforts of several experts in British history and archaeology, his shortcomings are now readily apparent to current scholarship. It is only a matter of time before this awareness transfers to the broader approach of dating early English history. Given several decades of discussion and refinement, a revision of how we see Bede will inevitably reach the lay person as well.

What is to replace the present place he holds in English history is another matter. Bede was the first scholar to put the history of Britain from the departure of the Romans to the Synod at Whitby into a single and easily understood context.

Because of his primacy, he was also the historian upon which standard medieval histories were based for centuries. Having shown his version to be inaccurate, it is necessary to start with what little primary source material we have and develop our own body of knowledge. That means that, for much of the fifth and sixth centuries, we are left only with Gildas.

In the study of post–Roman Britain, Gildas is perhaps the most thoroughly studied source. He is without doubt the least trusted among them.

Unfortunately, he is the only firsthand speaker who gives us information about all of fifth-century Britain. That fact has proven endlessly tantalizing; it keeps bringing the best scholars of the period back to him.

That he wrote the relevant material as nothing more than a prelude to a legal argument has hardly slowed historians down. That he gives no indications of where personal memory blends into living memory and then transitions into an oral tradition has meant nothing either. If anything, the additional difficulties have only given these scholars more nooks and crannies in which to work their innumerable theories as to his time and place of writing.

Several scholars in recent years have studied his geographical bias, the specific functions of his letter and other non-chronological aspects of his writing. Others, such as Professor Sims-Williams and Professor Higham, have pointed out the flaws in trying to recover even a relative chronology from an examination of his writings. Instead, these scholars have sought to independently understand exactly how Roman Britain collapsed into a sub–Roman island invaded by three different culture groups while a fourth attempted to reinvent itself from the shadow of Roman rule.[1]

A very few have attempted to reconstruct the chronology of the fifth century despite the obvious difficulties. Thompson examined the problem with his characteristic flare and, using the year of 446 as his anchor, decided that all the events from Aetius to Badon and Gildas' birth could have taken place in little more than a decade. His proposal can be summarized as follows:

446	Aetius
451–453	Raiding and famine
455–457	Guerrilla warfare
458–461	Prosperity

And while this timeline most definitely qualifies as a possibility, several potential flaws do emerge from such a conclusion. Gildas was notoriously unspecific in many different areas, including giving any absolute dates. The amount of time between and of each separate incident he spoke of was left vague as well. Thompson himself only offered that the above was a feasible chronology given what Gildas tells us in the straightforward language and the nuances of what he wrote. Even for him, the above made use of a minimal length of time.

Dumville's dates were derived by reading the material and then using the context of the language to guess at a range of dates of and between each event. His approach gave him the following:

446–454	Aetius
c. 450–455	Raiding and famine
c. 455–480	Peace and abundance
	Kingship?
c. 480	Plague, invasion, and introduction of the *superbus tyrannus*
c. 480–490	Saxon mercenaries and their rebellion
c. 490	Cities destroyed, migrations, emergence of Ambrosius
c. 495	Ambrosius wins a battle
c. 495–500	War
c. 500	Badon
c. 500–545	Gildas' lifetime up to the letter

As thorough as Professor Dumville normally is, the specific dates he gives seem to be wholly likely at first glance. The only cause for raised eyebrow is his uncharacteristic acceptance of the traditional date for Badon. It does seem curious, and convenient, that it is here dated to right around 500, the date generally given for Badon in every major history. As has been seen, it is a date based on deeply flawed material and assumptions.

As one looks more closely at the results of both scholars, one recognizes that though the layouts given by both of them seem to be plausible, they also have their individual and shared problems. The horizon of living memory falls roughly to the episode involving the letter to Aetius. If the letter was within living memory of the people Gildas had been around in his childhood, an exact date for the event would be feasible. If not, then the dating then it could not be. Both scholars assumed that Gildas' word could be taken at face value here and thus that the information on Aetius was perfectly correct. But they never presented a case for such an assumption.

On the other hand, the odd form of Aetius' name would argue otherwise. It is neither correct nor an interpretation of what it sounds like. It is clearly a name that was improperly remembered by a generation that had not been alive when Aetius was active.

Even working under the assumption that the Aetius entry and all later relative chronology is accurate creates problems. The very fact that the widely varying chronologies produced by Thompson and Dumville are possible serves to show the potential flaws of each theoretical model. While Thompson seems to rush through events almost too quickly, Dumville could well be needlessly lengthening the time frames; why would there need to be twenty-five years of peace? Why not ten? His dating of Badon does seem rather oddly in line with Geoffrey and later pseudo-historians. That agreement does nothing to help his credibility.

More specifically, Thompson seems to be streamlining not only the intervals between events, but Gildas' passage itself. He allows for only one cycle of devastation, recovery, and prosperity. Dumville is the more faithful to the source here. Whether it is a rhetorical device or an honest recounting of history, Gildas laid out two distinct periods of raiding followed by the Britons rising up, fighting back the foreigners, and falling into a period of peace and political decay.

Despite the fundamental differences Thompson and Dumville have in their approaches, both men were consistent in one important aspect of their approach—they all follow Gildas forward in time. I believe that this has led to fallacies of perception. Taking the same approach also has the disadvantage of making it easier to fall into the assumptions of previous scholars. To counter these potential errors in the reconstruction process, I propose to work with Gildas' post–Roman chronology in reverse. At worst, the approach will have the benefit of providing support for one or more of the previous attempts to understand Gildasian chronology. At best, perhaps a few of the unlikely assumptions created in the process will become more visible.

Let us begin where he finishes. Gildas says that for the forty-three years between his birth and the time of his writing, the Germanic peoples have attacked only in raids and skirmishes. In those years shortly after his birth the British maintained their vigil against them. The generation that has followed, who knew nothing of the horrors of the Germanic invaders, has grown less attentive. Worse, without understanding the threat they represent, the Britons have fallen to warring among themselves.

Accepting Gildas' words to the letter we can begin to break down the events of his life-span. In a period when 32 was the average life expectancy for men,[2] the life-span for participants could not have been another twenty years for the warriors who fought at Badon. Assuming that at least some of the participants at Gildas' singular battle were already veterans at the time of the battle, the period of vigilance may have been considerably less than two decades. Because of these facts, it is safe to assume that internecine conflicts were rife among the Britons within that period of time.

However, two items must be taken into account when studying this passage. First, Gildas would have received only random information from whatever travelers happened to come to the monastery he was at until he had completed his education. So, unless war directly affected him or those he had daily interactions with during this time, he would not have known that there were constant intra–British wars throughout the island during the first couple of decades of his life.

Second, it must never be forgotten that Gildas was writing a legal argument and not a history. As such, his biases become clear. It served his purposes to write an account of the past in which the actions of the present generation could be compared with the previous one. The results of the earlier cycle could then be used as a teaching tool for the people of his own time. The problems, their recovery, and their overwhelming victory against a powerful Germanic people did just that. In laying out what had happened and giving a clear path of cause and effect he was able to demonstrate the rewards of unity. In detailing how close the Britons had come to annihilation, he showed his readers the direction their civilization was heading.

For Gildas, Badon itself had been a decisive battle and the last real confrontation with the Germanic peoples. However, Gildas does clearly state that it was not the greatest battle. Nor does he give the name of the victorious general of the engagement. It might have been Ambrosius, but it may also have been someone else such as Arthur. And, knowing that the fighting season was short enough that an army could have participated in only a very small number of meaningful engagements, the war likely took some time. Twenty years, the probable maximum career of any chieftain, is likely on the short end of any reasonable estimate.

Ambrosius, whose career had occurred mainly before the battle, was the man who began the resurgence of British military power. He had emerged from a society that had been torn apart and was only recently plundered. In his lifetime, the Germanic mercenaries had swept over many areas of Britain and destroyed or taken anything they had wanted. Ambrosius united the Britons and focused all their energy into a campaign against the Germanic peoples. He gave them hope and a connection to a more secure past.

Ambrosius' rise to power had been as a result of the incursions of Germanic mercenaries or *foederati*. As the Roman presence in Britain had weakened over their last century of rule, the Irish, Picts, and Germanic peoples had all been raiding the Britons with increasing intensity and frequency. Gildas tells us that by the first few decades after 410 the raiding had become intolerable. The overking of the Britons, whom he labels *superbus tyrannus*, had hired the *foederati* in order to counter this threat. In Roman tradition, they were paid in food and goods. And when they were successful, he permitted more of them to land on the island.

Unfortunately, the Briton leader was unable or unwilling to pay all of his *foederati* enough to satisfy them. Or perhaps the *foederati* realized that they were not being paid by a true Roman. In any event it was only a matter of years before the mercenary bands had revolted and made what is described as an islandwide raid.

We know that their assault was made in 446 or later because of what Gildas says, that a letter was written to an Agitius, who was consul three times. Aetius is the only figure of the Roman Empire during the fifth century to have a name resembling Agitius, and he had his third term in 446. However, the use of the word Agitius instead of the proper Latin Aetius, and especially coming from a scholar of impeccable writing indicates a weak oral memory, one that has been described as on the boundaries of living memory.[3]

Other evidence that this is the limits of believable information may be seen as the narrative is looked at backwards. The appeal to Agitius was the third such request. The first two, according to Gildas, were Hadrian's and Antonine's walls, which history says were built over two centuries earlier.

The entire Late Roman and early post–Roman history he lays out can be seen as an attempt to rationalize the Roman remains that were still prominent on the island but whose origins had been forgotten. The election of three emperors from 406 to 407 is not mentioned because there was nothing in the landscape or the oral records to suggest that those events had ever occurred. To him there had been attacks in the past, there were walls, and the Romans had protected the British. These were made to fit together and work around his goal. The result was a cause and effect outline; his people had foolishly pushed the Romans out, the British had then been attacked from the north, and the Romans had rescued them. In their kindness, the Romans had told the British to build a wall, Antonine's Wall, and then left. When it proved insufficient after another widescale attack, the Romans had returned and built a second and stronger wall for them, Hadrian's Wall. The pattern he created in telling the history fit in well with what Gildas knew; that once the British had requested aid from the Romans and the Romans had been beneficent.

Their third request, to Aetius, had been refused because the Romans had tired of rescuing them. It is also the last time Rome is mentioned. Suspiciously, this is also where Vortigern enters the history. He is introduced solely to forward the history by explaining the presence of the Germanic peoples in Britain and the traditions his people had of the *foederati*.

The British intellect opens his ending of Roman history section with the Roman withdrawals which have been associated with 410. As can be seen clearly, there is a marked degeneration in the quality of the information he gives before Aetius. The explanations of the walls are only two examples. And since that is so, one standard assumption of historians seems much weakened—that the letter was sent to Aetius at precisely the year he was consul for the third time, or even within the range of dates from Aetius' third election to his death. The historian must not feel at all compelled to mark 446 as the year of the appeal, or even to work Gildas' chronology around the idea that the Germanic revolt took place at some time after that year.

Fortunately, the continent has preserved two other primary sources which speak of the Saxon revolt. They are the *Gallic Chronicle of 452* and the *Gallic Chronicle of 511*. With corrections to the dating schemes they use, both sources place the incident to roughly 441.[4] Their inconsistency with Gildas' chronology has caused some obvious problems in better understanding mid–century British history, so that generally speaking they have simply been glossed over by noting their internal and external inconsistencies. Several historians have simply ignored them. However, realizing that the original *foederati* may have been hired at any time during Aetius's years as one of the most prominent generals in Western Europe, other options reveal themselves.

Aetius was an active and noteworthy figure in the Roman Empire for many years before and after the year 446. In fact, between 433 and 454 he was the most significant Roman citizen. As he was a general of the Western Roman Empire, he spent a majority of those decades in Western Europe. If the British did write their request for help to him, it could have been at any point during that twenty-two year period. And, given that Gildas' relative history seems mostly accurate till at least this point and the continent's version does give a date for the Germanic uprising, it seems most likely that the letter was written at some before 441. More will be made of this derivation later in this chapter.

Gildas' history before 410 is so clearly flawed that nothing there should be accepted. For the period between then and the middle of the sixth century, there are no corroboratory sources apart from the Gallic Chronicles. This leaves no absolute year for any event between the withdrawal of the Roman presence by Constantine in 407 and well after Gildas wrote his historical preface. For that entire expanse of time, including as it does two Pictish and Irish raids, two returns of the Romans with their two wall formations, the appeal to Aetius, the Germanic mercenaries, their revolt, the emergence of Ambrosius, the Battle of Badon, the formation of kingships, and Gildas' entire life, we must guess about dates based on the clues this angry but well-read scholar left in his monologue.

Even more unfortunately, as the events prior to Aetius are nothing more than Gildas' attempts to rationalize what he knows with what he sees and build a theme that will culminate with the Germanic invaders, the range of believable historical events begins with the letter to him.

To the wild guesses, then. The barbarian incursions may well have taken place immediately after the letter to Aetius, but considering what easy targets the Britons appear to have been, there could hardly have been a delay of as much as ten years. A response to the threat in the form of Germanic mercenaries would have been swift and certain, perhaps within the same year but no longer than two or three years after the letter had failed to bring Roman legions back to the island. There, strongest indications are that these were settled along the southern and eastern coast, though there are suggestions that several may have been stationed closer to modern Scotland.

The mercenaries would have required food and supplies for their war-bands, but by Gildas' account they had brought over too many people to be supported by the native population. Within a few years, five at the most, the Britons would have been unable to pay and their employees would have been forced to act.

The revolt of the Germanic mercenaries would have followed as soon as they began to see their supplies diminishing. It makes the best sense that they would have raided those villages nearest them where they could most easily obtain what they needed and transport the materials home with them. For a majority of the *foederati*, this appears to have been the coastline extending from Kent. Ironically, this area had been responsible for a majority of the island's communications with the continent. With tribesmen controlling it and the sea between them and the continent, those communications quickly would have become inconsistent and incoherent.

By Gildas' account, there was no immediate resistance to the Germanic attack. That one was allowed to develop suggests that the Germanic peoples had no interest in conquest, only in the immediate interests of plunder and filling their stomachs. This agrees with the limited political structure to be found in the early Germanic record.[5] Within anywhere from a year to twenty, Ambrosius would emerge as the Briton leader, spearheading a campaign against the Germanic peoples that would eventually lead to Badon. If Gildas can be taken at his word here (as seems likely given the proximity of Gildas' audience to the events) and the British had begun as nothing more than a resistance group, then at least a decade but certainly no more than thirty years would have been required for a small band to develop into a military force capable of fighting a pitched battle. We have then:

X	Letter to Aetius
X+0–10	Picts resume attacks
X+0–13	Germanic tribesmen hired as mercenaries
X+2–18	Germanic revolt
X+3–38	Ambrosius becomes the Briton leader
X+13–68	Battle of Badon

This is a rather broad relative chronology, but it can hardly be claimed that it is inaccurate. It has in its favor a flexibility not to be found in either Thompson or Dumville, and it is not contingent on any absolute dates.

With a relative chronology laid out, the date that has been developed may be inserted, with 441 as the year of the revolt. Although it is not possible amid the difficulties of oral history to precisely time the appeal to Aetius, Gildas' testimony does indicate that it happened before the revolt. This gives us a second range of 433–439.

The Aetius time frame also helps with regards to the dating of Gildas's life. It has been determined that the appeal happened in 433–439, and it has been argued that the event occurred at the very edge of living history as that horizon stood during Gildas' childhood. Because of these truths we can safely make an estimate about the latest year at which Gildas may have been born. The very rare monk of later centuries has been known to have lived to eighty, and several ecclesiastics of the period are credited with the same unlikely lifespan. If Gildas was exposed to an octogenarian, and if that person had been told about the letter even if they were born some fifteen years after it occurred, he might well have remembered it. If that person then had occasion to tell a five-year-old Gildas about the letter at the end of his own life, then Gildas may have been born as late as 529. This would, however, be an extreme set of circumstances unlikely to be matched in a period of time where heavy Germanic raids and nearly constant internecine warfare were a part of everyday life, and the economy as well as food supplies would have been inconsistent at best.[6] Still, it is possible.

For the sake of argument, we will take the slightly more likely approach that Gildas must have been born by about 525 to have had any significant chance of hearing about the incident with the name of the recipient intact as well as the information that he had been a consul three times. To have received the name in so badly mangled a condition, he must have come across it closer to the beginning of his life, at the extreme range of his source's life, or more likely both. There seems no way that the form of Aetius' name, the place in his career Aetius was, and the events leading up to the letter to him could have been misheard while still comfortably within the common memory.

On the other extreme, it is possible that as a political event the letter might only have been remembered in the secular realm. In that case, any person born in or before 428 may have heard of the letter as it occurred, and a person of that birth-year would have died off by 483. Shortly thereafter, the event would have been forgotten. The memory of the event through secular means alone would give a lower extreme of as much as fifty years between event and Gildas' birth. By that reckoning Gildas could have been born no earlier than 478 to have heard about it as the last vestiges of the common memory were being forgotten; 478 to 525 is not a tight range of dates, but it is something to work with, and accepting that he must have been born within that range is worth the inexactness of the date itself. It means that Badon took place within that time period as well. The loose time frame for Gildas' birth-year also gives us a third date, albeit a second soft one, to contrast and work off of the hard date of 441. With the knowledge provided by those three points and plugged into the relative chronology already assembled for the events between Aetius and the writing of *De Excidio Britanniae*, we are left with:

433–439	Letter to Aetius
433–441	Picts resume attacks
433–441	Germanic tribesmen hired as mercenaries
441	Germanic revolt
448–461	Ambrosius becomes Briton leader
478–491	Battle of Badon
522–534	*De Excidio Britanniae*

Even if we are to assume for the moment that Ambrosius was another of Gildas' calculated exaggerations, that he was not the first and greatest leader in the counterattack against the invaders, it seems reasonable that chieftains such as Arthur would not have emerged till several years after the Germanic revolt and as a response to the same immediate need for protection as the one Gildas associated with Ambrosius; 448–461 is the earliest time at which Arthur could have been active.

A second possibility is that, as Ambrosius and Arthur are not placed together in all of the earliest literature, either Arthur did not emerge till after Ambrosius' career, or he was active in a different region than Ambrosius.[7] If the latter option was the case, as seems likely, Arthur would have been a leader who came to power as early as less than a decade after the Germanic revolt.

Alternatively, Arthur might well have been present at the Battle of Badon some forty years later. He might have been one of the better rulers of the time, and Gildas might have felt that were much easier targets. It is even a possibility, though there is no way to know, that Gildas was in Arthur's kingdom when he wrote. All we can determine for certain from the clues of Gildas' historical prelude is that the lower limit of Arthur's possible floruit is roughly 450. Though Gildas does not help to further refine the date range already established, he does provide a context for Arthur's career.

CHAPTER 23

Arthur's Expanding Orbit

In Chapter 13, those characters who are earliest associated with Arthur were studied individually in order to more accurately locate our subject's area of activity. Making use of a general rule of oral heroic literature that the central character will attract famous people from an ever widening area as the literature develops, it was hoped that studying the geographies associated with the earliest Arthurian heroes would suggest a rough central location for Arthur. The oral literary effect is something like what is seen in a black hole, with individuals living closest to the most famous king being sucked in quicker, while the more distant heroes may take centuries to be drawn into the literature associated with him. Given the right set of circumstance, an individual might never fully become a part of the cycle. Elsewhere, Tristan has made for a good example of the means and circumstances necessary to resist this generally inevitable process.[1]

Arthur is a somewhat vague character in the earliest British historical traditions, and the locations of his men were little more help. Still, the discussion did broadly point the reader in the same direction as the other approaches, and therefore was of some use in corroborating the finds of other discussions. Here a similar method will be employed, with a concentration on chronology instead of geography. It can only be hoped that the effort will bear more tangible fruit.

Gildas and Hueil sons of Caw

As has already been noted, Gildas is inserted in the aftermath of a tragic raid made by Hueil on Arthur in the *Vita Gildae* of Caradoc of Llancarfan, which may well possess early and accurate materials involving Arthur's inter-

164

actions and geography. Additionally, Hueil's encounter is mentioned in *Culhwch ac Olwen* and *Chwedl Huail ap Caw ac Arthur* with the same two kings present. These additional versions show the story to be traditional and associated solely with Arthur. As far as may be determined, Hueil's raid on Arthur belongs to the oldest stratum of Arthurian literature.

All three versions are in agreement that Hueil came from somewhere in Scotland. However, it is the Caradoc version that is of the most importance here. The actual details of the event are not as fully documented as in *Chwedl Huail ap Caw ac Arthur*, nor does it appear in as ancient an edition as can be found in *Culhwch ac Olwen*. Knowledge of the event is assumed in this version, which is perhaps an indication that it is not as traditional an account as the other two. Additionally, the *vita* adaptation focuses on a meeting between Arthur and Hueil's brother, Gildas. This Gildas, author of the *De Excidio Britanniae*, is regularly listed as the brother of Hueil and son of Caw in several sources.

Gildas' education with Illtud is consistently mentioned in other *vitae* traditions coming from different monasteries. It is suggested by Gildas himself in the *De Excidio Britanniae* studied above, so his association with the revered master is likely historical. Accepting Gildas' presence in the story and his association with Illtud during this time as historical, and placing that knowledge into context with the birth range that was derived for Gildas in the previous chapter, 483–491, then Arthur was an active and powerful chieftain between the years 488 and perhaps 511.

Gwynnliw, Gwlad, Brychan and Cadoc

These four characters are to be found in the *Vita Cadoci*, as was reviewed while studying the geographical aspect of Arthur. Arthur takes part in two episodes of the story. The first is the reconciliation between the abductor Gwynnliw, the abducted Gwlad, and the father Brychan. This would lead to the birth of Cadoc. The second was a confrontation between Cadoc and Arthur over an issue of sanctuary. This would have taken place over twenty-five years later for Cadoc to have been an adult abbot of a monastery.

Cadoc's death has been placed at roughly 580 in several annals.[2] Knowing that he could not have lived beyond eighty from the data compiled above, this puts the events surrounding his conception at anywhere from several years before 500 up to possibly the third quarter of the sixth century. Arthur's interaction with him at least twenty-five years later gives a career for Arthur of at least that long. According to the information to be found there, his career spanned at least a twenty-five year stretch of roughly 495–585.

Illtud

Illtud has been introduced above only as the teacher of Gildas. However, he is known to have had an intriguing career of his own. It is unfortunate that so little of his career has been recorded. His *vita* was written in the twelfth or thirteenth century and is nearly infamous for its devolved state.[3] Anachronisms abound in its pages, so it should come as no surprise that sections of his story are difficult to interpret. This, and the *vita*'s general habit of avoiding older name-forms especially pertaining to Arthur are why I have been tentative about making use of it in the discussions above. None of the information it gives about Illtud may be accurate.

The *vita* speaks of Illtud going to Arthur's court and being a member of his household. In time he would become a captain there before losing interest in the life of a warrior and allowing a monk to convert him to Christianity. He would eventually come to found his own monastery where he would become a famous teacher. As with Cadoc, Illtud's *vita* is tantalizing to any chronologist in that he interacts with Arthur at two separate points during his career, during his early adulthood and into middle age. The episodes are likely not as far apart as is the case with Cadoc, still they are potentially of some use.

Illtud is also a unique case in that many of his students achieved some level of fame during their own careers. Not only was Gildas important to British affairs, but Samson, Paul Aurelian, David, and Leonorus are all mentioned in various sources in conjunction with one or more events. Their obits are all roughly known as well. For instance, Samson was active and a significant leader in Gaul during the Third Council of Paris (c. 557) and took part in the events that brought Iudwal back to the Dumnonie kingship in Brittany (c. 560). Continental sources say that Samson died in 562. If he was a minimum of thirty years old at the Third Council of Paris, he was born no later than perhaps 530, and as he is not noted as dying young, he was probably born decades earlier.

David was present at the Synod of Victoria (c. 569), where he was elected archbishop. *Annales Cambriae* records his death in 589. If he was a minimum of thirty-five years old during the synod he was born no later than 540, and most likely several decades earlier than that.

Gildas crossed over to Ireland after being asked to help restore order there (c. 565), and died in roughly 570. He was born not after 535 and likely decades before then. The chapter above has determined his birth year as occurring in the last two decades of the fifth century. Leonorus died shortly after Iudwal's restoration around 560 at the age of fifty-one. He was therefore born in either 508 or 509 and was in Illtud's school by 514.

Taken together, the known lives of Illtud's students are consistent in showing an education beginning within a couple of decades of 500. This in turn suggests that Illtud's military career, if he had one, took place some time before then. If there is any truth in the Illtud connection to Arthur, it would be safe to say that the famed king was active in the decade before 500.

Urien

This character is the single secular figure connected to Arthur who has in turn been linked to any solid historical dates. In direct form this connection has come mainly from the romantic literature of the continent but began with Geoffrey of Monmouth's *Historia Regum Britanniae*. There Urien was made an older contemporary of Arthur. His son, Owain, appears to have been a standard member of Arthur's court from the first work of Chrétien de Troyes in the middle of the next century, while there is a good deal of evidence that he was already affixed to Arthur in the works of the troubadours and trouvères in the years before that.

Traditionally, work on the *Historia Brittonum* assumed a date of several years before 600 for Urien's obit, with a relatively long floruit (one of the body of poems attributed to his cousin Llywarch Hen refers to Urien's white head). However, a relatively recent suggestion by Professor Alcock has been supported by Dumville and taken up by Professor Koch. All of their arguments center on the political dynamics of Northumbria; *Historia Ecclesiastica* points to about 605 as the year that the kingdom was united into one central and powerful kingdom. It therefore seems unlikely that the Northumbrians could have been so close to annihilation only a handful of years earlier. For this reason, the above scholars now believe that Urien may have been active as early as 540 and probably was at the end of his career by 570.[4]

Although there is no direct connection with Arthur here, something can be gained from a study of Urien. His area of activity was Reged, and he is occasionally called Urien Reged in the bardic poetry. As dominant as he appears to have been, gaining for an epithet the region he ruled, it is highly doubtful that he and Arthur could have been active during the same span of time. With this in mind, Arthur's career took place either before 540 or after 570. The evidence up to this point has clearly indicated the former limitation.

The Twelve Battles

First recorded in *Historia Brittonum*, the twelve battles associated with Arthur are given as a summation of his military career. Their locations had long been studied before Professor Jackson was finally able to associate most of them with place-names using his linguistic expertise.[5] Unfortunately, two problems were defined due to his work. The first was that the distance between several of them made it nearly impossible that Arthur could have participated in all of them, and in fact at least one was shown to have been stolen from the career of another king.

Second was that he was not able to give a time frame for a vast majority of the battles. Badon belonged to the last part of the sixth century or the first part of the sixth century, based on the now-disputed dates as given in *Annales Cambriae*. Another battle, Chesters, he associated with a battle that took place in 616.[6] Recent scholarship would put that battle several years earlier. Cat Coit Caledon, the seventh battle, translates as the forest of Scotland. It could mean anything, but traditionally the Picts are not known to have fought pitched battles among themselves. It is possible that what was meant was the Roman battle fought there hundreds of years before, the Mons Graupius of Agricola.

As Jackson once pointed out, it looks as though the editor of the *Historia Brittonum* knew that Arthur had fought twelve battles, but for whatever reason did not have access to the names of those battles. To overcome this deficiency, he unscrupulously gathered together what place-names from the scraps of history that were available to him. The result was an eclectic group of battles that seem to have taken place all over Britain. Because of the suspect nature of several of the battles, all of those place-names in *Historia Brittonum*'s list are unreliable.

As in the previous chapters, there are sources which have proven unhistorical or at the very least unreliable. Of those that seem trustworthy, the indications all point to Arthur's career centering around the year 500. The persons associated directly with him and who are connected to fixed dates have indicated that he was likely active for some time before 500, and may have extended his career for a decade or so into the sixth century. Those individuals with a more vague chronology have allowed for this possibility as well. There have been no valid witnesses presented here whose testimony would require any modification of that assessment.

CHAPTER 24

Rough Archaeological Dates for Arthur

It should seem unlikely that archaeology would provide in any way a useful tool in determining the chronology of a specific individual. As was discussed at the beginning of the book, that particular social science makes use of hard science to locate and understand the period better, but it can be precise only when the artifacts it uncovers offer fixed dates. This is rare, however. Instead relative dates are normally used. Coins give an indication of the year a site was occupied, and their wear shows how old they may have been when they were lost or buried. Clothing, designs, and tools were often used within specific time frames, and so finding them at a site can give a range of dates for occupation as well.

No specific dates are feasible with regards to Arthur, and in fact it is doubtful if Arthur's life accomplishments will ever be chronologically mapped out to any extent no matter what materials are unearthed. The period he lived in was nearly bereft of all records and he was likely only one of a large number of nearly anonymous British chieftains. However, archaeology can be useful in providing a broad outline for the period in which he may have lived, and that will be its use here.

As was mentioned above, it should be noted that the occupation and activity of several fortifications in northern England around 500 contradicts the general nature of sub–Roman defensive structures. As a rule, it has been observed by Professor Alcock and other archaeological experts of the period that most pre-and post–Roman military sites in Britain were developed from the natural terrain and rock formations to give them a defensive and psychological advantage over the surrounding area.[1] These places have been labeled hill-forts because of their predilection to higher ground. The fact that the Roman forts were occupied around the Hadrian's Wall area during the post–Roman period implies a native presence that had retained strong Roman culture. This in turn leads to a couple of possible lines of study that I would like to point out at this time, but for which I do not have the expertise to elaborate upon.

First of all it is a fact in British studies that Arthur's name is Roman (see above). There is no record or myth of an Arthur in Britain before the Roman landings to suggest any other derivation, and the roots of the word are specific to the Latin language. This is of great interest because Arthur and Ambrosius are the only Latin lay names in Britain that can be placed after the middle of the fifth century.

Secondly, it has been established in previous chapters that Arthur was most likely a ruler based around the Carlisle area. With the known biases of the relevant historical, pseudo-historical, legendary, folkloric, and romantic sources accounted for, there is a near-unanimous agreement on this point among the source materials.

Chapter 15 also made a suggestion based on that conclusion: that Arthur may have been an influence in the repair work done on and around Hadrian's Wall at various times on either side of the year 500. It might, perhaps, be worth the time and space to go over the specific dateable finds of each site here so that a better understanding of what occurred may be developed.[2]

Moving from west to east, the first fortress that looks to have been occupied after the Roman withdrawal is Benwell. Germanic pottery and brooches have been recovered from the site, though they have never been satisfactorily dated. This is noteworthy because the Mercian kingdom did not emerge until the last decade or so of the sixth century, and it would appear that much smaller kingdoms did not develop until the middle of the sixth century. There has never been any connection drawn between these early kingships and Roman military sites, nor have any independent Germanic settlements shown indicators of having adopted a single aspect of the Roman culture. By the mid–sixth century, when the Germanic people were developing political units larger than the village, Roman thinking was long dead in Britain and had been for some time. Because of these realities, it may be determined that the Germanic finds at Benwell come from a time when the Romano-British controlled the area. In conjunction with the dating of the other finds and their respective contexts, it is likely that the Germanic population at Benwell consisted of mercenaries.

The next occupation is at Chesters. It contains annular brooches of Celtic design inside the fort.[3] These may date to the fourth century or the fifth. As the finds are not associated with Roman artifacts, the latter option seems more likely. Because there is no evidence that the fortifications were repaired and no sub–Roman finds have otherwise been located, it is likely that this settlement was composed of squatters.

Housesteads contains evidence of internal occupation and refortification, so that the site was clearly in use well after the Roman withdrawal. The re-use of the site as a living entity suggests occupation by Romanized Britons. Spearheads have been found within the walls, and these are similar to those found at Carvoran (see below). Like them, they are likely of fifth century provenance,[4] not only because of their style but because of the military nature of the occupation.

The remains at Chesterholm contain evidence of internal occupation and refortification as well, also suggesting settlement by Romanized Britons.[5] In addition, there is also a Class-I inscribed stone within a reasonable proximity of the structure,[6] and that class is generally associated with the fifth century.[7] The site's finds also include annular brooches inside the fort.[8]

The Birdoswald site includes several halls of the post–Roman type. This firmly places the occupation in the fifth century, most likely in the latter half. As has been seen, Dark Age halls were not needed until then because the primitive kingships from which they developed had not emerged yet.

Castleheads contains what is possibly a Class I stone, though it has been generally discounted as such.[9] This is the only real evidence of post–Roman occupation, and therefore it cannot be used in any paper attempting to find a pattern in the structures of the fifth-century landscape.

Of non–Hadrian's Wall forts, the South Shields site has revealed some evidence that its structure may have been refortified; there is a post–Roman ditch and possible evidence that the entrance was rebuilt. Outside the fort, there is also an inhumation cemetery indicative of Romanized Britons. One spearhead has been recovered, and it appears to be Germanic.[10] The fort itself seems to have been occupied but not by several consecutive individuals who understood the original function of the various buildings, or by a very small group that was unable to make use of the entire area. It seems most likely that Britons settled there, but decades after the Roman withdrawal.

The fort at Binchester has several early Germanic burials.[11] As with Benwell, the area is known to have been under British authority for nearly a century after the dating of the finds, so that it is likely the inhabitants there were either *foederati* or more passive Germanic settlers who submitted to some higher Briton authority.

Carvoran has Anglo-Saxon graves from the fourth or possibly the fifth century.[12] These burials have spearheads associated with them, which suggests either *foederati* occupation, post–Roman occupation by Germanic warriors, or both. It is possible that the issue of food and supplies that appear to have forced the *foederati* of other parts of the island were not an issue here, or that it was a problem that was resolved without the cataclysmic Germanic raid that the eastern coast of England suffered.

Without a doubt, the evidence presented above does not amount to much, and what there is hardly makes for an airtight case. However, the era being spoken of is notable for its sparcity of remains. Archaeologists have suggested the turmoil of the period caused many potentially useful artifacts to be destroyed. Historians have pointed out that the culture shock of losing contact with Rome caused many items to be used long after their normal period of service, thus potentially degrading even more evidence beyond the point of recovery by modern scholarship. However the reader would like to approach the difficulties inherent in these finds, there is little evidence within any of the sites from this time frame. The fact that there is as much to be found as there is in such an easily-themed area, and with as much consistency of date as there is, is remarkable.

Taken together, what the above finds seem to indicate is that at some point towards the end of the fifth century, someone was not only in control of an area that extended from one end of Britain to another, but that they considered themselves to be a continuation of the Roman presence. They used the in-place fortress system to their own ends and filled them with warriors or the same *foederati* the Romans had used. What little information that has been recovered of his power, floruit, and location suggests that the individual in question was the Latin-named Arthur.

CHAPTER 25

The Development of the Historical Horizon

Despite the fact that men wrote before him, and that their writings have proven to be of use in British historical studies, Bede is the first real historian of the British Isles. Perhaps he lived in the first era that could have produced one. Working out of Lindisfarne, he was able to look back on the transition from Roman to British to Germanic culture, and to see the development of Christianity with an eye not possible during its growth and the controversy between the Irish monks and the Roman priests.[1]

It has been seen that he made use of Gildas. We also know that he was able to access information from local monasteries within his native kingdom, from Canterbury, and possibly from the other occasional religious establishment outside of Northumbria. However, the breadth of his sources could not have countered one limitation; nothing he might have used could have been accurate much earlier than 597. That was the year that Kent had received the first official Christian missionaries, and the dignitaries that had initiated the resulting conversion would have been the first literate people to have been exposed to the legends, myths, and history of the Germanic peoples in Britain.

Bede suggests that Northumbria was contacted before Kent, and this is certainly possible. However, the difference could only be one of a few years. Historical records among the English could not have been kept much before 590 and could not have been accurately recorded using living memory for more than a few decades before that.

Bede admits as much in his writings. He is certain of himself when using Gildas. In writing of the fifth century he is even bold enough to offer dates where perhaps only relative dating would have been more appropriate. But when Gildas stops feeding him information around the middle of the next century, his writing changes dramatically. At that point he becomes vague in his dates, offering no more than a few scattered events for the scholar to fit between *De Excidio Britanniae* and nearly the end of the sixth century. It is only with the Roman interest in converting his people to Christianity that he becomes more certain again.

In contrast to *Historia Ecclesiastica*, *Annales Cambriae* or *The Welsh Annals* is not the work of a single historian, but rather the result of the efforts of several antiquarians and an editor who worked centuries after the time period under study here. *Annales Cambriae* offers two types of dates for the period from 410 to 600, neither of them particularly reliable or complete; these are the obits of major saints and the placement of major battles. As has been seen with the Arthurian events, examples of the latter category have been derived from guesswork that makes use of unsubstantiated assumptions about other sources of the period; even the 573 date for the relatively late Battle of Arfderydd is questionable.

The death years for the major ecclesiastics of the period are just as much in doubt. Each of the individuals listed in the *Welsh Annals* may be assigned alternate obit years if one employs the generally older Irish annals. The source does not even begin to become accurate till the beginning of the seventh century, where it borrowed from Irish annals and a derivative of the *Northern Memorandum*.[2] It is not contemporary till 795 when it was first recorded at St. David's.[3]

As has been noted above, *Historia Brittonum* gives no dates, and is vague in chronology as well. However, certain details in its pages give some indication as to its original source. The focus on Urien's family, and in particular Urien with regard to the northern alliance, is intriguing and unique in its insights into the political situation of the time. That the supplemental literature gives no primacy of place to the Reged hero is a second indication of *Historia Brittonum*'s bias. That his son Rhun is credited with converting the Northumbrians and Edwin, in direct contradiction to Bede's testimony, suggests the nature of that bias—Rhun himself or one of the monks who served him must originally have recorded the information being given. If this conclusion is the right one, the materials relating to Urien here may date to as far back as the beginning of the seventh century.

The Anglo-Saxon Chronicle has the same initial drawback as Bede's work, that it could not possibly have accurate information dating much before 597. However, there are additional issues with the materials it provides as well. The first problem is that *The Anglo-Saxon Chronicle* was put into its final form in the reign of Alfred the Great, who was at that time a rival to Mercia. Both kingdoms were in the midst of fighting against the Norse who had invaded the island and had by then all but conquered it. This means that the final editor would have had multiple objectives. He would have needed to put Wessex in the best possible light. He would have needed to undermine Mercia in particular. He needed to stress the longevity and strength of all the English people.

A second concern arises in a closer look at the earliest entries relating to the Germanic settlements. There are several details here of note. The first is an absence of Mercia. Both the initial landing and the establishment of its kingdom are entirely overlooked. This may well have been one way of saying that it was somehow illegitimate, in which case it would have been another way of undermining Mercia. Alternatively, the fact that Mercia has no access along the North Sea may have helped to obscure that event anyway. We may never know what the reason was.

Another item is that the original landing of every other dynasty active into the ninth century is recorded. As a rule, each appearance is assigned a date corresponding to the political stature of their kingdom in the ninth century; the earliest are the ancestors of the most powerful contemporary sovereignty. The one exception to this guideline, apart from Mercia, is Kent. It is intriguing to note that the landing of Hengest and Horsa, who would eventually settle in Kent, is clearly designated as the earliest appearance of Germanic settlers in Britain. Hengest is credited with putting the Welsh on the defensive and beating them back. Even in this highly nationalistic history, Hengest is solely named as being responsible for creating a vacuum for later tribes to make their own settlements. This suggests that at least one influence on the final version of the chronicle derived from Kent.

Several years after the Kent settlement, Wessex's initial landing is recorded as the second Germanic group on the island. The material of that kingdom has its own set of difficulties. As has seemed obvious to at least one scholar, the activities of their kings seem to focus on two separate regions, and until later on in Wessex's history, no king is active in both. The evidence suggests that the material was trying to assimilate two dynasties into the historical record. They had likely spent the early part of their existence fighting one another and by now had united into the ruling house of both kingdoms.[4]

That the historicity of the document is highly questionable at this point is generally accepted. The relative chronologies of the kingdoms, the impossibly early dates given for Kent and Wessex's settlement all point to some extensive manipulation of chronology and events. Still, the resource offers a key date. In 597, Æthelberht invited the Christians from Rome into his kingdom for the purpose of teaching himself and his people about the religion. If that date is to be assumed as the point at which living history was recorded, then the possible historical horizon should extend roughly fifty years before that point.[5]

The Pictish King-Lists are also a cornucopia of information about the period, and secondarily about Arthur. Because of their limited nature, however, of simply naming kings and dates, study of them has been largely restricted in its scope. What has been learned can be summed up as follows. The length of Drest I's hundred-year reign marks it and the period before him as strictly pseudo-historical. The period 662–668 is the horizon of the living history.[6] The span between Drest's death and the living history horizon is annalistic history.

However, Dr. Miller came up with an interesting and likely theory to explain much of the received chronology before Drest I. She first noted that the reigns of every one to four kings prior to Drest I always added up to some multiple of fourteen, the number of years included in one full cycle of Easter dating during the medieval period. Realizing the significance of the number, she continued her calculations forward. It was only when she got to the two Drests starting in 526 that the trend finally ended.[7] From this she concluded that the claimed historical horizon, the year from which all dates were accurate, was 526. She made comparison to Gwynedd's claim of 534 and Bernicia's of 547 to point out the likelihood of that date.[8] I would note that the Christianization of the Picts occurred well after Gwynedd and only a couple of decades before Bernicia, suggesting that it was not a factor. On the other hand, Gwynedd and Bernicia wrote official histories well before the Picts, meaning that there was an interest in history in those two kingdoms long before there was one in Pictland and its historical horizon cannot be before that of either kingdom. The Pictish King-Lists may only be consistently cross-referenced with the Irish annals, the *vita* of Columba, and Bede from the reign of Brude son of Maelgwn onwards.

As can be clearly seen, the historical horizon for native records seems in all cases to come into focus towards the middle of the sixth century. This is for several reasons. The Germanic peoples would only just begin to accept Christianity around 600, and only with their conversion would the Easter tables become necessary; it was the calculation of Easter each year which would provide the catalyst for the remembrance of political and social events in the first place. The Picts would accept the same religion only years before in the north through the efforts Uinniau and Columba. Their king-list stretches back well before this, but it is not till the middle of the sixth century that the years it supplies for those records begin to match up consistently with other records.

Wales' development was only slightly earlier. In the middle of the century, Samson's life records a coven, while David's speaks of a pagan king. Monasteries were the primary vehicles of the Christian religion in Britain, and monasteries by definition were to be found far away from settlements. Without the benefit of soldiers to protect them, they could not hope to maintain any semblance of consistent historical records until non–Christians could no longer intrude upon them. The historical horizon begins in the last decades of the sixth century because accurate historical records could not have been recorded sooner. The necessary recording aids were not present and the landscape to maintain them was simply not stable enough.

Conclusion

The above chapters have demonstrated first that Arthur existed. Examining every aspect of the evidence used in the traditional arguments and determining where and in which way they might be credible, it was the most economical conclusion. It has been seen that Arthur was scarce in the pseudo-historical records because they were put in final form during the ninth century, at least three centuries after his death. It has also been observed that there was a severe linguistic shift around the mid–sixth century which would have impeded the preservation of the praise poems as they had been sung in his hall. Unlike Urien and Gwrtheyrn, Arthur had no ninth-century descendants who could have used him to further their designs. As a result, there was no one with any political motivation to keep his name and accomplishments alive. Further, it has been demonstrated that Arthur lived at the beginnings of a heroic age, and that these periods are notorious for having little historical material on their earliest heroes. Finally, the region in which he lived was conquered within a century after his death by individuals of a different culture and language. They would eventually eradicate all Celtic culture, and with it the invaders would collaterally destroy many of the Cumberland folk memories pertaining to Arthur.

In other chapters, Arthur's remote connection to Fionn has been proven to be the product of volume and luck, not the result of similar beginnings. A new and fresh look at *De Excidio Britanniae* has revealed that the *superbus tyrannus* whom Gildas names may have been Arthur himself and not the Powysian king Gwrtheyrn.

It is quite possible that Arthur had a bard or bards in his household, and that they created many of the tales we now possess about Arthur. It is they who would have been the most likely creators of the legend of Arthur. In fact, the prominence of the bards in the late fifth century and throughout the sixth and the comparative wealth of information regarding British literary heroes in this period are probably not coincidental. In the British Heroic Age we have a historical context and a potential origination point for the transmission of the Arthurian legend.[1]

In the middle portion of the book, evidence was presented that Arthur was a figure of the north. This was done first by seeking to understand the varying pressures that were placed on the legend of Arthur as it was treated by the English and on the continent. Primarily, the two influences with the most impact were Geoffrey of Monmouth's *Historia Regum Britanniae* and Glastonbury's various enterprises. Each of them affected thinking on the subject to a degree not to be undervalued. They both established Arthur as a Somerset hero, a belief that persists to this day even in some academic and many pseudo-academic circles.[2] With their influences laid out, and the political and economic motivations behind the authority of their claims explained as well, they were left behind. In their place, an assessment of the less influential sources that named Arthur was made for the purpose of gaining a fresh perspective on the subject.

The investigation began with those materials that were generally agreed to be pre–Galfridic. Arthur's location in them was inconsistent, but favored the Old North. The *vitae* proved nearly useless for the study, except that in realizing there are only three *vitae* for northern saints one recognizes the tremendous bias against *Y Hen Ogled* that this genre has. Regardless of Arthur's location, it came as no surprise that he was placed mostly in Wales, followed by Cornwall, and that references to him in the north were almost nonexistent. The normal approach, of finding direct references to him and plotting his geographical location, was demonstrably inconclusive and so secondary associations were examined.

The fact that every one of the known bards of this period lived in either Gwynedd or *Y Hen Ogled* was a conclusion that was come to in the process of better understanding the nature of bardic activity in the period. It suggested that Arthur, their most popular subject, was from the north.

In studying the people with whom Arthur was most associated in the earliest sources, a tendency for northern figures was prominent as well. This study was followed by an examination of *Culhwch ac Olwen*. Here it was determined that there was a large amount of material deriving from the Old North that could not be accounted for except if the material was transferred, with Arthur, to Wales. Finally, a survey of the continental romance writers not only agreed that Arthur was a part of *Y Hen Ogled*, but placed him specifically in Carlisle. The last chapter was devoted to expanding on this result with the use of historical and archaeological knowledge. It was seen that there are reasonable grounds for locating Arthur's hall at Old Carlisle, probably the Roman fort known as Luguvalium.

Associating himself with the Romans, a kingdom that by the late fifth century would have taken on mythic proportions, might have served a variety of purposes. Generally speaking, however, it would have connected him to a time and a culture that gave hope and confidence to the people he ruled. It might also be seen as giving him a moral advantage over other British chieftains of the time. From a psychological standpoint, it was brilliant.

The Germanic presence may also have influence locating a capital in that particular location. Whereas it has been seen that the British chieftains would conduct raids on each other for the purpose of proving their valor and gaining more warriors,[3] the migrated Germanic tribes of the time were more interested in acquiring land than adding to the prestige of their warriors. If Cumbria was feeling a threat from the east during his floruit, Arthur would have been more conscious of the defensibility of his home than any of his contemporaries throughout Britain. Even a half-dilapidated Roman fortress would have served his purposes better than the best hill-fort of the time. The string of Hadrian's Wall strongholds that appear to have been reoccupied under his rule would have provided for a secure defense against any incursion.

Seeing Arthur in Carlisle, some other pieces of the puzzle seemed to fall into place. Old Carlisle, as Luguvalium, had been the command post for at least part of the wall. As such it had access to a nearby harbor. For a post–Roman chieftain, the harbor provided a possible point of trade and a base for any warships he might feel the need to have.

With Arthur's historicity established and his region of activity determined, the next logical concern was in determining the years in which he was active as precisely as possible. It has long been held that Arthur ruled in the years around 500. However, even an initial examination of the earliest sources shows clearly that this particular date was first presented by Geoffrey of Monmouth, and he was hardly a credible source for any information from the post–Roman period.

Eliminating Geoffrey and those influenced by him as a valid source of information on Arthur's chronology, the *Historia Brittonum* and *Annales Cambriae* were the two remaining early sources that influenced later thinking. The first was so vague in dating most of its other characters that it had only placed Arthur around 500 by influence from *The Anglo-Saxon Chronicle*. The latter's dates were easily shown to be the product of guesswork and were therefore invalid.

With no set dates for Arthur between 410 and perhaps 600, there was a need to start with a basic foundation, a set of limits within which Arthur must have fit. First, a cursory examination of the decline of *Romanitas* was made.

It was found that a significant portion of the names of known British leaders were Latin up to around 500 or a decade later. Patrick, whose Latin was good, and Gildas, whose Latin was unrivaled in his time, both were born before that cut-off as well. And with the tapering off of things Latin in the secular world, so would the sense of being Roman have declined after that point as well.

Another point of departure for the earliest possible date was the bards. All the earliest known bards were again listed and dated where possible. It was found that, though the earliest individuals who could be securely placed were active no earlier than 535, the evidence suggested that several could have been active up to a quarter century before 500.

This was followed by a look at one of the hagiographic authors, Caradoc of Llancarfan. In the examination of the body of *vitae* naming Arthur, it had been noted that although there were very few northern saints who had been subjects, Arthur was associated with northern figures in a relatively large proportion out of those he was in. The commonality between all of those Arthurian *vitae* with northern characters was Caradoc, their author. In examining Caradoc more closely, it was shown that all of his extant *vitae* contained northern figures. Nothing in any of his works suggest that his patron there had any reason for giving their hero a northern affinity. Even if something was missed with one of them, he did work for several different patrons during his career. All of his extant work contains northern references, making it most unlikely that any patron-driven reason existed. This conclusion implied first that Caradoc must have had access to the information about the northern figures himself, and second that the information likely came from a native and therefore relatively more reliable source than *vitae* are normally composed of. Both suppositions meant that the information Caradoc provided was valuable.

Arthur was named twice in the *Vita Cadoci*. In the first he was the peacemaker that allowed the saint's parents to come to an accord. In the second instance, his only purpose was to legitimize the monastery's claims on fishing rights.

He was also named twice in Caradoc's *vita* of Gildas. He was of interest there because of the work that Gildas has left us and particularly the vague chronology that he used as a preface. A chapter devoted to *De Excidio Britanniae* has already concluded that the reliable information it contains shows that British leaders began emerging soon after the middle of the fifth century and in response to Germanic incursions. Arthur would likely have begun his career at this point or shortly thereafter.

The next topic of discussion was the individuals and events that have been associated with Arthur and are roughly dateable. In this Arthur's oldest warriors could not factor because by the time their episodes were written down they no longer had enough of an independent existence to offer any clues.

```
    410 430 450 470 490 510 530 550 570 590 610 630 650
400 420 440 460 480 500 520 540 560 580 600 620 640 660
```

Romanitas   ├───────────────────┤

Bards   ├───────────────┤

Gildas   ├──┤

Arthur's orbit   ───

Archaeology   ├────┤

DATE RANGES OF ARTHUR BY CHAPTER. The range of dates when Arthur was most likely born or active according to the various techniques used in the above chapters. The reader will note that, despite the independent approaches used, there is a significant overlap between them if one remembers that *Romanitas of Arthur* determined a range of birth years for Arthur, while the balance of chapters were primarily interested in his period of activity.

However, the individuals found in the *vitae* tradition, Urien, and the twelve battles did have something more to offer. Though all of the individuals apart from Urien have only been roughly placed in the history of the late fifth and early sixth centuries, the ranges that could be determined for all of them matched up well with what had been previously determined regarding Arthur's chronology. Urien, as a ruler so prominent that his epithet was taken from the name of his kingdom, could not possibly have been Arthur's contemporary if they both ruled in the same region. Thus his floruit in the middle and later sixth century could not overlap Arthur's and thus its beginning serves as a *post quem*, or latest possible date for Arthur.

Archaeology was also employed in the search for Arthur. His placement in the Carlisle area and his possible association with several Hadrian's Wall fortresses were studied again from a chronological perspective. Looking at the finds discovered at these locations, the same basic pattern that had emerged elsewhere surfaced here; all those sites that could be dated with any certainty belonged roughly in the decade or two around 500.

It was tempting from this point to date Arthur with a little more specificity. In the past, less careful scholars have often done so. However, dates are not possible when dealing with Arthur at this time. A review of the source materials relating to that period confirmed why; the historical horizon is some half a century after his floruit. Despite the incredible assumptions of Geoffrey of Monmouth, and the blind faith of those who followed him, they were essentially correct. Based on the results of the above chapters, Arthur's period of activity was probably somewhere in the last two decades of the fifth century and extending into the first quarter of the sixth.

What has been learned is that Arthur was a historical entity who was based in the Old Carlisle area and was active in the period between the initial rise of kingship and the establishment of dynasties. Little can be known specifically of his career, but the extent of the range of refortified Roman installments suggests that he might have fought against Germanic tribesmen as well as Picts and other Britons. He would have been remembered initially not for nationalistic reasons but because his activities and his bard or bards captured the imagination of those who followed better than anyone of his era. Arthur was a famous king, but likely not a resistance leader or any conquering hero — he just performed the function of a heroic age king better than any of his contemporaries.

Appendices

Appendix A: The Location of Gildas

The location of Gildas has long been a source of great interest. This is primarily because that information would have a strong bearing on the geographical context of his one pseudo-historical work, *De Excidio Britanniae*. If Gildas wrote in the home region of one of his targets such as Gwynedd, for instance, why is there no indication in Gildas' *vitae* or any secular record that Maelgwn attempted to punish him? If he wrote from a location not ruled by any of the kings he berates, was there a political motivation? Was the castigation of so many powerful leaders supported or even suggested by the resident ruler? Speculation around Gildas' letter could be endless, and equally pointless, until it is known from where Gildas composed his letter.

There have, therefore, been many hundreds of hours focused on answering that question. However, the resulting essays have mainly been devoted to proving where in southwestern Britain Gildas may have been when he wrote his tirade. While it is true that all of his subjects were most probably Welsh and Cornish figures, this should not exclude Gildas as a northern writer. In fact, that Gildas was not in Cornwall or Wales while he was writing makes good sense for several reasons.

Living in northern Britain complements what is known of his family. As has been seen, Gildas' father is known as Caw "of Pictland" in all sources that bother to name his point of origin. This includes one of two *vitae* written about Gildas as well as the genealogical tradition. The former source also states that Gildas was born in Strathclyde,[1] which is at least on the borders of Pictish territories. It has been noted above that Hueil, one of Gildas' brothers in every known genealogy of Gildas, is mentioned in several different sources as making his raids from Scotland. Just as important, Gildas insults no northern kings, which seems odd considering the Britain he would have known contained several northern British kingdoms.[2]

It also seems irrational to argue that Gildas would have been writing in a region that was ruled by a person he was insulting. The *vitae* tradition is filled with holy men bringing powerful kings to their knees, but the reality of early medieval Britain was much different. In an area where Christianity had become the dominant religion a very short time before and kingship was the only bulwark between civilization as Britons knew it and the further incursions of Germanic peoples, it is difficult to believe that churchmen held a great deal of political power.[3]

If one accepts this point, then Gildas' life might well have been in danger if he had been living in most of Wales and Cornwall. Along those same lines, it would have been foolhardy for him to write in a region that was close to an offended king either, especially Gwynedd. In fact her king, Gildas' dragon Maelgwn, appears to have attacked all the more powerful kingdoms of southwestern Britain during his career. Gildas could not have hid behind the borders of any kingdom in Wales if he had attacked that particular king. To a lesser extent, it can be assumed that all of the kings he berates would have taken retribution on what he had to say about them. For that reason, British-controlled England east of Wales would also have been too dangerous.

Nor would it have been wise for Gildas to write in territories ruled by Germanic kings. The fire and brimstone bishop used a thinly veiled language of literary symbolism to describe them, an imagery that would have fooled no one. And in the midst of pagans, he wouldn't have had the influence of his religion to protect himself. In fact it seems unlikely that the non–Christian immigrants who occupied western Britain would have even allowed a Christian leader to live among them or their British subjects.

Evidence to be derived from his letter, in particular the *historia* section, suggests that he was from or at least was speaking of the history of the north. The perspective has a very clear northern bias.[4] Time and again he tells us that the Britons are harassed by the Picts and Irish, the former of which would reasonably have come from the north, while the latter could have as well if he was raised Pictish.[5] In response, he tells us that the British hired Germanic-speaking tribes to fight against them. Logically, these mercenaries would have been stationed in the north.[6] Knowledge of this situation implies a northern viewpoint.

It has been argued that Gildas' lack of knowledge regarding the building of Hadrian's and Antonine's walls is a strong argument against a northern perspective. The traditions regarding the walls should have been strong enough, so the argument goes, that at around 500 a vague idea of its date of composition and context of construction would have been common knowledge for anyone who had access to the north's local traditions. However, it has been seen that Gildas was writing over a century after he dated the creation of the walls, and he was born nearly three generations after the last Roman government broke down in Britain. Gildas was well beyond the range of living memory regarding both walls, and so could not be expected to know the details of their construction no matter where in Britain he was born or was active.

Gildas also mentions the Germanic revolt, which he dates to the middle of the fifth century. If it was as dramatic an event as Gildas would have us believe, and the continental sources do corroborate him here, it would have been a watershed in British history. Not only would people have died in the large-scale plundering that resulted but villages, local cultures, and many oral traditions would have been fractured by the devastation as well. There is no reason why any person born a full generation after that event would have had any idea as to the year or even the century in which Hadrian's Wall was built, no matter where they were born or were active.

With the basic arguments out of the way, let us take a look at what comes out in the *vitae* and other early materials and attempt to identify where Gildas might have received his information regarding the north.

What precipitates the migration of the Germanic peoples are repeated attacks by the Picts, the cultural group of the Scottish Highlands. Gildas' father, Caw, was a Pict, and neither he nor his family are ever placed anywhere other than in the Highlands of Scotland. If Gildas was from that region, he would have vaguely known of Pictish attacks on the still–Roman Britons from the oral traditions of his people. Even Strathclyde, which was his supposed birthplace in the Caradoc *vita* of Gildas, would have been on the borders of Pictland and possibly the recipient of such attacks.[7] Short of an unlikely Pictish marine attack into Wales or Cornwall itself, there would have been no reason for the southern Britons to have remembered Pictish attacks roughly a century after they were over. As a Welshman, Gildas would have felt no need to mention Hadrian or Antonine's walls, either. Only as a Pict, for whom the walls had served as a traditional barrier, would he have found their origins aesthetically necessary to a history of Britain.

Consistent tradition names Illtud as Gildas' teacher. This Illtud, famed for his learning, had most likely lived through a good portion of the events that Gildas catalogued, and especially those events that occurred after the letter to Aetius. With the education he received in Illtud's school, Llanilltud, Gildas would have been able to gather information about Roman culture and military protocols along with the basics of the Latin language. His background is why he seems to understand that the Britons were unarmed and had to be given weapons and training by the Romans; Illtud would have informed his students that Roman citizens never bore arms. Illtud would also have taught him about the Germanic mercenaries who had been used in the last days of the Roman occupation. Such had been standard Roman practices. It is possible that Illtud may have been his source about the letter to Aetius, though if Gildas received it from as careful a scholar as Illtud, he must have never seen it in written form.

Finally, there is Ambrosius. Little effort has ever been made to locate him as he founded no dynasty that was recorded. However, an Ambrosius is named in *Annales Cambriae*. There he is named as a leader in the battle at Gueleph. The conflict is listed as taking place in 437 and against Guitolin. The site has normally been taken as modern Wallop in Hampshire. Guitolin belongs to the same family as Gwrtheyrn, which ruled Gwrtheyrnion in Powys. As a native of Wales, Illtud may well have known of Ambrosius. However, as a leader in the church during this time, he would have had a wider perspective of British affairs than that and would have understood, as we do, that Ambrosius' successes were only local in scale. Gildas considers him a national hero by the way in which he presents the rebel leader. Most likely Gildas received his information as a youth from the local population. The method seems to have been largely informal.

Appendix B: The Transformation of Praise Poetry into Medieval Romances

Despite individual explanations as to why many sources have given such different locations for Arthur's capital, the sheer number of regions and sites has been described as a source of distrust in trying to determine his point of origin. As well it should be at first glance. However, the explanation for the wide variety is a simple one. The author has elsewhere shown that many of the Arthurian romances' sources stretch back to the ninth century and possibly to the fifth century where the poetry first began.[1] The romances would have developed as follows.

First, a large collection of praise poetry and legendary material would have survived Arthur, just as oral recollections of various kinds survive most heroic chiefs. Towards the end of the British Heroic Age (c. 600–700), this material would have been gathered into a loose cycle of tales around Arthur and possibly other British figures.[2] This can be seen in various states of development among Greek and Germanic cycles. As the culture continued, the group of stories surrounding the British heroes continued to develop, introducing new characters and adventures from easily accessible sources. Some characters were created.[3] They were molded into secondary beings within the cycles.[4] In the case of the Arthurian stories, most of the heroes of the cycle eventually became the vassals of Arthur. Such is what may be seen in *Hrolf Kraki's Saga*,[5] and more traditionally the Trojan War cycle.

Occasionally, a lucky combination of social, political, and economic factors may allow independent tales to be forged into works of epic literature. This is a long and complex process which there is no need to expound upon here.[6] The development is only notable for two reasons. First, these regenerations of the original stories inevitably result in the crystallization of the tales. Second, it is a near-certainty that the hero of such an epic or cycle did exist. This is because the person himself was the initial impetus. Hrolf Kraki, Attila the Hun, Theodoric the Great, and Siegfried of the Germanic heroic age, and Prince Yamato, Vladimir I, Gilgamesh,[7] Conchobar, and Agamemnon or Achilles[8] of the Japanese, Russian, Sumerian, Irish, and Greek heroic ages, respectively, were all historical figures and all were at the center of their particular epic.

These developments are all highly fortuitous to the historical scholar, because they present a natural progression of the stories from a form which is earlier than what might otherwise be hoped for. However, the absence of such an epic or cycle does not argue that the raw materials did not want for one. Unlike the good fortune that caused the epic for the *Iliad* to be written, one great eighth-century scholar such as Bede or even sixth-century Taliesin did not write the definitive volume on Arthur's life based on the original praise poetry of Arthur.[9] In its place, there are instead several Arthurian tales that appear to be degenerated forms of Arthur's exploits.[10] These are the results of praise poetry which was not crystallized at the end of the heroic age. Instead bards, *latimari*, soldiers, pilgrims, and traders all told different versions of the basic plots for centuries and in the process each version lost much of its original detail and meaning as the stories were retold and different authors found different points of importance and decided others were not as important.

Appendix C: Origins of All Proper Nouns in *Culhwch ac Olwen*

Below are the persons, places and tasks summarized in Chapter 14, designated as they are in the chapter. The numbers assigned below represent the line where each subject can be located in *Culhwch ac Olwen*.

Personal Names

Name	Origin	Line numbers
Achen[1]	Uncertain (France?)	200
Aed brenhin Iwerdon	Ireland	passim
Aethlem	Animal	728, 1202

Name	Origin	Line numbers
Alar	Literary	199
Alun Dyuet	Wales	185, 725
Amaethon mab Don	Myth	579
Amren mab Bedwyr	British	285
Anet	Animal	728, 1202
Angawd mab Kaw	Uncertain (*Y Hen Ogled*)	207
Anlawd Wledic	British (thirteenth century)	2, 15, 169, 453
Anoeth Ueidawc	Literary	322
Anwas Eidinawc	British	193, 233, 237
Anynnawc mab Menw	Uncertain	217
Ardwyat mab Kaw	Literary	210
Arthur	British	passim
Arwy Hir	British	365
Atleudor mab Naf	Uncertain	296
Baedan	Ireland	178
Banw	Animal	1149
Bedwyr	British	passim
Bedyw mab Seithuet	Literary	194
Beli	Myth	224
Bennwic	Animal	1149
Berth mab Kado	Dumnonia	224
Berwynn mab Kyrenyr	Wales	277
Bitwini Escob	Dumnonia	356
Bratwen mab Iaen	British	203
Bratwen mab Moren Mynawc	*Y Hen Ogled*	184
Brathach mab Gwawrdur	Literary	188
Bronllauyn Uerllydan	Object	279
Brys mab Bryssethach	Wales	332
Bryssethach	British	331
Bwlch	Literary	333, 736
Cacamwri (and variants)	Uncertain	passim
Kadarn	Literary	200
Kadellin Tal Aryant	Uncertain	289
Cadwy mab Gereint	Dumnonia	182
Kauall	Animal	1015, 1021, 1108
Kauall	Animal	337, 739
Kalcas mab Kaw	Uncertain (*Y Hen Ogled*)	212
Caletuwlch	Object	159, 1051
Call	Animal (Literary)	336, 739
Canhastyr Canllaw	Literary	190, 679
Carnedyr mab Gouynyon	Uncertain	250
Carnwenhan	Object	161, 1226
Karw Redynure	British	859, 868
Cas mab Saidi	British	293
Casnar Wledic	Myth (Wales)	215

Name	*Origin*	*Line numbers*
Kaw o Brydein	*Y Hen Ogled*	passim
Kei	British	passim
Ket Coet	Wales	287, 1055
Kelli	British	298
Kelemon merch Kei	Uncertain	360
Celyn mab Kaw	Uncertain (*Y Hen Ogled*)	207
Kethtrwn Offeirad	Uncertain	347
Kibdar	British	395
Kilyd mab Kyledon Wledic	*Y Hen Ogled*	1
Cilyd Canhastyr	*Y Hen Ogled*	190, 681
Kimin Cof	Wales	184
Kledyf Kyuwlch	Object	334, 737, 1110
Clememyl	Uncertain	359
Clust mab Clustueinat	Literary	347
Clustueinat	Literary	347
Clydno Eidin	*Y Hen Ogled*	362
Cnychwr mab Nes	Ireland	178
Coch mab Kaw	Literary	209
Conul Bernach	Ireland	179
Connyn mab Kaw	Literary	208
Cors Cant Ewin	Literary	190, 676, 1006
Cradawc mab laen	Uncertain	204
Creidylat uerch Lud Law	*Y Hen Ogled*	367, 988
Kuall	Animal (Literary)	337, 739
Cuan Cum Kawlwyt	Animal (Wales)	871, 872
Cubert mab Daere	Ireland	178
Cuel	British	298
Kulhwch	Myth	passim
Kuluanawyt mab Goryon	*Y Hen Ogled*	253
Custenhin Anhynwyedic	Wales (Dumnonia)	passim
Kyledon Wledic	*Y Hen Ogled*	1, 168, 453
Cyledyr Wyllt	*Y Hen Ogled*	994, 996, 1012, 1186
Kynan	Uncertain	1129–1130
Cyndelic Kyuarwyd	*Y Hen Ogled*	177, 399
Cyndrwyn mab Ermit	Wales	220
Kynedyr Wyllt mab Hettwn	British	344, 708
Kynuelyn Keudawc	Myth	342
Kynlas mab Kynan	Uncertain	1129–1130
Cynwal mab Kaw	Uncertain (*Y Hen Ogled*)	210
Kynwal Canhwch	Uncertain	361
Cynwas Curyuagyl	British	186, 1101
Cynwyl Sant	Wales	230
Kynyr Keinuarvawc	Wales	264
Kyrenyr	Wales	277
Daere	Ireland	178

Name	Origin	Line numbers
Dalldaf eil Kimin Cof	Wales	184
Datweir Dallpenn	Dumnonia	197
Diaspat	Literary	338, 741
Digon mab Alar	Literary	199
Dillus Uarruawc uab Eurei	Wales, probably	700, 960, 963, 976, 980
Dirmyc mab Kaw	Literary	206
Diwmach Wydel	British	635, 1037, 1038, 1042, 1052
Houndet Urenhin	Wales	31
Don	Myth	579, 584
Dorath	*Y Hen Ogled*	183
Drem mab Dremidyd	Literary	261
Dremidyd	Literary	261
Drutwas mab Tryffin	Wales	200
Drustwyn Hayarn	*Y Hen Ogled*	191
Drutwyn	Animal	673, 964, 986, 1014, 1106
Drwc	Literary	340, 742
Drwc Dydwc	Literary	337, 740
Drych eil Kibdar	British	395
Du	Animal	718
Duach (mab Gwawrdur)	Literary	188
Ducum	Brittany	124
Dunart	*Y Hen Ogled*	254, 993
Dwnn Diessic Unben	British	343
Dygyflwng	Literary	322
Dyuel mab Erbin	Dumnonia	219
Dyuynwal Moel	*Y Hen Ogled*	254
Ebrei	Uncertain	256
Echel Uordvyt Twll	Wales	195, 196, 1154
Edern mab Nud	Myth	182
Ehangwen	Object	264
Eheubryt mab Kyuwlch	*Y Hen Ogled*	341
Ehawc Llyn Lliw	Wales	902, 909
Eidoel mab Aer	Wales	passim
Eidon Uawrurydic	British	221
Eiladar mab Penn Llarcan	Ireland	343
Eissywed	Literary	339, 742
Eli	British	286, 1159
Eli Atuer	British	1115
Elidir Gyuarwyd	British	329
Ely	British	285, 1105–1106
Ellylw merch Neol Kyn Croc	British	371
Eneuawc merch Uedwyr	Uncertain	362
Enrydrec merch Tutuathar	Uncertain	362
Erbin	Dumnonia	219
Erduduyl merch Tryffin	Wales	364

Name	Origin	Line numbers
Ergyrat mab Kaw	*Y Hen Ogled*	211
Eri	British	passim
Erim	British	passim
Errnid mab Erbin	Dunmonia	219
Ermit	Dumnonia	220
Erw	British	217
Eryr Gwern Abwy	British	882, 883, 886, 901
Eskeir Gulhwch gonyn Cawn	British	191
Esni	British	181
Essylt Uyngul	post–1000	372
Essylt Vynwen	post–1000	372
Etmic mab Kaw	Literary	206
Eurei	Wales, probably	979
Eurneit merch Clydno Eidin	*Y Hen Ogled*	361
Euryawn Pennlloran	Uncertain	1128
Eus mab Erim	Uncertain	233
Eurolvyn merch Wdolwyn	British	364
Fergus mab Poch	Ireland	179
Fferis brenhin Freinc	France	277
Fflam mab Nwywre	Literary	218
Fflergant brenhin Llydaw	Brittany (post–1000)	216
Fflewdwr Flam Wledic	British	182
Gallcoit Gouynnyat	British	187–188, 274
Garanwyn mab Kei	British	284
Garselit Wydel	pan-Celtic	295, 697, 1117
Garwyli eil Gwythawc Gwyr	Uncertain	197, 1155
Garym	Literary	338, 741
Gereint mab Erbin	Dumnonia	182, 219
Gildas mab Kaw	*Y Hen Ogled*	219
Gilla Goeshyd	British (high-sounding)	298
Glas	Animal (Literary)	336, 739
Gleis mab Merin	British	123
Glesic	Animal (Literary)	336, 739
Gleissat	Animal (Literary)	336, 739
Glew mab Yscawt	Myth	1117
Glewlwyt Gauaeluawr	British	111, 114, 139, 192, 1121
Glinneu eil Taran	Myth	992
Gliui	Wales	831, 832
Gluydyn Saer	Uncertain	263, 1124–1125
Glythmyr Ledewic	Wales (Brittany)	1009, 1014, 1107–1108
Glythwyr	Literary	216
Gobrwy mab Echel Uordvyt	British	195
Gouannon mab Don	Myth	584
Gouynyon Hen	Uncertain	250
Gogiwr	Literary	86, 1120

Name	Origin	Line numbers
Goleudyt merch Anlawd	Wales (thirteenth century)	2, 14, 169, 453
Gorascwrn mab Nerth	Literary	341
Goreu mab Custennin	Dumnonia	811, 1178, 1230, 1239
Gormant mab Ricca	Dumnonia	198, 221
Goryon	*Y Hen Ogled*	253
Greit mab Eri	British	passim
Greidawl Galldouyt	*Y Hen Ogled*	passim
Grugyn Gwrych Ereint	Animal (*Y Hen Ogled*)	passim
Guilenhin brenhin Freinc	France	294, 720, 1130
Gusc mab Achen	Uncertain	200
Guyn Mygtwn merch Gwedw	Animal	689, 1006, 1177
Gwadyn Odeith	Literary	300, 303
Gwadyn Ossol	Literary	300, 301
Gwaedan mab Kynuelyn	Wales	342
Gwaeth	Literary	340, 743
Gwaethaf Oll	Literary	340, 743
Gwalchmei mab Gwyar	*Y Hen Ogled*	345, 404
Gwalhauet mab Gwyar	*Y Hen Ogled*	345
Gwarae Gwallt Eurin	Myth	315, 1008
Gwarthegyt mab Kaw	Uncertain (*Y Hen Ogled*)	1107, 1114
Gwastat	British	324
Gwawrdur Kyruach	Literary	188, 189, 363
Gwdolwyn Gorr	British	333, 364, 657
Gwedw	Animal	689, 1006, 1177
Gweuyl mab Gwastat	post–1000	324
Gweir Dathar Wenidawc	Gweir emanation	288, 360
Gweir Gwrhyd Enwir	Gweir emanation	290
Gweir Gwyn Paladyr	Gweir emanation	290
Gweir mab Kadellin	Uncertain	289
Gwen Alarch merch Kynwal	Uncertain	361
Gwenabwy merch Kaw	Uncertain (*Y Hen Ogled*)	258
Gwenhwyach	Uncertain	358
Gwenhvyfuar	Uncertain	161, 330, 358
Gwenlliant Tec	British	366
Gwenwledyr merch Waredur	Literary	363
Gwenwynwyn mab Naf	British	194, 250
Gweuyl mab Gwastat	British	324
Gwiawn Llygat Cath	Literary	351
Gwidon Ordu	*Y Hen Ogled*	652, 1206, 1228
Gwittart mab Aed	France	295
Gwlgawt Y Hen Ogled	*Y Hen Ogled*	624
Gwlwlyd Wineu	British	589
Gwrbothu, Hen	Wales	252, 1164
Gwrdiual mab Ebrei	British	256
Gwruan Gwallt Auwyn	British	294

Name	Origin	Line numbers
Gwrgi Seueri	Wales	1010
Gwrgwst Letlwm	*Y Hen Ogled*	993
Gwrhyr Gwalstawd Ieithoed	Uncertain	passim
Gwrhyr Gwarthecuras	Uncertain	186
Gwryon	Uncertain (Greek myth)	185, 288
Gwyar	British	345, 404
Gwydawc Gwyr	Uncertain	197, 1155
Gwydawc mab Menester	Uncertain	283
Gwyden Astrus	Animal	316
Gwydneu Garanhir	*Y Hen Ogled*	618
Gwydre mab Arthur	Uncertain	1116
Gwydre mab Lluydeu	British	258
Gwydrut	Animal	316
Gwydyl	British	1069
Gwyngat mab Kaw	Uncertain (*Y Hen Ogled*?)	208
Gwyngelli	Uncertain	1182
Gwynham	Wales	245
Gwynn Gotyuron	British	288
Gwynn Hyuar	British	296
Gwynn mab Ermit	Dumnonia (Wales)	220
Gwynn mab Esni	Gwyn mab Nud emanation	181
Gwynn mab Nud	Myth	passim
Gwynn mab Nwyvre	Gwyn mab Nud emanation	181, 218
Gwyn mab Tringat	Wales (Irish in Carmarthen)	1127
Gwynn Mygdwn	Animal	689, 1006, 1177
Gwryon	British	288
Gwys	Animal	1148
Gwystyl mab Nwython	*Y Hen Ogled*	256
Gwythawc Gwyr	British	197, 1155
Gwythyr uab Greidawl	*Y Hen Ogled*	passim
Halwn	Uncertain	312
Hen Vyneb	Uncertain	274
Henbedestyr mab Erim	Literary	234, 236
Hengedymdeith	Uncertain	274
Hengroen	Animal (Literary)	232
Hettwn Clauyryawc	Uncertain	708
Hettwn Tal Aryant	Uncertain	344
Hir Amren	Uncertain	323, 1221
Hir Atrwm	Literary	306
Hir Erwm	Uncertain	305
Hir Eidyl	Uncertain	323, 1221
Hir Peissawc brenhin Llydaw	Wales (Brittany)	1163–1164
Hu[n]abwy mab Gwryon	British	288
Huandaw	Literary	86, 1120
Huarwar mab Halwm	British	312

Name	Origin	Line numbers
Hueil mab Kaw	*Y Hen Ogled*	212, 259, 260
Hwyr Dydwc	Literary	337, 740
Hygwyd	Uncertain	1048, 1210, 1212, 1215
Hyueid Unllenn	Wales (myth?)	220
Iaen	Literary	202, 203, 204
Indec merch Arwy Hir	Uncertain	365
Iona urenhin Freinc	Literary	202
Iscawyn mab Panon	British	225, 1118
Iscouan Hael	Uncertain	224, 1115
Isperyr Ewingath	Uncertain	187
Iustic mab Kaw	Uncertain (*Y Hen Ogled*)	206
Llaeskemyn	Literary	86, 1123
Llamrei	Animal	1016, 1225
Llary mab Casnar Wledic	Wales	215
Llawin	Animal	1147
Llawurodet Uaruawc	British	223
Llawr eil Erw	British	217
Llenlleawc Wydel	Ireland	253, 293, 1051
Lloch Llawwynnyawc	British	192, 291
Lluber Beuthach	Ireland	179
Lluchet	Literary	339, 742
Llud Llaw Ereint	Myth	367, 916, 988–989
Lluydeu mab Kelcoet	Myth	287, 1055
Lluydeu mab Nwython	*Y Hen Ogled*	257
Lluydeu	Wales	258
Llwybyr mab Kaw	Literary	209
Llwng	Literary	322
Llwydawc Gouynnyat	Animal	1137, 1140, 1151, 1162
Llwyr Dydwc	Literary	338, 613, 740
Llwyryon	Literary	613
Llygatrud Emys	Literary	251, 1164
Llyr	Myth	215, 1181
Mahon mab Modron	Myth (*Y Hen Ogled*)	passim
Mabon mab Mellt	Myth	1007–1008, 1013
Mabsant mab Kaw	Literary	208
Madawc mab Teithyon	Uncertain	1126–1127
Mael mab Roycol	Literary	196
Manawedan mab Llyr	Myth	215, 1181
Maylwys mab Baedan	Ireland	178
Medyr mab Methredyd	Literary	349
Meilic mab Kaw	*Y Hen Ogled*	209
Melyn Gwanhwyn	Animal	593
Mellt	Myth	1007–1008, 1013
Menestyr	Title	283
Menw mab Teirgwaed	Uncertain	passim

Name	*Origin*	*Line numbers*
Merin	British	123
Methredyd	Literary	349
Mil Du mab Ducum	Brittany	123
Modron	Myth (*Y Hen Ogled*)	passim
Moren mab Iaen	Uncertain	203
Moren Mynawc	*Y Hen Ogled*	183, 184
Morgant Hael	*Y Hen Ogled*	256
Moro Oeruedawc	Uncertain	718
Moruran eil Tegit	Wales	225
Moruyd merch Uryen Reget	*Y Hen Ogled*	366
Mwyalch Gilgwri	Animal	847, 850
Myr	Uncertain	285
Naw mab Seithuet	Literary	194
Neb mab Kaw	Uncertain (*Y Hen Ogled*)	211
Neol Kyn Croc	British	371
Ner	British	263, 694, 828
Nerth mab Kadarn	Literary	200, 341
Nerthach mab Gwawrdur	Literary	188
Nes	Ireland	178
Neuet	Literary	339, 742, 1127
Nodawl Uaryf Trwch	Uncertain	223
Nud	Myth	passim
Nwython	*Y Hen Ogled*	256, 257, 994, 995
Nwywre	Cognate of Nudd	181, 218
Nynhyaw	Animal (Wales)	599
Och	Literary	338, 741
Odgar mab Aed	France (post–1000)	passim
Ol mab Olwyd	Literary	353
Olwen merch Yspadaden	Possibly myth	passim
Olwyd	Literary	353
Osla	British	278, 1180–1181, 1193–1194
Ouan mab Kaw	Uncertain (*Y Hen Ogled*)	207
Panawr Penbagat	British	296
Panon	Uncertain	225, 1118
Peibyaw	Animal (Wales)	599
Penn Llarcan	Ireland	343
Penn mab Nethawc	*Y Hen Ogled*	993–994
Penpingyon	British	86, 1121
Perif	Animal	201
Peris brenhin Freinc	France	277
Peul	Wales	365
Poch	Ireland	179
Prytwenn	Object	938, 1041, 1096
Pwyll Hanner Dyn	Myth	342
Rathtyen merch Vnic	Uncertain	359

Name	Origin	Line numbers
Reidwn Arwy	Uncertain	221
Reidwn mab Beli	Myth	224
Reidwn uab Eli Atuer	British	1114–1115
Reu Rwyddyrys	British	286
Rianhon	pan-Celtic	632
Ricca	Uncertain	198, 221
Rinnon Rin Barwuawc	Uncertain	663
Rongomynyat	Object	160
Roycol	Literary	196
Ruawn Pebyr mab Dorath	*Y Hen Ogled* (Uncertain)	183
Ruduyw Rys	British	1161
Run Rudwern	British	286
Run mab Nwython	*Y Hen Ogled*	257
Rymhi	Animal	315, 931
Saidi	Uncertain	185, 293
Samson Uinsych	Wales	214
Sande Pryt Angel	*Y Hen Ogled*	228
Saranhon mab Glythwyr	Literary	216–217
Sawyl Penn Uchel	*Y Hen Ogled*	344
Sberin mab Flergant Llydaw	Brittany (twelfth century)	216
Scilti Scawntroet mab Erim	Ireland	234, 239
Seithuet	Literary	193, 194, 195
Sel mab Selgi	Literary	202
Selgi	Literary	202
Selyf mab Sinoit	Uncertain	199
Seuwlch	Uncertain	333, 736
Siawn mab Iaen	British	204
Sinnoch mab Seithuet	Literary	193
Sinoit	Uncertain	199
Sol	Literary	300
Sucgen mab Sucnedut	Literary	316
Sucnedut	Literary	316
Sulyen mab Iaen	Wales (eleventh century)	203
Taran	Myth	992
Tarawc Allt Clwyt	*Y Hen Ogled*	1114
Tared Wledic	pan-Celtic	670
Tathal Twyll Goleu	Ireland	177
Tecuan Glof	British	255
Tegit	Wales	225
Tegyr Talgellawc	Uncertain	255
Teirgwaed	Uncertain	199, 408, 538
Teirtu	*Y Hen Ogled*	627
Teithi Hen mab Gwynham	Wales	245
Teithyon	Uncertain	1126–1127
Teleri merch Peul	Uncertain	365

Name	Origin	Line numbers
Teliesin Penn Beird	*Y Hen Ogled*	214
Teregut mab Iaen	Uncertain	202
Teyrnon Twr Bliant	Myth	255
Thangwen merch Weir	Uncertain	360
Trachmyr	Uncertain	286, 1106, 1159
Tringat mab Neuet	Wales (Irish in Carmarthen)	933, 1127
Tryffin	Wales	200, 364
Tutuathar	pan-Celtic	362
Twrch Llawin	Animal (Wales)	1147
Twrch Trwyth mab Tared	Animal (pan–Celtic)	passim
Twrch mab Anwas	Literary	201
Twrch mab Perif	Literary	201
Vchdryt Ardwyat Kat	British	186
Vchdryt Uaryf Draws	British	327
Uchdryt mab Erim	British	233
Uedwyr	Uncertain	362
Vnic Clememyl	Uncertain	359
Uryen Reget	*Y Hen Ogled*	366
Watu mab Seithuet	Literary	194
Weir Dathar	Uncertain	360
Waredur Kyruach	Uncertain	363
Wrnach Gawr	*Y Hen Ogled*	passim
Wyneb Gwrthucher	Object	160
Ych Brych	Animal	593
Ynyr	*Y Hen Ogled*	119
Yscawin mab Panon	British	225, 1118
Yscawt	Myth	1117
Yscudyd	British	329
Yskithrwyn Penn Beid	Animal	639, 1013, 1023, 1111
Yskyrdaf	British	329
Yspadaden Penkawr	British	passim

PLACE-NAMES

Name	Origin	Line numbers
Aber Cledyf	Wales	932, 933, 936, 1101
Aber Gwy	Wales	1179
Aber Hafren	Wales	1168
Aber Tywi	Wales	1128
Affric	Africa (Fabulous)	121
Allt Clwyt	*Y Hen Ogled*	1114
Annwuyn	*Y Hen Ogled*	714
Banawc	*Y Hen Ogled*	597
Caer Anoeth	British	125
Caer Brytwch	Literary	122

Name	Origin	Line numbers
Caer Brythach	Literary	122
Kaer Loyw	Wales	906, 923
Caer Neuenhyr Naw Nawt	Uncertain	126
Caer Oeth	Uncertain	125
Kaer Paris	France	278
Caer Se ac Asse	Literary	117
Kaer Tathal	Myth (Wales)	204
Camlan	British, probably *Y Hen*	226, 229, 231, 297
Cam Gwylathyr	Wales	954
Celli Wic y Gherniw	Cornwall	261, 351, 975, 1024, 1204
Keredigyawn	Wales	1159
Kernyw	Cornwall	passim
Cilgwri	British	847
Corsica	Europe	121
Cwm Kawlwyt	British	871, 872
Cwm Kerwyn	Wales	1112
Cymry	pan-Celtic	1095
Din Tywi	Wales	1158
Dinsol	*Y Hen Ogled*	106
Dyfneint	Cornwall	297, 313, 1167
Dyffryn Amanw	Wales	1149
Dyffryn Llychwr	Wales	1136
Dyuet	Wales	1056, 1098
Egrop	Europe	120
Eskeir Oeruel un lwerdon	Ireland	107, 350, 1030, 1066
Euyas	Wales	1166, 1174
Ewin	British	1152
Fotor	Literary	118
Freinc	France	passim
Gamon	Ireland	253–254
Garth Grugyn	Wales (secondary location)	1160
Glynn Ystu	Wales	1131
Gogled	*Y Hen Ogled*	107, 997, 1012, 1208
Groec	Uncertain	124
Gwern Abwy	British	882, 883
India Uawr	India (Fabulous)	118
India Uechan	India (Fabulous)	118
Lwerdon	Ireland	passim
Lotor	Literary	117
Lliwan	Wales	891, 902, 1179
Llwch Ewin	Wales?	1152
Llwch Tawy	Wales	1156
Llychlyn	Europe	120
Llydaw	Wales (Brittany)	216, 1007, 1058, 1163, 1164
Mor Terwyn	Europe	292

Name	*Origin*	*Line numbers*
Mynyd Amanw	British	1145
Mynyw	Wales	1099
Nerthach	Literary	122
Normandi	France	1059
Nyuer	Wales	1109, 1112
Pelunyawc	Wales	1126
Penn Blathaon ym Predein	*Y Hen Ogled*	262
Penn Pengwaed	Cornwall	106
Pennant Gouut	*Y Hen Ogled*	653, 1207
Porth Cleis	Wales	1098
Porth Kerdin yn Dyuet	Wales	1055–1056
Prydein	British	passim
Presseleu	Wales	1104
Pumlumon	Wales	953
Redynure	British	859, 860
Rydynawc Du o Brydein	British, probably Y Hen	332
Sach	Literary	117
Salach	Literary	117
Tawy	Wales	1156, 1166
Teir ynys Prydein	British	282, 368, 1057–1058
Uffern	Literary (*Y Hen Ogled*)	189, 653, 1208
Ystrat Yw	Wales	1162

TASKS

In response to Culhwch's request of Olwen as his bride, Yspadadden assigns him 40 tasks; two more are added as the story progresses. For the sake of simplicity these have been numbered as they are given in the story and the settings have been assigned a geographical, chronological, and/or literary classification.

1. Universal
2. Myth
3. Myth
4. British
5. Uncertain
6. Wales, but placed in *Y Hen Ogled*
7. Universal
8. Universal
9. Literary
10. *Y Hen Ogled*
11. *Y Hen Ogled*
12. *Y Hen Ogled*
13. Wales (Myth)
14. Ireland
15. Uncertain
16. Ireland
17. *Y Hen Ogled*
18. *Y Hen Ogled*
19. Pan-Celtic
20. Uncertain
21. Pan-Celtic (Animal)
22. Uncertain (Animal)
23. Literary
24. Literary
25. *Y Hen Ogled*
26. Myth (*Y Hen Ogled*)
27. Animal
28. Wales
29. Ireland
30. Animal[2]
31. Wales
32. Uncertain
33. Myth (*Y Hen Ogled*)
34. Animal
35. France
36. Wales
37. Animal
38. Universal
39. Literary
40. Pan-Celtic
41. Brittany
42. British

FINAL CALIBRATION

This list represents all persons and places that were not eliminated as unlikely or definitely nonexistent during an examination of the sources and influences of the story.

PERSONAL NAMES

Name	Origin	Line numbers
Aed brenhin lwerdon	Ireland	passim
Arthur	British	passim
Bedwyr	British	passim
Cacamwri (and variants)	Uncertain	passim
Kauall	Animal	1015, 1021, 1108
Caletuwlch	Object	159, 1051
Carnwenhan	Object	161, 1226
Kaw o Brydein	*Y Hen Ogled*	passim
Kei	British	passim
Kledyf Kyuwlch	Object	334, 737, 1110
Creidylat uerch Lud Law	*Y Hen Ogled*	367, 988
Custenhin Anhynwyedic	Wales (Dumnonia)	passim
Cyledyr Wyllt	*Y Hen Ogled*	994, 996, 1012, 1186
Cynwas Curyuagyl	British	186, 1101
Dillus Uarruawc uab Eurei	Wales, probably	700, 960, 963, 976, 980
Diwrnach Wydel	British	635, 1037, 1038, 1042, 1052
Drutwyn	Animal	673, 964, 986, 1014, 1106
Dunart	*Y Hen Ogled*	254, 993
Eidoel mab Aer	Wales	passim
Eri	British	passim
Erim	British	passim
Eurei	Wales, probably	979
Garselit Wydel	Pan-Celtic	295, 697, 1117
Gliui	Wales	831, 832
Glythmyr Ledewic	Wales (Brittany)	1009, 1014, 1107–1108
Goreu mab Custennin	Dumnonia	811, 1178, 1230, 1239
Greit mab Eri	British	passim
Greidawl Galldouyt	*Y Hen Ogled*	passim
Grugyn Gwrych Ereint	Animal (*Y Hen Ogled*)	passim
Guyn Mygtwn march Gwedw	Animal	689, 1006, 1177
Gwedw	Animal	689, 1006, 1177
Gwidon Ordu	*Y Hen Ogled*	652, 1206, 1228
Gwrgi Seueri	Wales	1010
Gwrgwst Letlwm	*Y Hen Ogled*	993
Gwrhyr Gwalstawd Ieithoed	Uncertain	passim
Gwynn Mygdwn	Animal	689, 1006, 1177
Gwythyr uab Greidawl	*Y Hen Ogled*	passim
Hygwyd	Uncertain	1048, 1210, 1212, 1215

Name	*Origin*	*Line numbers*
Llamrei	Animal	1016, 1225
Llenlleawc Wydel	Ireland	253, 293, 1051
Menw mab Teirgwaed	Uncertain	passim
Ner	British	263, 694, 828
Nwython	*Y Hen Ogled*	256, 257, 994, 995
Penn mab Nethawc	*Y Hen Ogled*	993–994
Prytwenn	Object	938, 1041, 1096
Rymhi	Animal	315, 931
Tringat mab Neuet	Wales (Irish in Carmarthen)	933, 1127
Wrnach Gawr	*Y Hen Ogled*	passim
Yscawin mab Panon	British	225, 1118
Yskithrwyn Penn Beid	Animal	639, 1013, 1023, 1111
Yspadaden Penkawr	British	passim

PLACE-NAMES

Name	*Origin*	*Line numbers*
Aber Cledyf	Wales	932, 933, 936, 1101
Kaer Loyw[3]	Wales	906, 923
Cam Gwylathyr	Wales	954
Celli Wic y Gherniw	Cornwall	261, 351, 975, 1024, 1204
Kernyw	Cornwall	passim
Eskeir Oeruel un lwerdon	Ireland	107, 350, 1030, 1066
Freinc	France	passim
Gogled	*Y Hen Ogled*	107, 997, 1012, 1208
Iwerdon	Ireland	passim
Llydaw	Wales (Brittany)	216, 1007, 1058, 1163, 1164
Pennant Gouut	*Y Hen Ogled*	653, 1207
Prydein	British	passim
Pumlumon	Wales	953

Appendix D: The Dating of Badon

As to how a year was derived, that is very much left to speculation at this time. The possibility of an alternate and now lost source cannot be overlooked, but at this point devoting time and effort to locating and describing the hypothetical material that might have composed it would be counterproductive. It is possible that a later contributor to the annals was attempting to synchronize the known history at his disposal with the event. If so, he may have been aware that an early version of *The Anglo-Saxon Chronicle* dates the beginning of Ceawlin's reign to 560, and credits him with a major expansion of Wessex under his direction. This hypothetical annalist might well have assumed (as many modern historians have done) that Badon had taken place in the south, so that Ceawlin's reign directly affected the peace Gildas spoke of. With those two assumptions in mind, he could simply have counted back Gildas' forty-three years from 560, deciding that 517 was a likely year for the Battle of Badon and that immediately after Gildas wrote the Germanic peoples began their expansion again. The above can be no more than conjecture, however. To my knowledge, no study has been done as to the developmental interrelationship between *Annales Cambriae* and *The Anglo-Saxon Chronicle* in this regard.

This leaves three major options for how 517 was come upon. As *Annales Cambriae* has been shown to have derived most of its early information from the *Northern Memorandum*, this may have been the initial reference point. However, as was seen in *Origins of the Arthurian Romances* and has been demonstrated by various authors over the last few decades, any hypothetical construction of the *Northern Memoranda* must assume vague dating.[1] If *Annales Cambriae*'s date of 517 was reached through that source, then even its initial material was deeply flawed.

The second option is that the information was derived through a reading of Gildas and a version of *The Anglo-Saxon Chronicle*. Leaving aside for a moment the issues facing the latter document, whatever annalist that could have worked out a date in this manner could have had no reference beyond a period of peace in the Germanic record that equated to that which Gildas claimed.

The third option is the most seductive, and the trickiest. While it is possible that the date comes from a now-lost source, and having even one secure date from so early in post–Roman history would be highly advantageous, there are two facts that argue against it. Several other events from the north are also listed before 600. In each case, even as late as the 573 entry for the Battle of Arfderydd,[2] the dates have been shown to be unsupportable, yet they have been connected to *Historia Brittonum* and therefore the *Northern Memorandum*, with no other scholar feeling compelled to suggest another source. The simple fact that Gildas' parochial history is unique in what had been the Roman Empire suggests that Britain likely produced no more individuals who could have provided more accurate contexts than what are now extant.

All three explanations for the date of 517 either rely on unreliable evidence or are simply hopeful. As has been seen above, 517 for his death would fit in nicely with the rough estimates that each chapter has generated regarding his career without upsetting any of the conclusions. However, it is unlikely that the date can have any bearing on historical fact as it now stands; it is no more likely than Geoffrey's 500, and for the same reasons.

Notes

Introduction

1. A point brought up by Professor Nicholas Higham in *King Arthur: Mythmaking and History* (New York, 2002), 117.

2. Chadwick, "Early Culture and Learning in North Wales," *Studies in the Early British Church*, ed. by Nora K. Chadwick (Cambridge, 1958), 29–120.

3. One will find Nennius used as the name of the *Historia Brittonum* author as rarely as possible. Though he has been generally accepted as the person who wrote what we know as the *Historia Brittonum*, Dumville has educated the academic community that this is not necessarily the case. Dumville, "Nennius and the *Historia Brittonum*," *SC* 10/11 (Cardiff, 1976), 78–95.

4. Higham, *King Arthur: Mythmaking and History* (New York, 2002), 118–129; Coe and Young, *The Celtic Sources of the Arthurian Legend* (Llanerch, 1995).

5. See Chapter 1, where Urien's literary prominence is more carefully explained.

6. This understanding is very clear in most of the writing. I must admit that I had had the same perception until reading through Professor Higham's recent series of books and Professor Koch's new interpretation of *Y Gododdin*. Higham, *Gildas and the Fifth Century* (Leicester, 1994), *An English Empire* (Leicester, 1996); *The Gododdin of Aneirin: Text and Context in Dark Age Britain*, ed. and trans. by John T. Koch (Cardiff, 1995), xxv–xli.

7. That this is clearly so may be made evident with a few examples. Ambrosius, the only Briton deemed worthy of Gildas in his intro-

duction, is hardly mentioned. Coel Hen, Pabo Post Prydein, and all Pictish heroes are altogether neglected. Arthur is given a separate chapter, to be sure, but only Urien has the privilege of leading British chieftains and the circumstance of only his death is given.

8. In this, Cunedda's presence would have been fundamental.

9. The works are described as being written in the ninth century because of the preponderance of evidence for the collection of many poems and records at this time. The majority of the above works were undoubtedly first written down in the ninth century, while the two Arthurian poems would have been most likely written in this period.

10. In fact, the addition of these materials may have been contrary to the propaganda Merfyn wished to portray. *Annales Cambriae* does not mention Urien, and most of the other literary records do not as well. Instead they emphasize the importance of Arthur as a political leader and warrior.

11. The *Northern Memorandum* and the *Northern Chronicle* have been heavily discussed over the years: Jackson, "On the North British section in Nennius," *Celt and Saxon*, ed. by Nora K. Chadwick (Cambridge, 1963); Dumville, "On the North British Section of the *Historia Brittonum*," *WHR* 8 (Cardiff, 1977); Hughes, "The Welsh Latin Chronicles: *Annales Cambriae* and Related Texts," *PBA* 59 (London, 1975); and Charles-Edwards, "The Authenticity of the Gododdin: An Historian's View," *Studies in Early Welsh Poetry: Astudiaethau ar yr Hengerdd*, ed. by Rachel Bromwich and R. Brinley Jones (Cardiff, rev. 1978). How-

ever, certain aspects of Gwrtheyrn's treatment derive from the tenth century and Dyfed's influence: Chadwick, "Early Culture and Learning in North *Wales*," *Studies in the Early British Church*, ed. by Nora K. Chadwick (Cambridge, 1958), 75–6, 90–120. As to *Y Gododdin*, scholars have quibbled over the past forty-five years about the date of composition, from 600 with Kenneth Jackson and Jarman to the eighth century with Charles-Edwards and back again to a reserved 550x640 by David Dumville and more specifically around 570 according to John Koch: *The Gododdin: The Oldest Scottish Poem*, trans. by Kenneth H. Jackson (Edinburgh, 1969) 58; *Aneirin: Y Gododdin, Britain's Oldest Heroic Poem*, trans. by Alfred O.H. Jarman (Llandysul, 1988), lxxiv; Charles-Edwards, "The Authenticity of the *Gododdin*: An Historian's View," *Studies in Early Welsh Poetry: Astudiaethau ar yr Hengerdd*, ed. by Rachel Bromwich and R. Brinley Jones (Cardiff, rev. 1978) 53; Dumville, "Early Welsh Poetry: Problems of Historicity," *Early Welsh Poetry: Studies in the "Book of Aneirin*," ed. by Brynley F. Roberts (Cardiff, 1988) 3–4; *The Gododdin of Aneirin: Text and Context in Dark Age Britain*, ed. and trans. by John T. Koch (Cardiff, 1995), xvi–xvii.

12. It might be contemplated that Arthur's absence from *Armes Prydein* compromises his position as a historical figure. However, neither Urien nor any of the northern heroes of the heroic age are mentioned, either.

13. Higham's suggestion that he is present only to be paired with Patrick suggests nothing more than a possible reason why he was included in the history. He would have made for a difficult addition in that regard if he was not already famous. Higham, *King Arthur: Mythmaking and History* (New York, 2002), 136–156.

14. What is of overwhelming importance to our knowledge of Urien are twelve extant poems from his bard, Taliesin.

15. *Pa gur?* and *Preiddeu Annwfn* are the only Arthurian poems which are demonstrably pre–Galfridic, but the innumerable allusions in the earliest twenty-six entries of *Trioedd Ynys Prydein* assume an overwhelming knowledge of Arthur which exceeds that of any other hero.

16. The next great leader in British politics was Urien, and we have much more specific dates and locations for his activities. The material is not large or tremendously useful in dating or placing the boundaries of his kingdom, but the cumulative knowledge to be gained from the authentic poetry of his chief bard, Tal-

iesin, gives a location, the rough center of the kingdom, and a general date of the late sixth century for his subject. It is indeed a twist of fate that Urien is as fully remembered as he is. It would seem the dynasty which took control of Gwynedd early in the ninth century claimed descent from Coel Hen through Llywarch Hael, his cousin. As Merfyn Frych, Rhodhri Mawr, and his sons peacefully acquired most of Wales, they tried to create a national consciousness by drawing on the common British heroes of the past: Chadwick, "Early Culture and Learning in North Wales," *Studies in the Early British Church*, ed. by Nora K. Chadwick (Cambridge, 1958), 29–120. As the family dynasty's most famous Saxon killer was Urien, he figured most prominently, and the poetry and stories of him were most often recorded. For Arthur, the few poems at hand are too mythologized and too broad in their placement of him to be of any use. He had no such descendants.

17. Though even the date for this event is not acceptable by any means. Professor Dumville's notes on the chronology of the *Historia Brittonum* unfortunately did not touch on Arthurian dates. However, Professor Dumville did establish the presence of an inconsistent 28-year discrepancy in both the *Annales Cambriae* and the historical section of the *Historia Brittonum* due to two different dating systems. It is possible that this same discrepancy may have occurred for the 537 entry. It is also possible that the date for Camlann is a product of antiquarian speculation, in which case it is only an approximation made as late as the ninth century: "Some Aspects of the Chronology of the *Historia Brittonum*" *BBCS* 25 (Cardiff, 1974), 439–445.

18. In fairness, there does not appear to have been any native coins minted between the end of the Roman occupation and the ninth century.

19. Cadbury-Camelot was the site for a series of digs by Professor Leslie Alcock during the 1960s conducted for the express purpose of locating Arthur's assumed home at Cadbury.

20. His most recent critics have been Professor Dumville and Dr. Padel: Dumville, "Sub-Roman history," *WHR* 8 (Cardiff, 1977), 188; Padel, "The Nature of Arthur," *CMCS* 27 (Cardiff, 1994), 1–32.

21. For the purposes of this paper, the Dark Ages are defined as existing between the end of the physical, substantial presence of the Roman Empire around 400 and the rise of Urien of Rheged in the last decades of the sixth century.

This is the period when the historical literary evidence is almost non-existent.

22. *Epistola ad Coroticum* is a letter by St. Patrick to a Coroticus (Ceredig) presumably of the Strathclyde region. It pertains to his slave raiding on the Irish coast. The letter itself makes so many assumptions of knowledge, however, that it is rarely used as evidence.

23. *The Life of St. Germanus* gives no dates and therefore this obstacle must be guessed through to be of any use. Gildas is notorious for giving no dates, and though he will indicate when an event occurred in conjunction with a more widely known event, his synchronisms have demonstrably been proven incorrect on more than one occasion. For instance, he claims that the Romans built Antonine's Wall and Hadrian's Wall after the Honorian rescript of around 410, though these walls are known to have existed for centuries before this time.

24. The archaeology has not proven effective even in this regard. The only certain difference between pre– and post–Roman occupation has often come down to amphorae from the Mediterranean, and the wine they contained was not a common product.

25. To some extent these are disputed, too: Anderson and Anderson, *Kings and Kingship in Early Scotland* (Edinburgh, 1973); Miller, "The Disputed Historical Horizon of the Pictish King-lists," *BBCS* 28 (Cardiff, 1978), 1–34.

26. Most recently by Professor Dumville, Dr. Padel, and Professor Higham: Dumville, "Sub-Roman Britain: History and Legend" in *History* 62, no. 205 (London, 1977), 188; Padel, "The Nature of Arthur," *CMCS* 27 (Cambridge, 1984), 1–32; Higham, *Gildas and the Fifth Century* (Manchester, 1994).

27. Ashe, "'A Certain Very Ancient Book'; Traces of an Arthurian Source," *S* 56.2 (1981), 301–23.

28. Professor Loomis wrote extensively on this, his favorite subject. For a list of his works on the topic see the bibliography.

29. Morris, *The Age of Arthur* (London, 1973).

30. Alcock, *Arthur's Britain* (New York, 1971), 81–5.

31. Jones, "Datblygiadau Cynnar Chwedl Arthur," trans. by Gerald Morgan, "The Early Evolution of Arthur" *NMS* 8 (Nottingham, 1963), 3–21; Jackson, "The Arthur of History," *Arthurian Literature in the Middle Ages*, ed. by Roger S. Loomis (Oxford, 1959), 1–11.

32. Bromwich, "Concepts of Arthur," *SC* 10/11 (Cardiff, 1976); Charles-Edwards, "The

Arthur of History," *The Arthur of the Welsh*, ed. by Rachel Bromwich, Brynley F. Roberts, and Alfred O.H. Jarman (Cardiff, 1991), 97–116.

33. This is because of the northerness of the people he is earliest connected to, and Arthur's presence in *Y Gododdin*: Jackson, "Again Arthur's Battles" *MP* 43 (Chicago, 1946), 57; Bromwich, "Concepts of Arthur," *SC* 10/11 (Cardiff, 1976); Charles-Edwards, "The Arthur of History," *The Arthur of the Welsh*, ed. by Bromwich, Brynley F. Roberts, and Alfred O.H. Jarman (Cardiff, 1991).

34. This said, Professor Koch's recent interpretation of *Y Gododdin*, in which he attempts to bring the poem back to its probable form in the sixth century, is a notable argument for the possibility of being able to date pre-ninth century poetry in the future.

35. *Teulu* is a permanent war-band and translates into Modern Welsh as "family." This development of an army personally tied to their leader represents Stage Two of Chadwick's levels of a heroic age. The first is defined by a raiding society that is dominated by one man with predatory habits. The second stage is marked by the development of the war-band. The third stage is one in which princes live removed from their people and are on more intimate terms with foreign princes than commoners: Chadwick and Chadwick, *The Development of Oral Literature*, vol. 3 (Cambridge, 1940) 732–4.

36. A suggestion followed in Chadwick, *The British Heroic Age* (Cardiff, 1976).

37. Johnson, *Origins of Arthurian Romance: Early Sources for the Legends of Tristan, the Grail and the Abduction of the Queen*, forthcoming.

38. In this sense some of the romances may be employed in the same context as the British *vitae*.

39. Though I am, with Miller and Dumville, hesitant to accept the father-son method of patrimony which appears in the dynastic genealogies. There is good evidence to follow Davies' lead and the implications of the Irish law texts in assuming a much more complex form of inheritance: Davies, *A Welsh Microcosm* (Leicester, 1982), 122–5; MacNeill, "The Irish Law of Dynastic Succession," *Studies* 8 (Oxford, 1919), 367–82, 640–53; Ó Corráin, "Irish Regnal Succession: A Reappraisal," *Studia Hibernia* 2 (Dublin, 1971), 7–39; Charles-Edwards, *Early Irish and Welsh Kinship* (Oxford, 1993).

40. In this Professor Dumville has perhaps been the leader of the movement. His clear insights into *Historia Brittonum*, *The Anglo-Saxon Chronicle*, and the writings of Patrick as

well as his appraisal of the period in general have made clear all the problems involved in studying the post–Roman era of Britain.

41. *The Gododdin of Aneirin; Text and Context in Dark Age Northern Britain*, ed. and trans. by John T. Koch (Cardiff, 1995).

42. Dark, *Civitas to Kingdom: British Political Continuity 300–800* (Leicester, 1994).

43. Higham, *Gildas and the Fifth Century* (Manchester, 1994); *An English Empire* (Manchester, 1995).

44. The author's efforts so far have indicated four traditional stories; abduction of Gwenhwyfar, destruction of a Celtic coven, Tristan's slaying of a dragon, and Gawain's adventures in Galloway. The first three have been thoroughly explored in *Origins of Arthurian Romance: Early Sources for the Legends of Tristan, the Grail and the Abduction of the Queen*, forthcoming.

45. Johnson, *Origins of Arthurian Romance: Early Sources for the Legends of Tristan, the Grail and the Abduction of the Queen*, forthcoming.

Chapter 1

1. Gildas says that he was born in the year of Badon, which is usually given as around 500.

2. Though it has long been suggested that Arthur was not necessarily the victor of Badon, Higham has been the first to postulate that the potentially later association of the two was an attempt to make the victory British and thus make it a source of national pride. Such a motivation would fit in well with the themes to be found in both the *Annales Cambriae* and *Historia Brittonum*. Higham, *King Arthur: Mythmaking and History* (New York, 2002), 58–9.

3. In fact, Giraldus Cambrensis states that this was the reason why Gildas denounced the Britons in *De Excidio Britanniae*. Gerald of Wales, *Descriptio Cambrensis* 2, trans. by Lewis G.M. Thorpe, 259.

4. However, if one wished to follow Professor Thomas Jones and argue that the text names Badon's victor, I would propose a date around 490 for the battle. This would still allow for a historic Arthur and be more in line with the lull in *The Anglo-Saxon Chronicle*. It would also be acceptable around Dumville's paper which assumes a great deal of birth-resurrection of Christ discrepancies, and Gildas himself, who died around 569 an old man. It would also align nicely with the current view that Gildas wrote in the early to mid–530s. The

postulated date would place the Arthurian period to the late fifth or early sixth centuries. Jones, "Datblygiadau Cynnar Chwedl Arthur," trans. by Morgan, "The Early Evolution of Arthur," *NMS* 8 (Nottingham, 1964), 5–6.

5. In particular, the stanza devoted to the Battle of Strathcarron (c. 642) dates the poem to centuries before the ninth century.

6. Arthur's traditional death has been placed at 537–9, while *Y Gododdin* has been traditionally been dated to about 600. Recent work on the poem has hypothesized a range from 540–570, while I will place Camlann to the decades after 500 later in the book.

7. *The Gododdin of Aneirin; Text and Context in Dark Age Northern Britain*, ed. and trans. by John T. Koch (Cardiff, 1995), 147.

8. Padel, "The Nature of Arthur," *CMCS* 27 (Cambridge, 1994), 14.

9. *The Vatican Recension of the Historia Brittonum*, ed. by David N. Dumville (Cambridge, 1985), 40–54.

10. Thurneysen, "Zimmer, Nennius vindicatus," *ZDP* 28 (Halle, 1896), 85, 87; Bruce, *The Evolution of Arthurian Romance from the Beginnings Down to the Year 1300* (Gottingen, 1923), 9; Jackson, "On the Northern British Section in Nennius," *Celt and Saxon: Studies in the Early British Border*, ed. by Nora K. Chadwick (Cambridge, 1963), 6; Hughes, "The Welsh Latin Chronicles: *Annales Cambriae* and Related Texts," *PBA* 59 (Oxford, 1975), 237–9; Bromwich, "Concepts of Arthur," *SC*, 10/11 (Cardiff, 1975–6), 175–6; Dumville, "The Anglian Collection of Royal Genealogies and Regnal Lists," *ASE* 5 (Cambridge, 1976), 23–50; Charles-Edwards, "The Authenticity of the *Gododdin*: An Historian's View," *Astudiaethau ar yr Hengerdd*, ed. by Rachel Bromwich, Brynley F. Roberts, and Alfred O.H. Jarman (Cardiff, rev. 1978), 63.

11. The purpose of *Historia Brittonum*, as Dr. Nora Chadwick long ago pointed out, was to validate the legitimacy of the royal house which came to power in Gwynedd during the early years of the ninth century. "Early Culture and Learning in North Wales," *Studies in the Early British Church*, ed. by Nora K. Chadwick (Cambridge, 1958), 29–120 and above.

12. Bromwich "Concepts of Arthur," *SC* 10/11 (1975–6) 175–6; Bruce, *The Evolution of Arthurian Romance from the Beginnings Down to the Year 1300* (Gottingen, 1923), 9; Thurneysen "Zimmer, Nennius vindicatus," *ZDP* 28 (Halle, 1896), 85, 87. Jackson opposed this conclusion on the grounds that a medieval scholar named Beulon requested a copy of *His-*

toria Brittonum with the Anglo-Saxon genealogies omitted and his copy did not contain the Arthurian section. As there is no way of proving Beulon had any more knowledge pertaining to the provenance of the Arthurian section than modern scholarship, Professor Jackson's theory is weak.

13. Notable because of its inclusion in *Pa gur?*, an account of Arthur's activities in summary form. See below.

14. Chadwick and Chadwick, *The Growth of Literature* (Cambridge, 1932), 155; Jackson, "The Arthur of History," *Arthurian Literature in the Middle Ages*, ed. by Roger S. Loomis (Chicago, 1959), 7–8; Bromwich, "Concepts of Arthur" (Cardiff, 1976), 169–72.

15. Hughes, "The Welsh Latin Chronicles: *Annales Cambriae* and related texts," *PBA* 59 (Oxford, 1975), 235–6.

16. Most notorious is the date of 449 for the arrival of the first group of Germanic-speaking mercenaries under Hengest and Horsa. This is clearly an unhistorical association that stems ultimately from a chronologically difficult passage in *Historia Ecclesiastica*. See below.

17. Higham, *King Arthur: Mythmaking and History* (New York, 2002), 58–9.

18. Padel's explanation that it was an afterthought to help historicize Arthur will be discussed in Chapter 2.

19. Most likely Camlann can be dated no closer than to the first third of the sixth century (and that in itself is a questionable association). Dumville, "Some Aspects of the Chronology of the Historia Brittonum," *BBCS* 25 (Cardiff, 1974), 439–45.

20. Hughes, "The Welsh Latin Chronicles: *Annales Cambriae* and related texts," *PBA* 59 (Oxford, 1975), 237–9; Bromwich, "Concepts of Arthur," *SC* 10/11 (1975–6), 175–6; Dumville "The Anglian Collection of Royal Genealogies and Regnal Lists," *ASE* 5 (Cambridge, 1976), 23–50; Charles-Edwards, "The Authenticity of the *Gododdin*: An Historian's View," *Astudiaethau ar yr Hengerdd*, ed. by Rachel Bromwich and R. Brinley Jones (Cardiff, 1978), 63.

21. Johnson, *Origins of Arthurian Romance: Early Sources for the Legends of Tristan, the Grail and the Abduction of the Queen*, forthcoming.

22. Dumville, "The Anglian Collection of Royal Genealogies and Regnal Lists," *ASE* 5 (Cambridge, 1976), 23–50; Hughes, "The Welsh Latin Chronicles: *Annales Cambriae* and related texts," *PBA* 59 (Oxford, 1975), 237–239.

23. Professor Chadwick was clear in indicating that some figures in heroic age literature may have been invented, though his assessment was that they tended to be lesser characters or were created by a series of unlikely events. Chadwick, *The Heroic Age* (Cambridge, 1912), 334.

24. Ker, *Epic and Romance: Essays on Medieval Literature* (Dover, 1957), 13–15.

25. If John Koch is correct, the raw elements of the Arthuriana section of the *Historia Brittonum* may have been in place as early as the late seventh century. If this is so, there is evidence that Arthur was being recorded as an historical character as little as a century and a half after his death. *The Gododdin of Aneirin; Text and Context in Dark Age Northern Britain*, ed. and trans. by John T. Koch (Cardiff, 1995), cxxi.

26. Alcock, *Arthur's Britain* (London, 1971), 153; Morris, *The Age of Arthur* (London, 1976), 146–7.

27. Roberts, "*Culhwch ac Olwen*, The Triads, and Saints' Lives," *The Arthur of the Welsh*, ed. by Rachel Bromwich, Brynley F. Roberts, and Alfred O.H. Jarman (Cardiff, 1991), 82.

28. Dr. Padel refers to Arthur's similarities with Fionn macCumhail, but here the folkloric hero can produce no parallel.

29. There is, of course, no way to be exactly certain when any of the saints were born, but there is such an intricate and fairly consistent amount of material based on different traditions that rough accuracy seems a possibility. Bartrum, *A Welsh Classical Dictionary: People in History and Legend up to about AD 1000*. (Cardiff, 1993), 26–7.

Chapter 2

1. In that respect, this paper is in direct response to Professor Dumville, who sagely if overconfidently reminded the Arthurian faithful "The fact of the matter is that there is no historical evidence about Arthur." Dumville, "Sub-Roman Britain: History and Legend," *WHR* 62 (London, 1977), 188.

2. Miller, "Historicity and Pedigrees of the Northcountrymen," *BBCS* 26 (Cardiff, 1976), 255–280.

3. Though if Koch's suggestions are right and Catraeth was a battle in which the men of Gododdin fought Urien and his allies, such an exemption is understandable. *The Gododdin of Aneirin: Text and Context in Dark Age Northern Britain*, ed. and trans. by John T. Koch (Cardiff, 1995).

4. Most probably 826. Dumville, "Some Aspects of the Chronology of the *Historia Brittonum*" *BBCS* 25 (Cardiff, 1974), 439–445.

5. Chadwick, "Early Culture and Learning in North Wales," *Studies in the Early British Church*, ed. by Nora K. Chadwick (Cambridge, 1958), 82.

6. And would now be assigned to the period of Rhodri Mawr, one of Llywarch's descendants and therefore a distant relative of Urien. Still, the poet would have been paid to be very sympathetic to the family's greatest warrior.

7. Rowland, *Early Welsh Saga Poetry* (Cambridge, 1990), 42–47.

8. Though the Llywarch poet could not help but compare the two opposing kings to a mouse scratching against a cliff. The clearest indication that the Llywarch Hen poems are more likely to be historically accurate than the *Historia Brittonum* is propaganda. The poems treat Llywarch Hen, progenitor of the Gwynedd House, as an old and impotent man. This is not a portrayal one would expect the royal family to have supported. And yet the poems are not obviously biased against the family. His sons and his cousin Urien are held in the highest esteem.

9. The Gwynedd kings most probably did not want the Llywarch Hen cycle to survive. As Dr. Williams has suggested, the cycle is most likely the result of *ad hoc* collections made by a person or persons to rescue them from oblivion once they had arrived in Wales; Williams, "Llywarch Hen and the Finn Cycle," *Astudiaethau ar yr Hengerdd*, ed. by Rachel Bromwich and R. Brinley Jones (Cardiff, 1978), 263–5).

10. Incidentally, all kings of different pedigrees and therefore individuals not recognized as leaders of other kings.

11. This point is particularly relevant to *Y Gododdin*. The fact that the Lothians fought and lost the battle without the alliance of any other British nation doomed the poem written thereafter to be the textbook example of what would happen to any king who fought alone.

12. John Koch's theoretical remodeling of *Y Gododdin* would allow for an entire historical reconstruction of the second half of the sixth century. *The Gododdin of Aneirin: Text and Context in Dark Age Northern Britain*, ed. and trans. by John T. Koch (Cardiff, 1995), xxxv–xli.

13. *Canu Taliesin*, 8, ln. 7, 9.

14. *Canu Llywarch Hen*, 8.

15. That is, if *Historia Brittonum* may be accepted at face value here.

16. Though Ambrosius does indisputably belong to the fifth century as a historical figure, as does Coroticus. Ambrosius' presence in *De Excidio Britanniae* and Coroticus' prominence in Patrick's *Epistola* are the most tangible pieces of evidence to be found for the century following Roman rule. See above in the Introduction.

17. The following few paragraphs are made using the basic assumptions associated with this figure so that his historical development and preservation may be presented without diversion. His true role in British history will be touched upon below.

18. Of course, archaeologically speaking, the Germanic speakers were present in significant numbers before the end of the fourth century, and therefore any tyrant whom Gildas would speak of should, historically speaking, be an emperor. This is incoherent with the floruit of Gwrtheyrn, who is generally assumed to have been some kind of overking in the fifth century. Dumville, "Sub-Roman: History and Legend," *History* 62 (Cardiff, 1977), 185.

19. "Gwrtheyrn," great king, is a linguistic parallel to "Vortigern." See Chapter 4 for a brief explanation, though I hope to write a more complete articulation of the relationship between these two very different characters in a future publication.

20. Bede, *A History of the English Church and People*, Book 1, trans. by Leo Sherley-Price, rev. by Ronald Edward Latham. (London, 1978), 15; Higham, *An English Empire* (Manchester, 1995), 40.

21. *The Vatican Recension of the 'Historia Brittonum,'* ed. by David N. Dumville (Cambridge, 1985), 40–54; Chadwick, "Early Culture and Learning in North Wales," *Studies in the Early British Church*, ed. by Nora K. Chadwick (Cambridge, 1958), 75–76.

22. Chadwick, "Early Culture and Learning in North Wales," *Studies in the Early British Church*, ed. by Nora K. Chadwick (Cambridge, 1958), 114.

23. Bede, *A History of the English Church and People*, Book 1, trans. by Leo Sherley-Price, rev. by Ronald Edward Latham (London, 1978), 15.

24. Chapters 31, 36–38, 43–44.

25. It is, unfortunately, impossible to know the extent of the damage done to Gwrtheyrn's reputation by the *Historia Brittonum*. If he was the *superbus tyrannus* of Gildas, then he was one of the British leaders who deployed Germanic speakers as mercenaries. But this may not have been such a foolish practice in itself—it was done throughout Europe during this period. Beyond the conjecture that this con-

nection is valid, there is only the persistent tradition that Gwrtheyrn was the ancestor of many of the Welsh royal families, in the face of the damning testimony of *Historia Brittonum*.

26. Chapter 61.

27. I have intentionally left out the *vitae* body, in which Maelgwn figures prominently. It is my belief that his regular inclusion there was the result of two non-political factors—his location near to many of the saints and his prominence during his lifetime.

28. Hughes, "The Welsh Latin Chronicles: *Annales Cambriae* and Related Texts," *PBA* 59 (London, 1975), 236–237.

29. Clan MacArthur puts him at the beginning of its pedigree. However, the clan system does not date before the twelfth century.

30. Geoffrey's belief that Constantine succeeded his uncle Arthur has no precedent, and for good reason. The king whom Geoffrey mentions, of Dumnonia, is to be found in Gildas' paper; he is the first king denounced. The following kings in Geoffrey's succession list precisely match the order of the successive rulers of the Britons as given by Geoffrey.

31. This phenomenon is most prominent in *Trioedd Ynys Prydein*, where Arthur and his men seem to invade the entire triadic system. *TYP*, lxix. He does overwhelm the triadic formula in the *White Book of Hergest*. *TYP*, lxxxi.

32. This is mainly seen by their sporadic appearance in British literature and their presence in *Trioedd Ynys Prydein*.

33. Comparatively speaking, of course. No scholar in his right mind would consider any early Welsh king an easy subject to study.

34. Taliesin engendered a dynastic hero for the new ruling house of Gwynedd and *Y Gododdin* is a beautiful example of the heroism against the common Germanic foe which the Gwynedd kings hoped to impress upon the other Welsh kingdoms of the ninth century. Apparently poetry pertaining to Arthur could not fulfill these functions. Incidentally, this may imply Arthur was not chiefly fighting German speakers in his lifetime but other British people as well.

35. As in the well-known *Y Gododdin* verse (B.38) of the oldest redaction. *The Gododdin: The Oldest Scottish Poem*, ed. and trans. by Kenneth H. Jackson (Edinburgh, 1969), 96–109; *The Gododdin: Text and Context for Dark Age North Britain*, ed. and trans. by John T. Koch (Cardiff, 1995). Koch's reconstruction of the poem suggests it can be dated prior to 638.

36. Though because *Annales Cambriae* is a tenth-century Dyfed document in its present form this judgment about Urien's absence may not be valid. Hywel Dda was a strong opponent to the Gwynedd dynasty, and any slight he could give it or the family from which it came would have been welcome.

Chapter 3

1. On the British Heroic Age, with general parameters from the early fifth to the late sixth centuries and beyond, see Chadwick and Chadwick, *The Development of Oral Literature*, vol. 1 (Cambridge, 1932), 16 et passim; *TYP*, lxvii, lxxvi; Chadwick, *The British Heroic Age* (Cambridge, 1976); *Aneirin: Y Gododdin*, Alfred O.H. Jarman (Cardiff, 1990), xlxivii.

2. Miller, "The Commanders at Arthuret" *TCWAAS* 75 (Kendall, 1975), 97. Dumville has argued that it was "maybe" 575–600, while Dr. Higham has concluded that there was no heroic age in Britain. I have argued here using the former date because of its traditional quality. However, both theories are equally untenable, as will be seen. "SubRoman Britain: History and Legend" *History* 62, no. 205 (London, 1977), 190 fn. 95; Higham, *Gildas and the Fifth Century* (Leicester, 1994).

3. Though Dumville, Koch, and Bartrum would dissent with this view. Both Dumville and Koch have argued that Urien's career may have centered about the mid-sixth century. Bartrum believes that Urien's date of birth was close to the end of the fifth century.

4. Pabo Post Prydein, Gwallog, Outigern, and Cynan Garwyn to name only a few.

5. Professor Dumville defines it here because it is a historical horizon of British history.

6. Dumville, "Sub-Roman Britain: History and Legend," *History* 62, no. 205 (London, 1977), 190 fn. 95.

7. We may say with certainty that the manner in which these cultures develop is consistent because of the studies of Hector and Nora Chadwick in *The Growth of Literature* (1932–40), a three-volume work which catalogued and discussed every major heroic age. They are still a seminal work in the field.

8. Chadwick and Chadwick, *The Growth of Literature*, vol. 3 (Cambridge, 1940), 733.

9. One must wonder how the very first heroic age society arose. The very existence of the heroic age assumes an alternative manner by which an heroic age could begin, one in which it develops without external influence. It must be admitted that this hypothetical al-

ternative could also have been the reason behind the British Heroic Age, but this seems unlikely and is unnecessary. It is well established that there were heroic societies in proximity to the fifth-century British, and that these societies probably were interacting with the British.

10. Indeed, there is good evidence that this is exactly what was happening in the late-fourth and early-fifth century Roman Empire. The triumphs of emperors is only the most obvious example of the weakening grip they had on Roman government.

11. These statements are in direct contrast to Dr. Dark's conclusions. He argues for a great deal of wealth in sub–Roman Britain. This is because a) the burden of Roman taxation was at an end; b) the non-producing but heavily using elite had vanished; and c) late Roman display strategies and temple donations were no longer in use. Dark, *From Civitas to Kingdom* (Leicester, 1994), 68. A historical example may well point out the flaws in his argument. One might, in the centuries to come, argue that the thirteen colonies of America went through a period of economic prosperity for many of the same reasons, and without the constant raiding of foreigners on U.S. soil. However, this is not the case. The political and economic structure of the U.S. initially struggled. Only because it remained united under one president was it able to correct many of its largest problems in the Constitution. Even this took over twenty years. The Britain of the fifth century had no unity, and it was under a similar kind of stress. Speaking of pre–446 sub–Roman Britain, Gildas tells us "Nam et ipsos mutuo, perexigui victus brevi sustenaculo miserrimorum civium, latrocinando temperabant: et augebantur externae clades domesticis motibus, quod huiuscemodi tam crebis direptionibus vacuaretur omnis regio totius cibi baculo, excepto venatoriae artis solacio." "For they resorted to looting each other, there being only a tiny amount of food to give brief sustenance to the wretched people; and the disasters from abroad were increased by internal disorders, for as a result of constant devastations of this kind the whole region came to lack the staff of any food, apart from such comfort as the art of the huntsman could procure them." Gildas, *The Ruin of Britain*, trans. by Michael Winterbottom (London, 1978), Chap. 19.4.

12. Dark, *From Civitas to Kingdom* (Leicester, 1994), 22.

13. This scenario has traditionally been associated with Vortigern's rise to power. However, it seems unlikely, as does any theory that

a military-based kingship developed without outside influences. Landowners would have no interest in changing a society in which they already held power. They would have sought to protect it and, failing in that, would have isolated themselves from the changing society. This is what occurred in Gaul and elsewhere during the fifth century.

14. This lesson was clearly a difficult one, Dr. Higham has noted that Gildas implies early kings were made and unmade regularly in the fifth century. Higham, *The Northern Counties to AD 1000* (Oxford, 1986), 251.

15. This has been discussed at length by Carney. Carney, *Studies in Irish Literature and History* (Dublin, 1955). As Strabo and others recorded, the bards were keepers of oral knowledge. This included oral tradition set forth in poems, origin legends, and cosmology. We know from medieval Irish and Welsh literature that bards were attached to kings and *teulus*, and that their function was to create and sing poems m praise of their king. One aspect of this function was most probably the preservation, and invention, of a suitable lineage for their patron. Strabo, *The Geography*, trans. by Leo H. Jones (New York, 1923), 4.5.4; Diodorus Siculus, *The Bibliotheca Historia of Diodorus Siculus.* trans. by John Skelton, ed. by Frederick M. Salter and H. L. K. Edward. (Oxford, 1968–71), 4.56.

16. Gildas, *The Ruin of Britain*, trans. by Michael Winterbottom (London, 1978), Ch. 34.6.

17. This may be implied by the extensive stanzas on simple warriors from *Y Gododdin* and elsewhere.

18. I would not dispute that bards were a part of British culture during the Roman centuries. However, this class of people was a part of the druidic order and therefore one of the hated aspects of British society. Their religion was perceived as a threat to the Roman government for many of the same reasons Christianity was. Their position within the Roman Empire would have left even the greatest of the bards to wander from town to town in southern Britain or move north. In this sense, the bard had a new function in sub–Roman British society.

19. A catalyst for the takeover by a heroic age-oriented group of soldiers can be seen in the Anglo-Saxon raid traditionally assigned to 449. It could not have happened before 441–446. The *Gallic Chronicles* attest that the Britons had been overrun in either 441 or 446, and Gildas states that the Britons suffered from a massive Germanic raid before managing to

build a stable society. It would not make sense that this attack would have been so successful after the Britons had been militarized. In fact, it probably forced the military element in society to the forefront. Thus, it took some years in which the new order may have stabilized and began to promote itself in the form of praise poetry. Using this means, a liberal date of 475 and a conservative estimate of 450 may be assumed for the onset of British Heroic Age society.

20. The following is only guess. However, in formulating it I have been as generous as possible in the amount of time certain events would take in order to occur. The intent is to show that there was a heroic age in full gear well before Dumville and Miller's proposed dates of 575 and 573, respectively.

21. Higham has judged that this had taken place "by about AD 450" in his regional history. Higham, *The Northern Counties to A.D. 1000* (London, 1986), 251.

22. Incidentally, these rough dates were arrived at without consultation with Professor Dumville's article "The Chronology of *De Excidio Britanniae*, Book I" yet, apart from focus, I agree fully with his estimations.

23. Chadwick and Chadwick, *The Development of Oral Literature*, vol. 3 (Cambridge, 1940), 732.

24. Clearly even replaced kings may not have been forgotten to history. A traveling bard might have remembered a story pertaining to him and continued his memory indefinitely. Such is maybe the case with such apparently well-respected heroes as Casnar Wledig and Llemenig ap Mawan.

25. *Y Gododdin* seems to have generated that motivation, even it was heavily damaged by time and the language shifts when it was written down three centuries after it was likely formed.

26. Jackson, *Language and History in Early Britain* (Edinburgh, 1953), 690; "The Britons in Southern Scotland," *Antiq* 29 (Gloucester, 1955), 77.

27. Bromwich. "Concepts of Arthur," *SC* 10–11 (Cardiff, 1976), 180–1.

Chapter 4

1. It should be said at the outset that Gerard Murphy, translator of several Fionn legends for the Irish Text Society, has directly denied any similarity of historicity or character development between Arthur and Fionn.

2. Dumville, "Sub-Roman: History and Legend," *History* 62, no. 205 (London, 1977), 188.

3. Contra Higham, *King Arthur: Mythmaking and History* (New York, 2002), 136–56.

4. Padel, "The Nature of Arthur," *CMCS* 27 (Cambridge, 1994), 19–23.

5. Ibid., 22.

6. *TYP*, triads 59 and 84.

7. This is most obvious in the triads, which name it four times.

8. The stories surrounding Fionn are littered with chronological difficulties. See Gerard Murphy's publications of the legends surrounding the Irish folkloric hero.

9. In particular *Pa gur?* There are also traces of appropriate behavior in *Preiddeu Annwn* and *Vita Cadoci*. Chadwick, *The Heroic Age* (Cambridge, 1912), 32.

10. After this, his name was found in *Hrolf Kraki's Saga* under Bjowulf.

11. Padel, "The Nature of Arthur," *CMCS* 27 (Cambridge, 1994), 20.

12. Unless, of course, one would care to argue that Fionn was also a historical character.

13. Padel, "The Nature of Arthur," *CMCS* 27 (Cambridge, 1994), 14, 20. Dr. Padel also claims this to lead to an "irresponsible atmosphere," a description of the heroic age society with which Professor Chadwick would agree. As to the remainder of Dr. Padel's statement, "whose main world is one of magical animals, giants, and other wonderful happenings," I find this to be only partially true, and then mostly for the later materials.

14. I have not dealt with several issues raised by Dr. Padel. Being a womanizer is a common trait of legend, as is being generous. As Dr. Padel himself says in the following pages, "many of which follow naturally from the basic similarities of form and setting." Padel, "The Nature of Arthur," *CMCS* 27 (Cambridge, 1994), 22.

15. If memory serves me, he was approximately forty feet tall.

16. His most notable possessions are his ship, spear, and sword. These objects have magical qualities, but Arthur does not. The best example of the supernatural qualities of his men is to be found in *Culhwch ac Olwen*.

17. Ó Hogáin, *Fionn macCumhail. Images of the Celtic Hero* (Dublin, 1988), 5.

18. Ibid., 4.

19. They are a judge and seer, and a king.

20. Ó Hogáin, *Fionn macCumhail. Images of the Celtic Hero* (Dublin, 1988), Chapter 1.

21. There is a strong tradition from the twelfth and thirteenth centuries for an alternate spelling of Arthur as Arcturus which Dr. Bromwich believes had a traditional authority. However, Arcturus was a star of the northern skies, and Lucan coined a term derived from this to describe the people of the north. The name also describes the bear-like qualities of the north. All this may be seen to naturally tie in with Arthur and his name, but of course has no mythological basis.

22. Professor Loomis spent much of his career in attempting to prove otherwise, but many of his stronger opinions on this subject have fallen to near-obscurity for good reason.

23. Except, of course, those legends which ascribe to the belief that Arthur is sleeping and will awaken someday to save the Welsh in their hour of greatest need. This appears to have been a legend developed well into the Middle Ages.

Chapter 5

1. Wright, "Gildas' prose style and its origins," *Gildas: New Approaches*, ed. by Michael Lapidge and David N. Dumville (Woodbridge, 1984), 107–28.

2. Dumville, "Sub-Roman Britain: History and Legend," *History* 62 (London, 1977), 173–92. Professor Dumville has since taken a more open approach to Gildas in *Gildas: New Approaches*, but I can empathize with the idea of tossing Gildas aside.

3. Clearly he was not fully aware of all fifth-century history. His belief that the two major defensive walls in Britain were created during the last years of Roman influence demonstrates his increasing ignorance and the heavier weight he must have given to fading oral memory as British history approached the fourth century. On the other hand, it must be assumed that Gildas did not totally rewrite the history of Britain up to his own time. His work was published and was intended to be read by his contemporaries; his audience would have known the recent history of Britain as well as he. It has been suggested that the wall stories were added to bring out a theme of the Britons being attacked by pagans whenever they regressed into actions insulting to God. The walls, and the two Roman returns associated with them, served only this purpose.

4. Gildas, *The Ruin of Britain*, trans. by Michael Winterbottom (London, 1978), Ch. 23.1.

5. These are the traditional dates for Ba-

don, which I would associate with Ambrosius for reasons which will become apparent as the argument presented in this chapter unfolds. Even if the reader does not agree with the explanation, changing the rough upper extreme of the given range does not affect the goals of the chapter.

6. This should be unsurprising, however. St. Patrick wrote to a man on the west coast of Scotland in the mid-fifth century, and the biography of St Germanus deals primarily with the second quarter of the fifth century, possibly in the region around London. The two areas of interest are much too specific to be of any use here.

7. Bede, *A History of the English Church and People*, trans. by Leo Sherley-Price, rev. by Ronald Edward Latham (London, 1978), Ch. 14.

8. In fact, two of Bede's purposes in writing *Historia Ecclesiastica* were to demonstrate the Germanic-speaking peoples' better right to sovereignty in Britain and to show the continuing superiority of the English church over that of the British one. Gildas only used the Germanic speakers in his prelude as the vengeful tools of God, not as godlike beings themselves. Higham, *An English Empire* (Leicester, 1994), 14–16.

9. Bede, *A History of the English Church and People*, Preface, trans. by Leo Sherley-Price, rev. by Ronald Edward Latham. (London, 1978). He notes in particular Abbot Albinus and Nothelm, who would become abbot in 735–736.

10. This evidences a primacy legend. Primacy, the superior right to rule all the English, would have been claimed by every early English nation. No country would voluntarily have superimposed Kent's foundation legend over its own; such an act would have been one of open inferiority. See the discussion below.

11. Miller "Bede's Use of Gildas," *EHR* 91 (London, 1976) 254 n. 1; Dumville, "Kingship, Genealogies, and Regnal Lists," *Early Medieval Kingship*, ed. by Peter S. Hayes and Ian N. Wood (Leeds, 1977), 78–79.

12. Higham, *An English Empire* (Manchester, 1995), 40.

13. I will follow current thinking in believing that the *superbus tyrannus* invited the last group of *foederati*, not the first. A Germanic cultural presence can be seen in Britain by the fourth century, long before Honorius' letter to the British people and the *superbus tyrannus* of Gildas. This opposes Gildas' statement that after the letter to Aegitus the first Germanic speakers arrived.

14. Alcock, *Arthur's Britain* (London, 1971), 24; Lapidge, "Gildas' Education and the Latin culture of subRoman Britain," *Gildas: New Approaches*, ed. by Michael Lapidge and David Dumville (Woodbridge, 1984), 27–50. The latter source proves this point by revealing that Gildas is here writing a carefully constructed legal argument in the Roman fashion of oratory.

15. For instance, Constantine, his direct predecessors, and St. Germanus' visits would otherwise deserve note in any thorough survey of sub–Roman Britain.

16. *Historia Brittonum*, ed. and trans. by John Morris (Chichester, 1978), Ch. 56.

17. Gildas, *The Ruin of Britain*, trans. by Michael Winterbottom (London, 1978), Chap. 23.

18. *TYP*, 395.

19. Another instance of greatly altered public opinion can be seen in the British government's treatment of Churchill's advice during World War I. Twenty years later he was elected prime minister and became the most trusted leader on the island.

20. It is also quite possible that Gildas, whether intentionally or not, altered the sequence of events to allow this particular figure to have been the traitor who allowed the Germanic speakers to settle in Britain. Again, if the *superbus tyrannus* was intended to be Arthur, this makes good sense. There is a clear literary tradition of animosity between Arthur and Gildas' clan, even if there is no historical evidence. The literary background of the stories named above is, as Dr. Clancy has informed me, of too diverse a nature to pinpoint any one or any group of sources. It is in fact conceivable that all three sources have been influenced by one common source. However, the fact that the plots and the treatment of Arthur vary considerably makes this an unlikely scenario.

21. Such as when he states that Maximus took all the soldiers of Britain with him. This hardly seems possible in light of the twenty-odd years of continued Roman government here.

22. Dumville, "The Chronology of *De Excidio Britanniae*," *Gildas: New Approaches*, ed. by Michael Lapidge and David N. Dumville (Woodbridge, 1985), 83.

23. *TYP*, 275.

Chapter 6

1. As it is generally accepted that Sir Ifor Williams was correct and the Llywarch Hen collection of poetry was composed in the mid-to late ninth century, it is safe to assume this allusion stretches back to material of the eighth century and possibly earlier.

2. Mostyn 146:1, Peniarth MS 215349, and the Iolo MSS 188.

3. It is a well-covered fact that prior to the historical horizon kings from outside the royal family who were renowned during their lifetimes were often pulled into a lineage to raise its prestige level.

4. *Early Welsh Genaeological Tracts*, ed. by Peter C. Bartrum (Cardiff, 1966), 10.

5. Ibid., 46.

6. Miller, "Date-guessing and Dyfed," *SC* 12 (Cardiff, 1977), 33–34.

7. Bartrum, *A Welsh Classical Dictionary: People in History and Legend up to about AD 1000* (Cardiff, 1993), 617; *Rhigyfarch's Life of David*, Chapter 5, gives Triphunus as the name of the local king when the saint was born in the mid-fifth century. There is additional but more complex evidence which I hope to present in a future work.

8. *TYP*, 275; "Concepts of Arthur," *SC* 10/11 (Cardiff, 1976), 175–181; Jackson, "Once again Arthur's Battles," *MP* 43 (Chicago, 1945), 44–57.

9. See below.

10. Chadwick, *The Heroic Age* (Cambridge, 1912), 350–351.

11. Nash-Williams, *The Early Christian Monuments of Wales* (Cardiff, 1950), nos. 87 and 176.

12. Morris, *The Age of Arthur* (London, 1976), 125; *Culhwch ac Olwen*, ed. and trans. by Rachel Bromwich and D. Simon Evans (Cardiff, 1992), 93; contra Sims-Williams, "The Significance of the Irish Personal Names in *Culhwch ac Olwen*," *BBCS* 29 (Cardiff, 1982), 615.

13. Alcock, *Arthur's Britain* (London, 1971), 94, 286, 357; Higham, *The English Conquest: Gildas and the Fifth Century* (Leicester, 1994), 40–41; Evison, "Distribution Map of England in the First Two Phases," *Angles, Saxons, and Jutes: Essays Presented to J. N. L. Myres*, ed. by Vera I. Evison (London, 1981), 143–144. Morris' conjecture that a Visigothic Theodoric may have been Arthur's admiral and was later rewarded with a country in Wales may be unprovable, but it is a possibility given what is known of the situation in the period. The same is true of Thomas' more recent suggestion about Merovingian mercenaries; Morris, *The Age of Arthur* (London, 1976), 127; Thomas, "'Gallici Nautae de Galliarum Provinciis'—A Sixth/Sev-

enth Century Trade with Gaul, Reconsidered," *Medieval Archaeology* 34 (London, 1990), 9 and 16.

14. As opposed to Cei, the hero most often considered the earliest associate of Arthur. There is evidence in several of the *Culhwch ac Olwen* episodes that he did, in fact, at one time exist apart from Arthur. Leaving aside for the moment a few episodes in which Cei, not Arthur, is the main hero, Cei does forcefully tell his supposed king to "get out of the way," so to speak. Cei was, in fact, such a strong force in the story that the narrator found it necessary to get rid of him so that Arthur could take part in some of the later episodes. Hence the englyn (poem) to Cei about Dillus which sends Cei off in a fury, such an act, satire, would have been the lowest form of insult to a heroic age warrior. Gowans, *Cei and the Arthurian Legend* (Cardiff, 1988).

15. The chronological congruity with Arthur's floruit is strong evidence that Drutwas was, in fact, a literary member of Arthur's court before Cei and Bedwyr. It is very possible that he was a historical member of the *teulu* or a one-time enemy.

16. Miller, "Date-guessing and Dyfed," *SC* 12 (Cardiff, 1977), 33–61.

17. *TYP*, 275–276.

18. For example, it is already accepted that Gildas was a contemporary of Arthur; it is further possible to delete many of the *Culhwch ac Olwen* from any connections with Arthur on the grounds of their mythical or jovial nature, their association with other, earlier Celtic works which connect them to other periods, or their obvious addition in the last compilation through the Norman or French influence.

19. Because of the vast body of Greek mythology, such connections will always be easier and more quickly found there. However, Germanic mythology and saga material have also been used.

20. Professor Alcock and Professor Morris both used the *vitae* to substantiate and help explain the period 480 to 570, though it has been generally agreed that the latter went much too far in trusting these sources. In addition, I have written one volume on the potential historical uses of the early Arthurian romances. See the bibliography for specific references.

Chapter 7

1. Lewis, "The Historical Background," *A Guide to Welsh Literature*, vol. 1, ed. by Alfred O.H. Jarman and Gwilym R. Jones (Swansea, 1976), 14–18.

2. The series of events are, of course, the same which produced the heroic age. The function of the bard at this time was modified due to the influence of Christianity.

3. Chadwick, "Early Culture and Learning in Wales," *Studies in the Early British Church*, ed. by Nora K. Chadwick (Cambridge, 1958), 85–6.

4. Dumville, "On the Northern British Section of the *Historia Brittonum*," *WHR* 8 (Cardiff, 1977), 345–54.

5. Dumville, "The Historical Value of the *Historia Brittonum*," *Arthurian Literature* 6, ed. by Richard Barber (Cambridge, 1986), 1–26.

6. I include in this list of chapters the "Arthuriana" section, in agreement with Bromwich, Thurneysen, and Bruce. Bromwich, "Concepts of Arthur," *SC* 10/11 (Cardiff, 1976), 175–6; Thurneysen, "Zimmer, Nennius Vindicatus," *ZDP* 28 (Halle, 1896), 85, 87; Bruce, *The Evolution of the Arthurian Romance from the Beginning Down to the Year 1300* (Gottingen, 1923), 9.

7. Bromwich, "Concepts of Arthur," *SC* 10/11 (Cardiff, 1976), 163–181; Hughes, "The Welsh Latin Chronicles: *Annales Cambriae* and related texts" *PBA* 59 (London, 1975), 233–259; Dumville, "On the North British Section of the *Historia Brittonum*," *WHR* 8 (Cardiff, 1977), 345–354.

8. There is here room for dispute; Professor Dumville and Dr. Miller have argued that his obit may have been as early as 534. Dumville, "Gildas and Maelgwn," *Gildas: New Approaches*, ed. by Michael Lapidge and David N. Dumville (Woodbridge, 1984), 51–9; Miller, "Relative and absolute publication dates," *BBCS* 26 (Cardiff, 1976), 169–74.

9. Miller, "Relative and Absolute Publication Dates," *BBCS* 26 (Cardiff, 1976), 169–74; Dumville, "The Chronology of *De Excidio Britanniae*, Book I," *Gildas: New Approaches*, ed. by Michael Lapidge and David N. Dumville (Woodbridge, 1984), 51–9.

10. Miller, "Relative and Absolute Publication Dates," *BBCS* 26 (Cardiff, 1976), 169–74; Dumville, "The Chronology of *De Excidio Britanniae*, Book I," *Gildas: New Approaches*, ed. by Michael Lapidge and David N. Dumville (Woodbridge, 1984), 51–9.

11. The idea that out of virtually nothing poetic masters suddenly appeared in Britain during a period of fifteen years is an outrageous one. It would be like placing Leonardo da Vinci, Raphael, Donatello, Rabelais, and Mi-

chelangelo in Greece during the Greek heroic age and expecting them to reach the level of art which they achieved during the Renaissance. However, there is the evidence to be had from *Trioedd Ynys Prydein,* whose earliest triads list several bards who may have lived from the late fifth to the late sixth centuries. This indicates a developing culture in the years preceding the British renaissance.

12. I include here the Arthuriana section and, based on Professor Dumville's computations, would estimate the *superbus tyrannus* (Arthur) flourished in the last two decades of the fifth century. Dumville, "The Chronology of *De Excidio Britanniae,* Book 1," *Gildas: New Approaches,* ed. by Michael Lapidge and David N. Dumville (Woodbridge, 1984), 84.

13. The three poets of this group who may be located were from *Y Hen Ogled,* therefore it seems reasonable that the remaining two were as well.

14. Gruffydd, "From Gododdin to Gwynedd: Reflections of the Story of Cunedda," *SC* 14–15 (Cambridge, 1989/1990), 10.

15. This is because of Gwrtheyrn's dates of activity. Kirby, "Vortigern," *BBCS* 23 (Cardiff, 1970), 37–59; Miller, "Date-guessing and Pedigrees," *SC* 11 (Cardiff, 1976d), 96–109.

16. *The Gododdin of Aneirin: Text and Context in Dark Age Britain,* ed. and trans. by John T. Koch (Cardiff, 1995), xlv.

17. Ibid., xvii–xxvi.

18. Bartrum, *A Welsh Classical Dictionary: People in History and Legend up to about AD 1000* (Cardiff, 1993), 16.

19. The Ciannachta came from central Ireland. Morris, *The Age of Arthur* (London, 1973), 159.

20. This is because of the place of composition, Gwynedd. Chadwick, "Early Culture and Learning in North Wales," *Studies in the Early British Church,* ed. by Nora K. Chadwick (Cambridge, 1958), 29–120.

21. Although it is unclear exactly when the various other regions of medieval Gwynedd were excised from Irish rule. Much of Gwynedd's early history is entirely unknown.

22. Having a bard of high stature at one's court could be seen by contemporaries as a status symbol. Only the wealthy could keep one and only an extremely successful raider could be wealthy.

23. *TYP,* 275

24. Ibid., triad no. 7.

25. Ibid., triad no. 10.

26. Ibid., triad no. I 1.

27. Ibid., triad no. 34.

28. *TYP,* lxx–lxxi; Williams and Jones, *Gramadegau'r Penceirddiaid* (Aberystwyth, 1934), lxxxviii, xci; Lloyd-Jones, *The Court Poets of the Welsh Princes* (London, 1948), 29 fn. 31.

29. Ibid., xi.

30. Taliesin is listed as the third poet.

31. Their sons, Elinwy and Cynhafal, are also otherwise unknown.

32. This premise is based entirely on pseudo-historical sources; however it may be externally validated to some extent. Chapter 2 has given strong evidence for the emergence of stable kingships as early as the mid-fifth century, which is in accordance with Professor Dumville's Gildas-based chronology. In addition, archaeology has provided support for the emergence of a Northumbrian presence by the mid-sixth century. Perhaps a corrected theory would be that the bard lived between the mid-fifth and early-sixth centuries, but the broader range helps ensure validity.

33. Gwilym ddu o Arfon, *Poetry from the Red Book of Hergest.* ed. by J. Gwenogrvyn Evans. (Llanbedrog, 1911), 1228.

34. It is generally assumed that Dunawt served as an eponym for the region he controlled, Dunotinga in modern Cumberland.

35. I include Gwynedd here because their ancestors were traditionally from *Y Hen Ogled,* so that it would have considered itself a part of northern British history. Powys extended well north of modern Wales.

36. These are Cian, Bluchbard, Cadegr, Argad, and Golydan.

37. The question then is, if the known bard served a reasonably powerful king, why has their relationship not been remembered. This may be for several reasons. The poet may have been so renowned that he surpassed his patron, as modern professionals occasionally surpass their trade. Poor fortune may have simply eliminated all of a given poet's works, leaving no indication of his patron; if the original works of Aneirin were not extant, his patron would be nearly unknown to us as well.

38. As I intend to show in a forthcoming book, even less is known than has been supposed. The eponymous rulers of Gwynedd, for instance, may not have been born till well into the *fifth* century, if they lived at all. Certainly they were not active till the final two or three decades of the fifth century.

39. I intend to pursue the connection between the North and the British Heroic Age more closely in an upcoming publication.

Chapter 8

1. This is another subject which I hope to explore further.

2. In fact, the first poems appear in the last third of the sixth century, and then only the poetry which served some political purpose. Again, this is because of the enormous political as well as linguistic changes which took place in *Y Hen Ogled* during the course of the seventh, eighth, and ninth centuries.

3. There is also a possibility that one or more of his poets' names survived and are recorded in *Historia Brittonum* or *Trioedd Ynys Prydein*. This person or persons would be the source of our main historical and pseudo-historical body of information on Arthur. The bard's existence would also explain the large amount of traditional material regarding Arthur. Arthur was such a successful chieftain in his lifetime that he was probably able to get the very best bards.

4. For instance, the famous lumberjack Paul Bunyan had a forty-foot ox named Blue, and he brushed his teeth each morning with a young pine tree.

5. I refer here to the two instances in *Mirabilia* and the Battle of Badon.

6. Geoffrey of Monmouth, *The History of the Kings of Britain*, trans. by Lewis G. M. Thorpe (New York, 1966), 256–7. This is only the most blatant instance; they are to be found throughout the account.

7. *TYP*, triad 20W.

8. There is no manner by which it may be certainly determined that any event dated so early is chronologically accurate and no way to prove or disprove the date. The only external support would be the argument of Professor Dumville, who places the *superbus tyrannus* at around 480.

9. Chadwick, "Early Culture and Learning in North Wales," *Studies in the Early British Church*, ed. by Nora K. Chadwick (Cambridge, 1958), 29–120; Miller, "Relative and absolute publication dates," *BBCS* 26 (Cardiff, 1976), 169–74; Dumville, "Gildas and Maelgwn," *Gildas: New Approaches*, ed. by Michael Lapidge and David N. Dumville (Woodbridge, 1984), 51–9; Dumville, "The Historical Value of the *Historia Brittonum*," *Arthurian Literature* 6, ed. by Richard Barber (Cambridge, 1986), 1–26.

Chapter 9

1. As Higham has pointed out, Amr likely derives from Middle and Old Welsh *amrant*,

eyelid. It is hardly likely as a personal name and is only connected to Arthur via superficial similarity. Higham, *King Arthur: Mythmaking and History* (New York, 2002), 89.

2. Though see Koch's translation and interpretation. *The Gododdin of Aneirin: Text and Context for Dark Age North Britain*, ed. and trans. by John T. Koch (Cardiff, 1995).

3. Jones, "Datblygiadau Cynnar Chwedl Arthur," trans. by Gerald Morgan, "The Early Evolution of Arthur," *NMS* 8 (Nottingham, 1964), 8.

4. Ibid., 8–9; Rachel Bromwich "Concepts of Arthur," *SC* 10–11 (Cardiff, 1975–6), 170–171.

5. *TYP*, 160.

6. Ibid., cxxxii.

7. Lloyd, *History of Wales: From the Earliest Times to the Edwardian Conquest* (Longmans, 1939), lxxxvii; Foster, "*Culhwch ac Olwen and Rhonabwy's Dream*," Arthurian Literature in the Middle Ages, ed. by Roger S. Loomis (New York, 1959), 39–40.

8. Bromwich, "Concepts of Arthur," *SC* 10–11 (Cardiff, 1975–6), 179–80.

9. Higham, *King Arthur: Mythmaking and History* (New York, 2002), 77.

10. Though it must be noted that in Professor Koch's reconstruction of the Gododdin poem, he finds no reason not to date the excerpt to "probably primary material, pre-638." *The Gododdin of Aneirin: Text and Context in Dark Age Britain*, ed. and trans. by John T. Koch (Cardiff, 1995), 147.

11. As usual, Dr. Bromwich is the exception to this rule. For nearly fifty years she saw Arthur as the first of a long list of northern heroes who were transferred, literarily, to Wales during the Middle Ages. This is because all of the British military heroes of the early medieval period seem to have come from the north, and because the Battle of Camlann most likely occurred on Hadrian's Wall. Professor Alcock and Professor Morris both placed Arthur in the Gloucester region because of the king's flimsy connection to the Battle of Badon and Geoffrey of Monmouth's connection of this battle to Bath.

Chapter 10

1. Evidence that Arthur was a creature of legend by this time may be seen in *Historia Brittonum* and *Y Gododdin*.

2. Parry and Caldwell, "Geoffrey of Monmouth," *Arthurian Literature in the Middle*

Ages, ed. by Roger S. Loomis (Chicago, 1959), 73; Roberts, "*Culhwch ac Olwen*, The Triads, and Saints' Lives," *The Arthur of the Welsh*, ed. by Rachel Bromwich, Brynley F. Roberts, and Alfred O.H. Jarman (Cardiff, 1991), 97–8.

3. *The History of the Kings of Britain*, trans. by Lewis G.M. Thorpe (New York, 1966), 13.

4. Tatlock, *The Legendary History of Britain* (Berkeley, 1950), 443.

5. Roberts, "*Culhwch ac Olwen*," *The Arthur of the Welsh*, ed. by Rachel Bromwich, Brynley F. Roberts, and Alfred O.H. Jarman (Cardiff, 1991), 99.

6. *The History of the Kings of Britain*, trans. by Lewis G.M. Thorpe (New York, 1966), 41.

7. Piggott, "The Sources of Geoffrey of Monmouth: The 'Pre-Roman King-List,'" *Antiq* 15 (Gloucester, 1941), 269–86.

8. Gildas, *The Ruin of Britain*, trans. by Michael Winterbottom (London, 1978), Chap. 28–36.

9. Most notably South Cadbury, known also as Cadbury-Camelot.

10. I have addressed Geoffrey before the traditionally pre–Galfridic sources because of a recurring problem in Middle Welsh literature and Arthurian literary studies, that most literature may be defined only as pre–1150, while Geoffrey wrote in 1136. There is a discrepancy here and it must be considered at least possible that Geoffrey influenced some of these pre–1150 sources.

11. Tatlock, *The Legendary History of Britain* (Berkeley, 1950), 22.

12. Ibid., 17–18.

13. Ibid., 34.

14. Ibid., 60.

15. Griscom, *The Historia Regum Britanniae of Geoffrey of Monmouth* (London, 1929), 211–14. Although Tatlock is most critical of this happenstance. *The Legendary History of Britain* (Berkeley, 1950), 31–3.

16. Atkinson, *Stonehenge* (London, 1956), 183–5. A more complete explanation for the comparison is given by Stuart Piggott, "The Sources of Geoffrey of Monmouth: II: The Stonehenge Story," *Antiq* 15 (Gloucester, 1941), 305–319.

17. Ibid., 305–319.

18. Goodrich, *King Arthur* (New York, 1985), 100.

19. Padel, "Geoffrey of Monmouth," *The Arthur of the Welsh*, ed. by Rachel Bromwich, Brynley Roberts, and Alfred O.H. Jarman. (Cardiff, 1991), 229–35. The exact dates are roughly 700 to 1207.

20. The best detailing of the pottery found in Britain, and especially Tintagel, is still Thomas, *A Provisional List of Imported Pottery in Post-Roman Western Britain and Ireland* (Redruth, 1981). This material is detailed to Tintagel specifically in "East and West: Tintagel, Mediterranean Imports and the Early Insular Church," *The Early Church in Western Britain and Ireland*. ed. by Susan M. Pearce (Oxford, 1982), 17–34.

21. Tatlock, *The Legendary History* (Berkeley, 1950), 46–7. Incidentally, Eldol, the only man to fight his way through Hengest's trap, is duke of this area.

22. Ibid., 436.

23. Ibid., 27.

24. Ibid., 28.

25. The Lincoln reference may be found in Tatlock, *The Legendary History* (Berkeley, 1950), 26, while the Winchester reference can be located in Tatlock, *The Legendary History* (Berkeley, 1950), 36–9.

26. Ibid., 49.

27. Ibid., 11–12. This was also the site of a major rebellion by Angus in 1130.

28. Ibid., 107.

29. With his evident literary training, it is very possible that Geoffrey guessed Camlann took place on the Camblam river and, for literary symmetry, decided to have Arthur's birth take place in the same region.

Chapter 11

1. Roberts, "*Culhwch ac Olwen*, the Triads, and Saints' Lives," *The Arthur of the Welsh*, ed. by Rachel Bromwich, Brynley Roberts, and Alfred O.H. Jarman (Cardiff, 1991), 73–96.

2. This has been well-expressed in Dr. Wendy Davies' article "Property Rights and Property Claims in Welsh '*Vitae*' of the Eleventh Century," *Hagiographie, culture et sociétiés ive–xiie*, ed. by Pierre Riché (Paris, 1981), 515–33.

3. Most notable in this regard was Glastonbury, whose meteoric rise during the century following the Norman invasion has been well documented.

4. The *vitae* are notorious for being chronologically inconsistent.

5. Roberts, "*Culhwch ac Olwen*, The Triads, and Saints' Lives," *The Arthur of the Welsh*, ed. by Rachel Bromwich, Brynley Roberts, and Alfred O.H. Jarman (Cardiff, 1991), 82.

6. Maelgwn is the only other British king mentioned in more than one *vita*. He, however, was a Gwynedd king and there are a relatively

large number of *vitae* devoted to Gwynedd saints.

7. Although Cadoc is associated with Glywising, it is possible he may be a composite with a southern Scottish figure, as evidenced with his episode with Caw of Pictland; *Vita Cadoci*, Chapter 26.

8. This is presumably because the Norman kings did not have as much control over the north.

9. It is worth noting here that all the *vitae* are quite vague in locating Arthur, not even deigning to name a city with which to associate him. This is a telltale sign that there was no tradition for Arthur as a Welsh figure, and that he was being relocated to Wales and other places in order to suit the needs of the monasteries which were producing the *vitae*.

10. For a full discussion of the matter see Rahtz, "Pagan and Christian by the Severn Sea," *The Archaeology and History of Glastonbury Abbey: Essays in Honour of the Ninetieth Birthday of C.A. Ralegh Radford*, ed. by Lesley Abrams and James P. Carley (Woodbridge, 1991), 32–33.

11. Foot, "Glastonbury's Early Abbots," *The Archaeology and History of Glastonbury Abbey: Essays in Honour of the Ninetieth Birthday of C.A. Ralegh Radford*, ed. by Lesley Abrams and James P. Carley (Woodbridge, 1991), 167 and 169; Finberg, "St. Patrick at Glastonbury," *The Irish Ecclesiastical Record* (Dublin, 1967), 346.

12. Glastonbury Abbey does claim it had such records, but timely fires have effectively erased any sign of habitation before its existence can be proved by outside evidence.

13. Abrams, *Anglo-Saxon Glastonbury: Church and Endowment* (Woodbridge, 1996), 335.

14. Ibid., 335–336.

15. Reasons for this have varied from royal disfavor to Viking devastation.

16. *Two Lives of Gildas*, ed. and trans. by Hugh Williams (Llanerch, rep. 1990), 98.

17. This is two be found in Caradoc's *Life of Gildas*, and involves Melvas' kidnapping of Arthur's queen.

18. As has been seen, this was done both because of Geoffrey's access to sources of the early medieval world and the influences of the political situation and the current state of affairs in the English church. His home region of Monmouth was also in roughly that area. Some or even all of his localized information might have come from stories he had heard as a child.

19. The clearest indication of this is that his nephew, the legitimate heir, was named Arthur.

20. Cadbury, for instance, is first linked to Arthur in the sixteenth century by Leland, *De Rebus Britannicis*, vol. 5, ed. by Thomas Hearne (London, 1970), 28–9.

21. We may even take the influence of Glastonbury back to 900. Here a Glastonbury entry may be found in the Glossary of Cormac about the site, indicating its prominence. The entry is linguistically most probably a part of the original text, "not much later than 900" according to David Binchy. Personal communication to Finberg, "St. Patrick at Glastonbury," *The Irish Ecclesiastical Record* (Dublin, 1967), 355, fn. 36.

22. Exception being made for *Culhwch ac Olwen*, which was deeply influenced by events current at St. David's around 1081. *Culhwch ac Olwen* also contains influences from Scotland, Ireland, and Brittany.

23. If we are to use place-name evidence in order to prove where an individual lived, a colonial scholar could claim that certain U.S. sites were dwelled in by seventeenth- and eighteenth-century figures whom we know never visited the cities. Such is the case with Georgia (George I), Virginia (Elizabeth), Maryland (Mary, Queen of Scots), Madison (fifth U.S. president), WI, and the state of Washington (first U.S. president).

Chapter 12

1. Though they, too, may have their own motivations, as will be seen in later chapters.

2. Jackson, "Arthur in Early Welsh Verse," *Arthurian Literature in the Middle Ages*, ed. by Roger S. Loomis (Chicago, 1959), 13; Sims-Williams, "The Early Welsh Arthurian Poems," *The Arthur of the Welsh*, ed. by Rachel Bromwich, Brynley Roberts, and Alfred O.H. Jarman (Cardiff, 1991), 35.

3. This battle has normally been placed in Catterick, in modern Yorkshire.

4. The form and level of maturation of the poem has been discussed by Professor Jackson, Professor Sims-Williams, and Professor Koch in their three interpretations of *Y Gododdin*.

5. *Y Gododdin: Text and Context in Dark Age Britain*, ed. and trans. by John T. Koch (Cardiff, 1995), 147.

6. Jackson, "Once Again Arthur's Battles," *MP* 43 (Chicago, 1945), 44–57.

7. Ibid.

8. Lloyd, *The History of Wales* (Cardiff, 1912), 126 fn. 6; Chadwick, *The Growth of Literature* (Cambridge, 1932), 155; Crawford,

"Arthur and his Battles," *Antiq* 9 (Gloucester, 1935), 279; Jackson, "The Arthur of History," *Arthurian Literature in the Middle Ages*, ed. by Roger S. Loomis (Chicago, 1959), 78; Bromwich, "Concepts," *SC* 10–11 (Cardiff, 1976), 169.

9. "Urbe Legionis" appears to be the only site which does not fall in the Old North. I shall have more to say about this in Chapter 16.

10. Hughes, "The Welsh Latin" *PBA* 9 (London, 1975); Dumville, "The Anglian Collection," *ASE* 5 (Cambridge, 1976), 23–50; Charles-Edwards, "The Authenticity of the *Gododdin*," *Astudiaethau ar yr Hengerdd* (Cardiff, 1978), 63.

11. This has already been discussed briefly in Chapter 1. However, for more information see Professor Jackson, "Once Again Arthur's Battles," *MP* 43 (MP (Chicago, 1945), 57. "The Site of Mount Badon," *Journal of Celtic Studies* 2 (Cardiff, 1958), 152–4; and Professor Alcock, *Arthur's Britain* (London, 1971), 62, 68–71, both place Badon in southwest Britain on historical grounds, while Jackson additionally used linguistic evidence. Dr. Charles-Edwards holds a dissenting view in "The Arthur of History," *The Arthur of the Welsh*, ed. by Rachel Bromwich, Brynley F. Roberts, and Alfred O.H. Jarman (Cardiff, 1991), 30.

12. Haycock, "'Preiddeu Annwn' and the figure of Taliesin," *SC* 14–15 (Cardiff, 1984), 52–77.

13. Sims-Williams has observed that this is the least reliable of the three place-names because of its property of being well-known. Sims-Williams, "The Early Welsh Arthurian Poems," *The Arthur of the Welsh*, ed. by Rachel Bromwich, Brynley F. Roberts, and Alfred O.H. Jarman (Cardiff, 1991), 39.

14. It has been suggested by Professor Thomas and Dr. Bollard that the "arthur" which precedes Disethach could be alternatively translated as a pronoun "he," in which case Disethach belongs to Cei. If so, this limited contradictory testimony belongs in the next chapter. Thomas, *Traddodiad Barddol* (Cardiff, 1976), 69; Bollard, "Arthur in the Early Welsh Tradition," *The Romance of Arthur*, ed. by James J. Wilhelm (New York, 1984), 19.

15. Rowland, *Early Welsh Saga Poetry* (Cardiff, 1990), 95.

16. Johnson, *Origins of Arthurian Romance: Early Sources for the Legends of Tristan, the Grail and the Abduction of the Queen*, forthcoming.

17. Haycock, "'Preiddeu Annwn' and the figure of Taliesin," *SC* 14–15 (Cardiff, 1984), 157–8.

18. Dr. Haycock has explained that all the castles named in *Preiddeu Annwn* are actually synonyms for the British Otherworld; Haycock, "'Preiddeu Annwn' and the figure of Taliesin," *SC* 14–15 (Cardiff, 1984), 163–177.

19. Sims-Williams, "The Early Welsh Arthurian Poems," *The Arthur of the Welsh*, ed. by Rachel Bromwich, Brynley F. Roberts, and Alfred O.H. Jarman (Cardiff, 1991), 46–7. The suggestion is that he is a combination of a fifth-century British general, a man lauded in *Y Gododdin*, an eighth-century Cornish king, and a Cornish saint. It is interesting that this text places the composite strongly in the southwestern regions of Britain.

20. Sims-Williams, "The Early Welsh Literature," *The Arthur of the Welsh*, ed. by Rachel Bromwich, Brynley F. Roberts, and Alfred O.H. Jarman (Cardiff, 1991), 46–7.

21. "An Early Ritual Poem in Welsh," ed. and trans. by Mary Williams, *S* 13 (Cambridge, 1938), 38–51.

22. Gowans, *Cei and the Arthurian Legend* (Cambridge, 1988).

23. Roberts, "*Culhwch ac Olwen*, The Triads, and Saints' Lives," *Arthur of the Welsh*, ed. by Rachel Bromwich, Brynley F. Roberts, and Alfred O.H. Jarman (Cardiff, 1991), 80.

24. *TYP*, lxx, cviii. Dr. Bromwich listed the early triads and explained her reasoning for her choices there.

25. These are triads 1–46 in Dr. Bromwich's edition (Cardiff, rev. 1978), xi.

26. Especially with regard to known and remembered place-names; it is interesting that Geoffrey's history places Arthur in Camlann, Cornwall, and London as well.

27. If this third possibility is the correct one, as I believe it is, it would have been originally molded into this pan–British state by the nature of heroic age literature. This form of memory regards specific geographic locations with little significance though, as will be seen, there are always hints in the material of the original locations.

Chapter 13

1. I have also included in this study the two figures who are consistent enemies of Arthur—Hueil ap Caw and Medrawt. The reasoning why this is so is the same as with his *teulu*: both are associated with Arthur by the ninth century and are consistently portrayed as such throughout all the literature in which they are mentioned.

2. Chadwick, *The Growth of Oral Literature*, vol. 3 (Cambridge, 1940), 201.

3. It is the author's assumption that the heroes who were earliest associated with Arthur and whose connection has remained were not originally of his *teulu*. They were probably, instead, heroes of the same generation and local affiliation. This also would be consistent with other heroic age materials.

4. Due to the nature of the Early Welsh literature, this is the earliest date from which any Welsh work can be certainly dated without the support of historical context.

5. *Pa gur?*, ln. 33.

6. Ibid., ln. 40.

7. Ibid., 1n. 42.

8. Ibid., 1n. 43.

9. Ibid., 1n. 64.

10. Ibid., 1n. 78.

11. Ibid., 1n. 81.

12. *Culhwch ac Olwen*, ll. 384–392.

13. Ibid., ll. 759–824.

14. *Culhwch ac Olwen*, l. 396.

15. *Pa gur?*, l. 48.

16. *Culhwch ac Olwen*, ll. 19 1.

17. *Trioedd Ynys Prydein*, ed. and trans. by Rachel Bromwich (Cardiff, rev. 1978), 329–32.

18. Johnson, *Origins of Arthurian Romance: Early Sources for the Legends of Tristan, the Grail and the Abduction of the Queen*, forthcoming.

19. Padel, "The Cornish Background of the Tristan Stories," *CMCS* 1 (Cambridge, 1982), 55.

20. *Trioedd Ynys Prydein*, ed. and trans. by Rachel Bromwich (Cardiff, rev. 1978), 312.

21. *Culhwch ac Olwen*, ln. 259–60.

22. Caradoc's *Vitae Gildae*, Chapter 5.

23. *Culhwch ac Olwen*, ln. 211.

24. Caradoc's *Vitae Gildae*, Chapter 5.

25. *Vita Cadoci*, Chapter 26.

26. Caradoc's *Vitae Gildae*, Chapter 1.

27. Jackson, "Once Again Arthur's Battles," *MP* 43 (Chicago, 1945), 56; Jones, "Datblygiadau Cynnar Chwedl Arthur," trans. by Gerald Morgan, "The Early Evolution of Arthur," *NMS* 8 (Nottingham, 1964), 6; *Trioedd Ynys Prydein*, ed. and trans. by Rachel Bromwich (Cardiff, rev. 1978), 160; Bromwich, "Concepts of Arthur," *SC* 10–11 (Cardiff, 1976), 173.

28. The author does not claim either of these two men as credible historians, not would he suggest that their works represent any historical or pseudo-historical reality. In supplement to the *Annales Cambriae* and local legend, however, they do provide ample evidence to reflect a Scottish Modred tradition.

29. Ross, *Pagan Celtic Britain* (London, 1967), 368–70. His name has also been found in the Beddau stanzas in Peniarth 98B, but this is most likely a case of a northern figure being relocated in Wales. Jones, "The Black Book," *PBA* 53 (London, 1969), 136.

30. Ibid., 1.11.

31. *Culhwch ac Olwen*, ed. by Rachel Bromwich and D. Simon Evans (Cardiff, 1992), ln. 224.

32. Johnson, *Origins of Arthurian Romance: Early Sources for the Legends of Tristan, the Grail and the Abduction of the Queen*, forthcoming. For his development into a Roman military god and its possible influences on the development of his British incarnation see Irby-Massie, *Military Religion in Roman Britain* (Boston, 1999), 108; Ross, *Pagan Celtic Britain* (London, 1967), 127; Webster, *The Pagan Celts and Their Gods under Rome* (London, 1986), 146, fn. 37.

33. Ross, *Pagan Celtic Britain* (London, 1967), 371.

34. *Pa gur?*, 1n. 28.

35. Ibid., 1n. 79.

36. To avoid giving unwarranted stress to one site, each location in an individual source is listed only once, despite the number of characters associated with that site in the sources.

37. More specifically, the *Vitae Cadoci* is known to have made use of the legends of at least one northern figure, Caw. The author has argued above for the tremendous impact that Glastonbury had on influencing Arthurian sites in Cornwall and Somerset, as happens in *Dialogue*. Because of this, it cannot be certain that the Arthurian episode has not also been transplanted. Twenty-six W of *Trioedd Ynys Prydein* is thought to have been a burlesque because of its untraditional character. Bromwich, "The Tristan of the Welsh," *The Arthur of the Welsh*, ed. by Rachel Bromwich, Brynley F. Roberts, and Alfred O.H. Jarman (Cardiff, 1991), 214.

38. This appears to have been a fairly common occurrence. *Trioedd Ynys Prydein*, ed. and trans. by Rachel Bromwich (Cardiff, rev. 1978), 331–2, 397400, 430–2, and 469–74.

39. Professor Jackson estimated in the latter years of the eleventh century. It is, of course, impossible to be certain. Jackson, *Language and History in Early Britain: A Chronological Survey of the Brittonic Languages 1st to 12th c. A.D.* (Edinburgh, 1953), 9.

40. I would like to stress that lineage in such a fluid society as this could mean very little.

41. Besides, it has long been recognized that many northern characters were transplanted to

Wales by the medieval Welsh. See *Trioedd Ynys Prydein*, ed. and trans. by Rachel Bromwich (Cardiff, rev. 1978), 331–2, 397–400, 430–2, 469–74.

42. As was elucidated in my previous book, the Hadrian's Wall god Belatucudros is also strongly associated with Arthur in the romance literature. This makes two gods who are associated with Arthur in the literature. Both have been uniquely placed in the Hadrian's Wall region through archaeological means.

Chapter 14

1. Jackson, *The International Popular Tale* (Cardiff, 1961), 77.

2. One of the irritations of the story, and of most stories of this nature, is that the missions given to the hero at the beginning of the story are not all achieved while other, unmentioned jobs seem to replace them. This is the result of a large story being kept in an oral environment. Various items and eventually major sections are forgotten and others replace them.

3. According to Dr. Bromwich, Culhwch definitely has mythological origins, possibly pre–Celtic. *Culhwch ac Olwen*, ed. by Rachel Bromwich and D. Simon Evans (Cardiff, 1992), 46–7. Also, Olwen may have mythological associations. Roberts seems to favor Olwen as a creation of the story and Culhwch as a saga figure. *Culhwch ac Olwen*, ed. by Rachel Bromwich and D. Simon Evans (Cardiff, 1992), 46–7 and 117–18, respectively; Roberts, *"Culhwch ac Olwen*, The Triads, and Saints' Lives," *The Arthur of the Welsh*, ed. by Rachel Bromwich, Brynley F. Roberts, and Alfred O.H. Jarman (Cardiff, 1991), 74.

4. *Culhwch ac Olwen*, ed. by Rachel Bromwich and D. Simon Evans (Cardiff, 1992), lxxix. The course of the boar strongly resembles William the Conqueror's path to St. David's in 1083.

5. This, in all probability, would have been at one stroke, though the association of various historical characters with Arthur would have been done over some time in the past.

6. *Culhwch ac Olwen*, ed. by Rachel Bromwich and D. Simon Evans (Cardiff, 1992), lxxxii.

7. These boundaries almost definitely do not fully represent the fluidity of this story's history.

8. Chadwick, *The Growth of literature*, vol. 3 (Cambridge, 1940), 201. It should also be noted that as this process is continuing, gener-

ally no figure outside of his heroic age is added to his cycle. When the literature ceases in its oral form, however, other additions may be made, such as in *Culhwch ac Olwen* itself.

9. As one may note, the category of post–1000s is entirely made up of characters from the court-list (ll. 175–373), including the category of Literary, which accounts for nearly all other figures apart from Arthur and those individuals attached to him elsewhere.

10. That this process often occurred may be amply demonstrated in the continental version of the Arthurian romance. Here, Arthur is still the center of court life and is still a figure of high esteem. It is, however, quickly his men who become the center of individual adventures, most probably because the adventures were originally those of the men who are now Arthur's heroes.

11. In the "Proper Nouns in *Culhwch ac Olwen*" appendix, all the personal names, place-names, and Tasks have been listed separately, with their corresponding geographical location and the line in *Culhwch ac Olwen* on which they may be found.

12. Jackson, *Language and History in Early Britain: A Chronological Survey of the Brittonic Languages 1st to 12th c. A.D.* (Edinburgh, 1953), 609.

13. It is feasible that some of the names and places may have come from British regions which were lost to the Germanic peoples in the first half of the fifth century, but there is little or no evidence in the extant literature that any specific memory of this period remains.

14. Bromwich, "Concepts of Arthur," *SC* 10–11 (Cardiff, 1976), 163–181.

15. It should also be noted that the study of the Tasks has shown which *anoethau* pre-dated Arthur and are therefore eligible to be eliminated in the second round of reduction. This also means that any persons or place-names located only in the mythological tasks will also be eliminated.

16. The category of Ireland consists of Aed and Llenlleawc. Aed was a common Irish name, and may very well be mythological, sixth century, or tenth century. Llenlleawc is also to be found in the pseudo–Taliesin work "Preiddeu Annwn," where he is called "die Irish," and *Historia Regum Brittaniae*. As there are no other instances of the name, and as his epithet has been variously translated, Ireland is not a secure placement for the character. The two remaining Dumnonian characters are Goreu and Custennin. Despite their entries in several genaeologies, neither character is to be found in any

other early British records, so their very existence as historical characters must be called into question, and thus there Dumnonian ties. There are two Breton entries, but both may also be associated with Wales (the Llydaw district). These are usually candidates for early associations as well.

17. As Dr. Wendy Davies does not feel it wise to suggest borders, I have here employed Dr. Dark's boundaries, which he has developed on the assumption that religious men would have kept within political limits as they administered their teachings. He looked at the dedications of the various Welsh saints and used them to establish borderlines. As a secondary proof, these are generally based on major riverways which have traditionally served to separate political units. Dark, *Civitas to Kingdom: British Political Continuity* (Leicester, 1994).

18. 2. Porth Cleis, 3. Mynyw, 4. Deu Gleddyf, 5. Presseleu, 6. Glyn Nyfer, 7. Cwm Cerwyn, 8. Peluniawg 9. Aber Tywi, 10. Glyn Ystun, 11. Diffryn Llychwr, 12. Mynydd Amanw, 14. Llwch Tawy, 15. Tawy and Ewyas, 16. Aber Gwy, 17. Aber Lliwan.

19. Again, I have made a full list available in the appendices.

20. Incidentally, it has been often remarked that the heroes of the British Heroic Age all lived north of Wales, apart from several Gwynedd exceptions.

21. It could also be postulated that the tale was formally turned to prose after Hywel Dda (949 or 950). This would explain the heavy influence of Dyfed and other kingdoms outside of Gwynedd. In the tenth century, Dyfed had influence throughout most of the rest of Wales. To Dyfed, *Culhwch ac Olwen* would have been a political document. This would further explain why Gwynedd is nearly absent in the story.

Chapter 15

1. In the pages below, I have only listed and scrutinized those works of literature which named Arthur as residing at his most common sites—Cardoel (Carlisle), Caerleon, Glastonbury, and London.

2. For the development of praise poetry into the romance, see the Appendices.

3. To be sure, this is not always the case; the Breton lais are notable exceptions. It is, however, true as a rule.

4. Certain romances are valid literary sources for this period as I have shown in *Ori-*

gins of Arthurian Romance: Early Sources for the Legends of Tristan, the Grail and the Abduction of the Queen, forthcoming.

5. I have provided a survey of the many different ways in which the material may have been transferred and the evidence that this may have happened in *Origins of Arthurian Romance: Early Sources for the Legends of Tristan, the Grail and the Abduction of the Queen*, forthcoming. However, the classic study is by Dr. Bromwich, "First Transmission to England and France," *The Arthur of the Welsh*, ed. by Rachel Bromwich, Brynley F. Roberts, and Alfred O.H. Jarman (Cardiff, 1991), 273–298.

6. Bulloch-Davies, *Professional Interpreters and the Matter of Britain* (Cardiff, 1966).

7. The first continental Tristan romance was patronized at the court of Henry of Anjou and Eleanor of Aquitaine, who owned Brittany. As was seen above, several Breton *vitae* manage to bring Arthur to them as well.

8. *Lanval*, 1n. 5. It is called Karduel.

9. In fact, it may have been because of David's researches into Cumbrian history that Carlisle was named. See Johnson, *Origins of Arthurian Romance: Early Sources for the Legends of Tristan, the Grail and the Abduction of the Queen*, forthcoming.

10. Ibid., Chapter 2.

11. *Le Conte du Graal*, ln. 336; Carlisle.

12. *Yvain*, ln.7; Dr. Owen says in his notes that this is to be translated as Carlisle.

13. *Yvain*, ln. 2680.

14. *Le Chevalier de la Charrette, l.* 29.

15. *Cliges*, ln. 275.

16. *Erec et Enide*, ln. 28.

17. Johnson, *Origins of Arthurian Romance: Early Sources for the Legends of Tristan, the Grail and the Abduction of the Queen*, forthcoming. In this volume I have also provided evidence that many of the pieces of literature which covered these two subjects were derived from a pre-ninth century period. This would give them added credibility. They have, therefore, been used in the arguments following.

18. Caradoc, *Vita Gildae*, Chapter 10.

19. *Perlesvaus*, ll. 6582 and 6787.

20. Robert de Boron, *Robert de Boron: Le Roman de L'Estoire dou Graal*, trans. by William Roach (Paris, 1927), 1046 and 1071.

21. Though this may well not have been his primary source. The reference implies only that it was being influenced by the so-called discovery of Arthur's body in 1191.

22. *Didot Perceval*, ll. 139, 285, 893, 999, 1905, 2162, 2649.

23. *Perlesvaus*, ll. 78, 159, 520,... 9455.

24. *Le Chevalier À L'Épée*, ln. 30.

25. *La Mule Sanz Frein*, ln. 22.

26. The site appears consistently throughout all his works.

27. *Meraugis de Portlesguez*, ln. 844.

28. *La Vengeance Raguidel*, ll. 3855 and 3895.

29. *Fergus*, 2.19, 9.13, 19.3, 20.20, 88.7, 145.33, 166.23.

30. *Gliglois*, ll. 42 and 2896.

31. *L'Âtre Pèrilleux*, ll. 988, 2526, 2558, 3434, 5212.

32. *Tristan*, ll. 650 and 684.

33. *Hunbaut*, ll. 3412 and 3413.

34. *Yder*, ll. 324, 4792, 6655, 6666.

35. There are several equally correct versions of the *First Continuation*, *Second Continuation*, ll. 23533, 24619; *Gerbert's Continuation*, ll. 6782, 7368; *Mannessier's Continuation*, ll. 38517, 39509, 45003.

36. The specific examples referred to have been explained in Johnson, *Origins of Arthurian Romance: Early Sources for the Legends of Tristan, the Grail and the Abduction of the Queen*, forthcoming.

37. Ibid., 162.

38. The most likely suggestion has been that Chrétien took materials from a traditional Gauvain story to form a counterpoint to Perceval's adventures.

39. Loomis, "Tristram and the House of Anjou," *MLR* 17 (Cambridge, 1922), 24–30.

40. In marrying Maud, Eleanor's husband Henry of Anjou may have been granted access to source material from that region.

41. Johnson, *Origins of Arthurian Romance: Early Sources for the Legends of Tristan, the Grail and the Abduction of the Queen*, forthcoming.

42. Lanval and Lancelot are not traditional heroes, and therefore do not have any geographic connections.

43. Perceval's patronymic in *Peredur*, mab Efrawg, has long been thought to connect him with Ebrauc, modern York. Tristan, in the form Drust, is a common Pictish name, even though it is known throughout the British world. Edern mab Nudd is a creature of mythology. Gauvain has traditionally been associated with Galloway in the romances. This begins in *Le Conte*, when Gauvain's family is to be found there. In addition, the name itself has been seen to have an ancient association with the region of Galloway. He is, however, not to be found in the earliest romances. *Le Conte*, ll. 8341–45; Newell, "Arthurian Notes," *MLN* 17 (Baltimore, 1902), 277–8.

44. For convenience, I have put an asterisk by each hero who is not known in Welsh legend and put each story which was based on traditional materials in bold so that the reader may more easily see the correlations between region on one hand and traditional hero, influences, and source access on the other.

45. Loomis, "Gawain and the Green Knight," *Arthurian Literature in the Middle Ages*, ed. by Roger S. Loomis (Oxford, 1959), 529.

46. This variation is in many different romances. Goodrich, *King Arthur* (New York, 1985), 270. However, it is important to remember that the sources which most commonly give the place-name Caerlion or Caerleon are either composites of earlier known romances or are filled with untraditional and therefore unreliable elements.

47. This is often done in Welsh literature. A prime example of this phenomenon can be seen in *Culhwch ac Olwen*. See *Culhwch ac Olwen*, trans. and ed. by Rachel Bromwich and D. Simon Evans (Cardiff, 1992), 271.

48. "E" version of *The Anglo-Saxon Chronicle* (1092).

49. *WR* (1100).

50. P (1130); Ekwall, *The Concise Dictionary of English Place-Names* (Oxford, 1936), 88.

51. *Le Lais du Cor*, ll. 1, 12, 586.

52. Goetinck, *Peredur* (Cardiff, 1975), 129–55.

53. Roberts, "Geoffrey of Monmouth," *NMS* 20 (Nottingham, 1976), 29–40.

Chapter 16

1. This is the location of ruins believed by some to be the remains of the Hadrian's Wall supply base, Luguvalium. McCarthy, "Thomas, Chadwick, and Post-Roman Britain," *The Early Church in Western Britain and Ireland*, ed. by Susan Pierce (1982), 241–256; McCarthy, "A Roman, Anglian and Medieval Site at Black Friar's Street, Carlisle" (1990), 368–372; McCarthy, "Carlisle," *Current Archaeology* 116 (Friary, 1989), 368–372; Selkirk, *Current Archaeology* 101 (Friary Press, 1986), 172–177; Keevil, Shotter, and McCarthy, "A Solidus of Valentinian II from Scotch Street, Carlisle," *Brit* 20 (Stroud, 1989), 254–255; Dark, "A Sub-Roman Defense of Hadrian's Wall," *Brit* 23 (Stroud, 1992), 112–113. It was probably also a part of the kingdom of Rheged, which seems to have no royal, historical genealogy before Urien and his sons. Miller, "Historicity and the Pedigrees of the Northcountrymen," *BBCS* 26 (Cardiff, 1976), 272.

2. In his defense, it was only a very few of them that he felt confident in locating. He also did not feel justified in locating Arthur on the basis of these battles, though his arguments have not been returned to in fifty years.

3. Jackson, "The Arthur of History," *Arthurian Literature in the Middle Ages*, ed. by Roger S. Loomis (Chicago, 1959), 1–11.

4. *The Gododdin of Aneirin; Text and Context in Dark Age Northern Britain*, ed. and trans. by John T. Koch (Cardiff, 1995), 147.

5. As with Professor Jackson, I would here also like to point out that this is intended by Dr. Bromwich as no more than loose conjecture. Bromwich, "Concepts of Arthur," *SC* 10/11 (Cardiff, 1976), 181.

6. Traditionally, Bamborough was captured in 547 or 549, creating the kingdom of Northumbria. However, as will be seen below, the traditional dating of Arthur's life and death are based on unsubstantiated evidence.

7. Rachel Bromwich, personal communication.

8. Higham, *An English Empire* (Manchester, 1995), 218–240.

9. This is a paraphrase of Triad 51 *of Trioedd Ynys Prydein*, ed. and trans. by Rachel Bromwich (Cardiff, rev. 1978).

10. The assumption that fighting was ethnically based is most probably due to the near-contemporary *Y Gododdin*. However, one must keep in mind that it was written down in the ninth century by the Gwynedd dynasty, and one of their express purposes in writing down northern history was to unite the Britons against the English. It was a ninth century version of "Remember the Alamo." For reasons of consistency, all signs that Britons had fought on the other side would have been erased.

11. Breeze and Dobson have termed it "ornamental rather than functional." Breeze and Dobson, *Hadrian's Wall* (London, 1978), 219.

12. See Evison, "Distribution Maps and England," *Angles, Jutes, and Saxons*, ed. by Vera I. Evison (London, 1981), 1434; Wacher, *The Towns of Roman Britain* (Los Angeles, 1974), 176–7; Ramm, "The End of Roman York," *Soldier and Civilian in Roman Yorkshire* (York, 1971), 178–99; Frere, Hassall, and Tomlin, "Roman Britain in 1989," *Brit* 19 (Stroud, 1990), 325–7. Germanic artifacts which have been collected in York indicate it may have been controlled by the Germanic speakers by the late fifth century, indicating dominance over the region.

13. As has been seen, the period in which Arthur lived was not a static one. Arthur would not have been born in an established royal family, nor would he necessarily have felt tied to the land as a member of a feudal system might. In other words, tradition would not have forced a location on him, so strategic sense may have played a large part in determining his location. In addition, as will be seen below, many of the forts along Hadrian's Wall were reoccupied or fortified in the fifth and sixth centuries, inviting speculation of a single authority, or several authorities acting in unison. Such a possibility also makes it unlikely that York was a capital; it was too far from the action.

14. Dark, "A Sub-Roman Defense of Hadrian's Wall," *Brit* 23 (Stroud, 1992), 119.

15. Breeze and Dobson, *Hadrian's Wall* (London, 1978), 225. Five seem concretely datable to the fifth or sixth century; the other three suggest that they may also belong to that period.

16. Dark, *From Civitas to Kingdom* (Leicester, 1994), 112.

17. Meaney, *A Gazetteer of Early Anglo-Saxon Burial Sites* (London, 1964), 198.

18. Wacher, *The Towns of Roman Britain* (Los Angeles, 1974), 32–3; Ramm, "The End of Roman York," *Soldier and Civilian in Roman York*, ed. by Ronald M. Butler (York, 1971), 178–9; Frere, Hassall, and Tomlin, "Roman Britain in 1989," *Brit* 19 (Stroud, 1990), 325–7.

19. Charlesworth, "The Defenses of Isurium Brigantum," *Soldier and Civilian in Roman Yorkshire*, ed. by Ronald M. Butler (York, 1971), 162–3.

20. Wenham, *Derventio (Malton) Roman Fort and Civilian Settlement* (York, 1974), 32–3; Robinson, *The Archaeology of Malton and Norton* (York, 1978).

21. 1. Stanwix, 2. Castleheads, 3. Birdoswald, 4. Carvoran, 5. Chesterhohn, 6. Housesteads, 7. Chesters, 8. Benwell, 9. South Shields, 10. Corbridge, 11. Binchester, 12. Carlisle, 13. Catterick, 14. York, 15. Aldborough, 16. Malton, 17. Ribchester.

22. Dark, "A Sub-Roman Defense of Hadrian's Wall," *Brit* 23 (Stroud, 1992), 116–119.

23. Ibid., 116–17.

24. The idea of a joint control of Hadrian's Wall is plausible but unlikely. The arrangement would be an awkward one. While it must be admitted that a direct control of the entire of Hadrian's Wall would be very difficult, it seems more feasible that there would be one dominant power.

25. Thomas, *Christianity in Britain up to about 500 A.D.* (London, 1981), 269.

26. As is well known, early Christian con-

verts would have converted simply because their chief had or because of economic convenience. An individual's beliefs would have been of no importance. Christian archaeological remains during this period may therefore be used to verify little more than the extent of a chieftain's influence.

27. Dark, "A Sub-Roman Defense of Hadrian's Wall," *Brit* 23 (Stroud, 1992), 112.

28. Ibid., 116.

29. The other possibility would be Yorkshire, though I have above shown reason for believing this possibility has its problems.

30. It is, of course, quite possible that there may have been two leaders. There may have been a confederation of individual chieftains who controlled all of Hadrian's Wall. It does, however, seem more likely to me that the fewer men involved, the more effective the control could have been.

31. It is at Carlisle where six Roman roads intersect. For comparison, York has four, and Canterbury six. The Romans had apparently deemed Carlisle an extremely important site in their overall control of Britain. Margary, *Roman Roads in Britain* (London, rev. 1967), 359, 428, and 36 respectively.

32. This list includes Cedig, Serwan mab Cedig, Eliman, Llyngesog Llawhir mab Eliman, Elinwyn mab Cadegr, and Mordaf Hael. For the most part, they are all but unknown. See Bartrum, *A Welsh Classical Dictionary: People in History and Legend up to about AD 1000* (Cardiff, 1993).

33. Chadwick, *The British Heroic Age* (Cardiff, 1976), 115–18. This is supported in Breeze and Dobson, *Hadrian's Wall* (London, 1978), 200.

34. Mabon appears in *Culhwch ac Olwen* and *Pa gur?*, indicating an ancient connection. As was demonstrated in *Origins of Arthurian Romance: Early Sources for the Legends of Tristan, the Grail and the Abduction of the Queen*, forthcoming, Beli is one manifestation of the grail king and as such has been connected with the figure of Arthur since at least before the ninth century.

35. Breeze and Dobson, *Hadrian's Wall* (London, 1978), 262–4.

Chapter 18

1. The Saxon Shore forts were built to deal with the heavy pirating of the Saxons during the Late Roman occupation of Britain. They began at the closest point to Gaul and progressively expanded north and west. The settlement of the Germanic mercenaries has been a point of contention between scholars. History knows that the Germanic peoples did not begin in the north and work their way south over the next few centuries; they began in the southeast and went northwest.

2. Thompson, "Gildas and the History of Britain," *Brit* 10 (Stroud, 1979), 207.

3. Ammianus Marcellinus, ed. by John C. Rolfe (Cambridge, 1971–2), 29.4.

4. I will have a great deal more to say about Vortigern-Gwrtheyrn in an upcoming book.

5. Recent scholarship has also established the extent of his library. Laister numbered his titles at over 200, while more recently Lapidge has estimated it at roughly 250, plus biblical and liturgical works. Brown has shown where and from whom the library was most likely developed. Laistner, *Thought and Letters in Western Europe AD 500–900* (Ithaca, 1957), 162; Lapidge, *The Anglo-Saxon Library* (Oxford, 2006), 60; Brown, *A Companion to Bede* (Woodbridge, 2009), 3–8.

6. As was demonstrated above, the bards listed later on do not all fit into the era they are roughly placed, suggesting that the author had managed to compile a list but had no real idea of when they had each been active and was simply placing them between major eras. This suggestion will gain more substance when, in a future book, I will show that Hengest and Horsa as well as Vortigern and St. Germanus (rect. Garmon) are chronologically misplaced

Chapter 19

1. *TYP*, 544.

2. Professor Thompson has perhaps covered the topic most thoroughly. It must also be noted that there is no overriding evidence that he needed to have come. There is no annalistic evidence, only the testimony of his personal *vita*. See *St. Germanus of Auxerre and the End of Roman Britain* (Woodbridge, 1984).

3. Miller, *Sicilian Colony Dates* (New York, 1972), 117–127.

4. The range is a broad one because of the variety of dates associated with Aneirin and Taliesin and their associated Battle of Catterick and reign of Urien and Gwallog, respectively. Traditional dates for both have centered around 600, while more recent scholarship has suggested dates much earlier. Alcock, *Economy, Society and Warfare among the Britons and Saxons* (Cardiff, 1987), 253; Dumville, "Early Welsh

Poetry: Problems of Historicity," *Early Welsh Poetry: Studies in the "Book of Aneirin,"* ed. by Brynley F. Roberts (Cardiff, 1988), 3–4; *The Gododdin of Aneirin,* ed. and trans. by John T. Koch (Cardiff, 1997), xiii–xxxiv.

5. Wright, "Gildas' prose style and its origins," *Gildas: New Approaches,* ed. by Michael Lapidge and David N. Dumville (Woodbridge, 1984), 107–28.

6. Lapidge, "Gildas' Education and the Latin Culture of Sub-Roman Britain," ed. by Michael Lapidge and David N. Dumville, *Gildas: New Approaches* (Woodbridge, 1984), 50.

7. Dumville, "The Death-Date of Patrick," *St. Patrick: AD 493–1993,* ed. by David N. Dumville (New York, 1993), 29–34; Dumville, "St. Patrick and Fifth-Century Irish Chronology: The Kings," *St. Patrick: AD 493–1993,* ed. by David N. Dumville (New York, 1993), 45–50; Dumville, "St. Patrick and Fifth-Century Irish Chronology: The Saints," *St. Patrick: AD 493–1993,* ed. by David N. Dumville (New York, 1993), 51–58.

8. Dumville, "Verba Militibus Mittenda Corotici: An Analysis of St Patrick's Tract on the Crimes of Coroticus," *St. Patrick: AD 493–1993,* ed. by David N. Dumville (New York, 1993), 117–128.

9. *TYP* 484.

10. Rhys, *Celtic Britain* (London, 1904), 118; *TYP* 484.

11. That this pattern is accurate may be cross-checked by the fact that southern Dyfed appears to have been the most Romanized area of Britain that would survive the mid-century upheavals, and therefore would most likely have retained their sense of Romanitas the longest.

12. Admittedly, all of the individuals active into the middle of the sixth century were from southern Wales as well, so that their geography might also account for their Latin names as well. However, that they were all born within a couple decades of 500 would not significantly affect the conclusions being arrived at here.

13. Mackreth, "Roman Public Buildings," *Urban Archaeology in Britain,* ed. by J. Schoefield and R.H. Leech (1987), 133–146.

14. Alcock, *Dinas Powys: An Iron Age, Dark Age and Early Medieval Settlement in Glamorgan* (Cardiff, 1963), 42; Alcock, *Economy, Society and Warfare among the Britons and Saxons* (Cardiff, 1987), 39.

15. Kent, "From Roman Britain to Saxon England," *Anglo-Saxon Coins,* ed. by Reginald H.M. Dolley (London, 1961), 1–22; Kent, "The End of Roman Britain: The Literary and Numismatic Evidence Reviewed," *The End of Roman Britain,* ed. by P. John Casey (Oxford, 1979), 15–28; Dark, *Civitas to Kingdom: British Political Continuity 300–800* (Leicester, 1994), 200–206.

Chapter 20

1. Bartrum, *A Welsh Classical Dictionary: People in History and Legend up to about AD 1000* (Cardiff, 1993).

2. Dumville, "On the North British Section of the *Historia Brittonum,*" *WHR* 8 (Cardiff, 1977c), 345–354; Jackson, "On the Northern British Section in Nennius," *Celt and Saxon: Studies in the Early British Border,* ed. by Nora K. Chadwick (Cambridge, 1963), 20–62.

3. For instance, several of Maelgwn's bards are known. If Talhaeran was active in Gwynedd he would have predated the infamous king.

4. The triads cannot be taken at face value here, that each king was an assassin. Such an activity would be well outside the range of acceptability for their class, and unlikely to succeed three times in any event. Two alleged victims, Gwrgi and Edwin, died in battle. Finally, there are perhaps two hundred miles and forty years between Edwin and Gwenddoleu.

Chapter 22

1. Sims-Williams, "Gildas and the Anglo-Saxons," *CMCS* 6 (Cambridge, 1983a), 1–30; "The Settlement of England in Bede and the *Chronicle,*" *ASE* 12 (London, 1983b), 1–41; Higham, *Gildas and the Fifth Century* (Leicester, 1994).

2. Miller, *Sicilian Colony Dates* (New York, 1970), 117–127.

3. Living memory at a given point in time is defined as any memory that a historian would have had access to throughout his life. Therefore, if Gildas was forty-three years old when he wrote *De Excidio Britanniae* and the oldest person he could have talked with as a child would have been eighty, living memory would extend up to one hundred and twenty years.

4. *Chronica Minora I* (Berlin, 1886), 515–660, ed. by Theodor Mommsen; Miller, "The Last British Entry in the 'Gallic Chronicles,' " *Brit* 9 (Stroud, 1978b), 315–318; Jones and Casey, "The Gallic Chronicle Restored: A Chronology for the Anglo-Saxon Invasions and the End of Roman Britain," *Brit* 19 (Stroud,

1978), 367–398; Burgess, "The Dark Ages Return to Fifth-Century Britain: The 'Restored' Gallic Chronicle Exploded," *Brit* 21 (Stroud, 1990), 185–195. These scholars have taken different approaches and have generally disagreed with each other about everything but this date.

5. Arnold, *An Archaeology of the Early Anglo-Saxon Kingdoms* (New York, 1988), 101–48, 176–230.

6. How many U.S. individuals born in 1980 or later know anything more than that Kennedy was assassinated in the past? In 1985 or later that we landed on the moon? This in an era of instant access to information and history courses with prescribed syllabi that cover such landmark events in U.S. history.

7. Ambrosius would appear to have been active in southwestern England or Wales for several reasons. Gildas says he was Roman and his name is clearly of Latin derivation. Southwestern England remained under direct Roman control the longest, thus making the four decades of relative peace that Gildas claims between Badon and his letter a historical possibility there. In contrast, the eastern portion would come under consistent Germanic control from immediately after the Germanic revolt. Finally, the single battle attributed to Ambrosius other than (possibly) Badon is Wallop. This is modern Guelleph in southwestern England.

Chapter 23

1. Johnson, *Origins of Arthurian Romance: Early Sources for the Legends of Tristan, the Grail and the Abduction of the Queen*, forthcoming.

2. From the last quarter of the sixth century, inconsistencies between the various annals and Bede of up to three years are common. However, none of more than eight years has been demonstrated.

3. Morris, *Arthurian Period Sources*. Vol. 3. *Persons: Ecclesiastics and Laypeople* (Chichester, 1995), 80.

4. *The Gododdin of Aneirin; Text and Context in Dark Age Northern Britain*, ed. and trans. by John T. Koch (Cardiff, 1995), xv–xviii; Dumville, "Early Welsh Poetry: Problems of Historicity," *Early Welsh Poetry: Studies in the Book of Aneirin*, ed. by Brynley F. Roberts (Aberystwyth, 1988), 3–4; Higham, *Kingdom of Northumbria, AD 350–1100* (Stroud, 1993), 83; Alcock, *Economy, Society, and Warfare*

among the Britons and Saxons (Cardiff, 1987), 253.

5. Jackson, "Once Again Arthur's Battles," *MP* 43 (Chicago, 1945), 44–57.

6. Ibid., 57.

Chapter 24

1. Alcock, *Arthur's Britain* (New York, 1971), 209–229.

2. Kenneth Dark has determined that western and northern Britain, which regardless of the findings of this paper were most likely where Arthur was active, were generally devoid of any activity during the fifth and sixth centuries. Dark, "High Status Sites, Kingship and State Formation in Post-Roman Western Britain AD 400–700," Unpublished Ph.D. thesis (Cambridge, 1990).

3. Miket, "A Re-Statement of Evidence for Bernician Anglo-Saxon Burials," *Anglo-Saxon Cemeteries 1979*, ed. by Phillip A. Rahtz (London, 1980), 289–305.

4. Swanton, *The Spearheads of the Anglo-Saxon Settlements* (London, 1973), 28–34.

5. Bidwell, *The Roman Fort of Vindolanda at Chesterholm Northumberland* (Carlisle, 1985), 75; Frere, Hassall, and Tomlin, "Roman Britain in 1987," *Brit* 19 (Stroud, 1988), 436–7; "Birdoswald. Dark Age Halls in a Roman Fort," *Current Archaeology* 116 (Friary, 1989), 288–91; Collingwood and Wright, *The Roman Inscriptions of Britain* (Oxford, 1965), 1722; Jackson, "Brigomaglos and St. B:log," *AA* 10 (Newcastle upon Tyne, 1982), 61–68.

6. Bidwell, *The Roman Fort of Vindolanda at Chesterholm Northumberland* (Carlisle, 1985), 38, 45–6.

7. Laing, "Archaeological Notes on some Scottish Early Christian Stones," *PSAS* 114 (Darking, 1985), 277–87.

8. Miket, "A Re-Statement of Evidence for Bernician Anglo-Saxon Burials," *Anglo-Saxon Cemeteries 1979*, ed. by Phillip A. Rahtz (Taunton, 1980), 289–305.

9. Collingwood and Wright, *The Roman Inscriptions of Britain* (Oxford, 1965), 2331.

10. Johnson, *Hadrian's Wall* (Carlisle, 1989), 115; Breeze and Dobson, *Hadrian's Wall* (New York, rev. 1978), 231.

11. Miket, "A Re-Statement of Evidence for Bernician Anglo-Saxon Burials," *Anglo-Saxon Cemeteries 1979*, ed. by Phillip Rahtz. (Taunton, 1980), 289–305.

12. Swanton, *The Spearheads of the Anglo-Saxon Settlements* (London, 1973), 28–34.

Chapter 25

1. Miller, "Bede's Use of Gildas," *EHR* 90 (London, 1975), 241–261; Higham, *An English Empire* (Manchester, 1996).

2. Hughes, "The Welsh Latin Chronicles: *Annales Cambriae and Related Texts*," *PBA* 59 (London, 1975), 242.

3. Ibid., 234–5.

4. Kirby, "Problems of Early West Saxon History," *EHR* 80 (London, 1965), 10–29.

5. If the maximum age was roughly fifty-five, then roughly 550 would have been about the year in which a person still alive in 597 would have able to recall as a small child.

6. Miller, "The Disputed Historical Horizon of the Pictish King-Lists," *BBCS* 28 (Cardiff, 1978), 1–11.

7. Ibid., 9–11.

8. Dumville, "Gildas and Maelgwn: Problems of Dating," ed. by David N. Dumville and Michael Lapidge, *Gildas: New Approaches* (Woodbridge, 1984), 51–9. For Northumbria's horizons see above.

Conclusion

1. As Professor Dumville has pointed out, a knowledge of the historical context and transmission of a source are two of the key elements in determining its value as a historical source. The third element is external validation, of which there is none. Dumville, "Early Welsh Poetry: Problems of Historicity," *Early Welsh History*, ed. by Brynley F. Roberts (Aberystwyth, 1988), 1.

2. Geoffrey Ashe presented what are perhaps the most convincing materials in this regard in *The Quest for Arthur's Britain*, ed. by Geoffrey Ashe (London, 1968).

3. In the heroic age mindset, land is not the most valuable of commodities; it is honor, fame, and prestige which are most sought after. Attila the Hun had no wish to rule the Roman Empire, only to show his power by making it pay tribute to him.

Appendix A

1. *Vita Gildae*, chapter 1. Again, *vitae* are not historical sources, but contain useful details when those details have not been used to forward the purpose of the author's patron.

2. I disagree with Professor Sims-Williams here. He argues that Gildas is not a known name from any language, while I would argue that we know extremely little about Pictish personal names in general. The limited traditional evidence would suggest he was a Pict. Sims-Williams, "Gildas and Vernacular Poetry," *Gildas: New Approaches* (Dover, 1984), 169 fn. 2.

3. An opinion shared by Sims-Williams and Thompson as well. Sims-Williams, "Gildas and the Anglo-Saxons" *CMCS* 6 (Cambridge, 1983), 3; Thompson, "Gildas and the History of Britain," *Brit* 10 (Stroud, 1979), 225.

4. Dr. Wright's article gives conclusive evidence that Gildas did not write solely of the northern part of Britain. However, I do not believe that anyone has ever argued that Gildas did. Wright, "Gildas' Geographical Perspective: Some Problems," *Gildas: New Approaches*, ed. by Michael Lapidge and David N. Dumville (Woodbridge, 1984), 85–105.

5. The Scottish kingdom of Dalriada was originally a den of thieves and marauders whose inhabitants came from Ireland.

6. That there were Germanic military installations in the north is demonstrated by the Germanic structural remains to be found at Catterick, and the artifactual remains at a number of the northern sites which were reoccupied during the fifth and sixth centuries. Several sites in northwestern Britain, most notably Dumfries, have at one time been thought to originally have been named after one Germanic tribe or another. Though their original names have been shown to be alternatively derived at this time, the fact that they all seem to be located along a perimeter is intriguing. Wacher, "Yorkshire Towns in the Fifth Century," *Soldier and Civilian in Roman Yorkshire*, ed. by Ronald M. Butler (York, 1971), 165–77.

7. The Britons had stigma against the Picts. Given the otherwise consistent association of Gildas with the Picts, it seems likely that Caradoc moved his subject's birthplace to avoid tarnishing his name.

Appendix B

1. In my thesis, evidence was presented that the abduction, grail, and Tristan stories were based on common heroic age literature, with indication that the former two were in existence and associated with Arthur by 900. Johnson, *The Origins of Arthurian Romance: Early Sources for the Legends of Tristan, the Grail and the Abduction of the Queen*, forthcoming.

2. Kei, Gwalchmei, and Bedwyr may each have been independent figures at an early stage

of this process but were soon added to the Arthurian material.

3. In the case of Arthurian literature, examples of this phenomenon would be Lancelot, Bors, and many of Lancelot's kin.

4. Page has claimed that the *Iliad*'s hero is in fact Achilles. If this is so, then the epic represents the stage of heroic age literature described above. Achilles is the first warrior among many. Page, *History and the Homeric Iliad* (California, 1959), 254.

5. In the main saga great pains are taken to counterpoint the fighting prowess of the warriors with the wisdom and intelligence of Hrolf. The internal evidence suggests that his two chief warriors may have been kings in their own right. A heroic age chieftain could not rule without the admiration of his men. These two facts suggest the absorption described above.

6. For a more detailed explanation of this phenomenon, see Ker, *From Epic to Romance* (New York, 1896), 6–7, 13–15.

7. Kramer, *The Sumerians: Their History, Culture, and Character* (Chicago, 1959), 45; Bottéro, *The Near East: The Early Civilization* (New York, 1967), 54.

8. Page, *History and the Homeric Iliad* (California, 1959), 254.

9. This task was left for Mallory to attempt. His effort is unsatisfactorily finished (from a historical standpoint), and was done without the use of the oldest sources.

10. The tales of Erec, Tristan, Lancelot, and Perceval all seem to be quite common, for instance.

Appendix C

1. An educated guess would be that this is in fact Aachen, capital of the Frankish empire under Charlemagne and his French heirs.

2. Here I follow Dr. Rachel Bromwich and Dr. David Simon Evans in inserting the two pups of the bitch Rhymhi. *Culhwch ac Olwen*, ed. by Rachel Bromwich and D. Simon Evans (Cardiff, 1992), xlviii.

3. This site is named in conjunction with Mabon ap Modron, a northern figure. Clearly this is a case of attempted relocation.

Appendix D

1. Jackson, "On the Northern British Section in Nennius," *Celt and Saxon: Studies in the Early British Border*, ed. by Nora K. Chadwick (Cambridge, 1963), 20–62; Hughes, "The Welsh Latin Chronicles: *Annales Cambriae and Related Texts*," *PBA* 59 (London, 1975), 233–259; Bromwich, "Concepts of Arthur," *SC* 10/11 (Cardiff, 1976), 163–181; Dumville, "The Anglian Collection of Royal Genealogies and Regnal Lists," *ASE* 5 (Cambridge, 1976b), 23–50.

2. Miller, "The Commanders of Arthuret," *TCWAAS* 75 (Kendall, 1975), 96–117.

Bibliography

Primary Sources

Aneirin. *The Gododdin: The Oldest Scottish Poem.* Trans. by Kenneth H. Jackson. Edinburgh, 1969.

Aneirin: Y Gododdin, Britain's Oldest Heroic Poem. Trans. by Alfred O.H. Jarman. Llandysul, 1990.

The Anglo-Saxon Chronicle. Trans. by George Norman Garmonsway. London, 1986.

Armes Prydein. Ed. by Sir Ifor Williams. Trans. by Rachel Bromwich. Dublin, 1982.

L'Atre périlleux. Ed. by Brian Woledge. Paris, 1936.

Aue, Hartmann von. *Iwein.* Ed. and trans. by Patrick M. McConeghy. New York, 1984.

Bede. *A History of the English Church and People.* Trans. by Leo Sherley-Price, rev. by Ronald Edward Latham. London, 1978.

Béroul. *Tristan.* Ed. by Alfred Ewert. Oxford, 1939.

Biquet, Robert. *Le Lai du Cor.* Ed. by Heinrich Dörner. Strassburg, 1907.

"*The Black Book of Carmarthen:* Stanzas of the Graves" (Englynion y Beddau.) Ed. and trans. by Gwyn Jones. *Proceedings of the British Academy* 53, 97–137. London, 1967.

Canu Llywarch Hen. Ed. by Sir Ifor Williams. Cardiff, 1935.

Chrétien de Troyes. *Arthurian Romances.* Trans. by Douglas David Roy Owen. London, 1989.

_____. *Les Chansons Courtoises de Chrétien de Troyes.* Ed. by Marie Claire Zai. Lang, 1974.

Chronica Minora I. Ed. by Theodor Mommsen. 515–660. Berlin, 1886.

The Continuations of the Old French Perceval of Chrétien de Troyes. Ed. by William Roach. Philadelphia, 1949.

Culhwch ac Olwen: An edition and study of the oldest Arthurian tale. Ed. by Rachel Bromwich and D. Simon Evans. Cardiff, 1992.

Didot Perceval. Trans. by William A. Nitze. Chicago, 1932–7.

The Didot Perceval, According to the Manuscript of Modena and Paris. Trans. by William Roach. Philadelphia, 1941.

"An Early Ritual Poem in Welsh" ("Ymddiddan Gwenhwyfar ac Arthur"). Ed. and trans. by Mary Williams. *Speculum* 13, 38–51. Cambridge, 1938.

Early Welsh Genaeological Tracts. Ed. by Peter C. Bartrum. Cardiff, 1966.

Eschenbach, Wolfram von. *Parzival.* Trans. by Helen M. Mustard and Charles E. Passage. New York, 1961.

_____. *Parzival.* Trans. by Arthur Thomas Hatto. Baltimore, 1980.

_____. *Wolfram von Eschenbach: Parzival.* Ed. by Gottfried Weber. Darmstadt, 1963.

Geoffrey of Monmouth. *The History of the Kings of Britain.* Trans. by Lewis G. M. Thorpe. New York, 1966.

Gerbert de Montreuil. *La Continuation de Chrétien de Troyes*. Ed. by Mary Williams. Paris, 1922–5.

Gildas. *The Ruin of Britain*. Trans. by Michael Winterbottom. London, 1978.

Giraldus Cambrensis. *Itinerarium Cambriae. English: The Journey through Wales and the Description of Wales*. Trans. by Lewis G.M. Thorpe. New York, 1978.

Gliglois. Ed. by Charles H. Livingston. *Harvard Studies in Romance Languages* 8. Cambridge, 1932.

The Gododdin of Aneirin: Text and Context for Dark Age North Britain. Ed. and trans. by John T. Koch. Cardiff, 1997.

Le Clerc, Guillaume. *Fergus*. Ed. by Ernst Martin. Halle, 1872.

Le Haut Livre du Graal: Perlesvaus. Ed. by William A. Nitze. Totowa, 1937.

Historia Brittonum. Ed. and trans. by John Morris. Chichester, 1978.

Hunbaut. Ed. by Jakob Stijrzinger-Hermann Breuer. Dresden, 1914.

Leland, John. *De Rebus Britannicis*. 6 vols. Ed. by Thomas Hearne. London, 1970.

The Lives of the British Saints, vol. 3. Ed. by Sabine Baring-Gould and John Fisher. London, 1907–13.

Manassier. *La Continuation de Perceval*. Ed. by Chaim Potvin. Mons, 1865–71.

Marcellinus, Ammianus. Trans. by John C. Rolfe. Cambridge, MA, 1971–72.

Marie de France. *The Lais of Marie de France*. Ed. By Glyn S. Burgess and Keith Busby. New York, 1986.

A Monk of Rhuys and Caradoc of Llancarfan. *Two Lives of Gildas*. Trans. by Hugh Williams. Llanerch, 1899, reprinted 1990.

Nibelungenlied. Trans. by Arthur Thomas Hatto. New York, 1970.

Paiens de Maisières. *Le Chevalier àl'épée*. Ed. by Edward Cooke Armstrong. Baltimore, 1900.

_____. *La Mule sans frain*. Ed. by Boleslaw Orlowski. Paris, 1911.

Poetry from the Red Book of Hergest. Ed. by J. Gwenogrvyn Evans. Llanbedrog, 1911.

"'Preiddeu Annwn' and the figure of Taliesin." Ed. by Marged Haycock. *Studia Celtica* 14/15, 52–77. Oxford, 1984.

Raoul de Houdenc. *Meraugis de Portlesguez*.

Ed. by Mathias Friedwagner. Halle, 1897–1907.

_____. *La Vengeance Raguidel*. Ed. by Mathias Friedwagner. Halle, 1909.

Rhigyfarch. *Rhigyfarch's Life of David*. Llanerch, 1989.

Robert de Boron. *Robert de Boron: Le Roman de L'Estoire dou Graal*. Trans. by William Roach. Paris, 1927.

Siculus, Diodorus. *The Bibliotheca Historia of Diodorus Siculus*. Trans. by John Skelton. Ed. by Frederick Millet Salter and H.L.K. Skelton Edward. Oxford, 1968–1971.

Strabo. *The Geography*. Trans. by Leo Horace Jones. New York, 1923.

Taliesin. *Canu Taliesin*. Ed. by Sir Ifor Williams. Cardiff, 1960.

Trioedd Ynys Prydein: The Welsh Triads. Ed. and trans. by Rachel Bromwich. Cardiff, rev. 1978.

The Vatican Recension of the Historia Brittonum. Ed. by David N. Dumville. Cambridge, 1985.

Vitae Sanctorum Britanniae et Genealogiae. Ed. by Arthur W. Wade-Evans. Cardiff, 1944.

The White Book: Welsh Tales and Romance Reproduced from the Peniarth Manuscripts. Ed. by J. Gwenogvryn Evans. Private press, 1907.

Zatzikhoven, Ulrich von. *Lanzelet*. Ed. by Roger Sherman Loomis. Trans. by Kenneth Grant Tremayne Webster. Ed. by Roger S. Loomis. New York, 1951.

Secondary Sources

Abrams, Leslie. *Anglo-Saxon Glastonbury: Church and Endowment*. Woodbridge, 1996.

_____, and James P. Carley, eds. *The Archaeology and History of Glastonbury Abbey. Essays in Honour of the Ninetieth birthday of C. A. Ralegh Radford*. Woodbridge, 1991.

Alcock, Leslie. *Arthur's Britain*. New York, 1971.

_____. *Dinas Powys: An Iron Age, Dark Age and Early Medieval Settlement in Glamorgan*. Cardiff, 1963.

_____. *Economy, Society and Warfare among the Britons and Saxons.* Cardiff, 1987.

Andersen, Ølvind, and Matthew Dickie, eds. *Homer's World: Fiction, Tradition, Reality.* Bergen, 1995.

Anderson, Marjorie, and Alan Orr Anderson. *Kings and Kingship in Early Scotland.* Edinburgh, 1973.

Arnold, Christopher J. *An Archaeology of the Early Anglo-Saxon Kingdoms.* New York, 1988.

Ashe, Geoffrey. "'A Certain Very Ancient Book'; Traces of an Arthurian Source in Geoffrey of Monmouth's *History.*" *Speculum* 56, no. 2, 301–23. Cambridge, 1981.

_____, ed. *The Quest for Arthur's Britain.* London, 1968.

Atkinson, Richard John Copland. *Stonehenge.* London, 1956.

Bartrum, Peter C. *A Welsh Classical Dictionary: People in History and Legend up to about AD 1000.* Cardiff, 1993.

Bengston, Hermann. *Einführung in die alte Geschichte.* München, 1953.

Bidwell, Paul T. *The Roman Fort of Vindolanda at Chesterholm Northumberland.* Carlisle, 1985.

Bollard, John K. "Arthur in the Early Welsh Tradition." *The Romance of Arthur,* 13–25. Ed. by James J. Wilhelm. New York, 1984.

Bottéro, James. *The Near East: The Early Civilization.* New York, 1967.

Bowen, Geraint. *The Settlements of the Celtic Saints in Wales.* Cardiff, 1956.

Breeze, David J., and Brian Dobson. *Hadrian's Wall.* London, rev. 1978.

Bromwich, Rachel. "Concepts of Arthur." *Studia Celtica* 10/11, 163–181. Cardiff, 1976.

_____. "Dwy Chwedl a Thair Rhamant." *Y Traddodiad Rhyddiaithyn yr Oesoedd Canol,* 143–175. Ed. by Geraint Bowen. Llandysul, 1974.

_____. "Transference to England and France." *The Arthur of the Welsh,* 273–98. Ed. by Rachel Bromwich, Brynley F. Roberts, and Alfred O.H. Jarman. Cardiff, 1991.

_____. "The Tristan of the Welsh." *The Arthur of the Welsh,* 209–28. Ed. by Rachel Bromwich, Brynley F. Roberts, and Alfred O.H. Jarman. Cardiff, 1991.

_____, Alfred O.H. Jarman and Brynley F. Roberts, eds. *The Arthur of the Welsh.* Cardiff, 1991.

_____, and R. Brinley Jones, eds. *Astudiaethau ar yr Hengerdd.* Cardiff, 1978.

Brown, George Hardin. *A Companion to Bede.* Woodbridge, 2009.

Bruce, James Douglas. *The Evolution of the Arthurian Romance from the Beginning Down to the Year 1300.* Gottingen, 1923.

Bulloch-Davies, Constance. *Professional Interpreters and the Matter of Britain.* Cardiff, 1966.

Burgess, Richard W. "The Dark Ages Return to Fifth-Century Britain: The 'Restored' Gallic Chronicle Exploded." *Britannia* 21, 185–195. Stroud, 1990.

Butler, Ronald Morley, ed. *Soldier and Civilian in Roman Yorkshire.* York, 1971.

Camden, William. *Camden's Britannia.* Trans. by Edmund Gibbon. London, 1695.

Carman, J. Neale. "The *Perlesvaus* and Bristol Channel." *Research Studies* 32, 85–105. 1964.

_____. "South Welsh Geography and British History in the *Perlesvaus.*" *A Medieval French Miscellany: Papers of the 1970 Kansas Conference on Medieval French Literature,* 37–59. Lawrence, 1972.

Carney, James. *Studies in Irish Literature and History.* Dublin, 1955.

Chadwick, Hector. *The Development of Oral Literature.* 3 vols. Cambridge, 1932–40.

_____. *The Heroic Age.* Cambridge, 1912.

Chadwick, Nora Kershaw, ed. *The British Heroic Age: The Welsh and the Men of the North.* Cardiff, 1976.

_____, ed. *Celt and Saxon: Studies in the Early British Border.* Cambridge, 1963.

_____, ed. "Early Culture and Learning in North Wales." *Studies in the Early British Church,* 29–120. Cambridge, 1958.

_____, ed. *Studies in the Early British Church.* Cambridge, 1958.

Charles-Edwards, Thomas. "The Arthur of History." *The Arthur of the Welsh.* Ed. by Rachel Bromwich, Brynley F. Roberts, and Alfred O.H. Jarman, 15–32. Cardiff, 1991.

_____. "The Authenticity of the Gododdin: An Historian's View." *Astudiaethau ar yr Hengerdd.* Ed. by Rachel Bromwich and R. Brinley Jones, 44–71. Cardiff, 1978.

_____. *Early Irish and Welsh Kinship*. Oxford, 1993.

Charlesworth, David. "The Defenses of Isurium Brigantum." *Soldier and Civilian in Roman Britain*. Ed. by Ronald M. Butler, 155–64. York, 1971.

Clucas, Philip. *Britain An Aerial Close-up*. New York, 1994.

Coe, J.G, and S. Young. *The Celtic Sources of the Arthurian Legend*. Llanerch, 1995.

Collingwood, Robin George, and Roger P. Wright. *The Roman Inscriptions of Britain*. Oxford, 1965.

Crawford, Osbert Guy Stanhope. "Arthur and his Battles." *Antiquity* 9, 217–91. Gloucester, 1935.

Crotch, Walter John Blyth. *The Prologues and Epilogues of William Caxton*. London, 1928.

Dark, Kenneth. *Civitas to Kingdom: British Political Continuity 300–800*. Leicester, 1994.

_____. "High Status Sites, Kingship and State Formation in Post-Roman Western Britain AD 400–700." Unpublished Ph.D. Thesis. Cambridge, 1990.

_____. "A Sub-Roman Defense of Hadrian's Wall." *Britannia* 23, 111–120. Stroud, 1992.

Davies, Wendy. *An Early Welsh Microcosm: Studies in the Llandaff Charters*. London, 1978.

_____. *The Llandaff Charters*. Aberystwyth, 1979.

_____. "Property Rights and Property Claims in Welsh '*Vitae*' of the Eleventh Century." *Hagiograaphie, Culture et Societiés ive–xiie sieclès*, 515–33. Ed. by Pierre Riché. Paris, 1981.

Doble, Gilbert Hunter. *Lives of the Cornish Saints*. Truro, 1960–70.

Dumville, David N. "The Anglian Collection of Royal Geneaologies and Regnal Lists." *Anglo-Saxon England* 5, 23–50. Cambridge, 1976.

_____. "The Chronology of *De Excidio Britanniae*, Book 1." Ed. by David N. Dumville and Michael Lapidge. *Gildas: New Approaches*, 61–84. Woodbridge, 1984.

_____. "The death-date of Patrick." *St. Patrick: AD 493–1993*. Ed. by David N. Dumville, 29–34. New York, 1993.

_____. "Early Welsh Poetry: Problems of Historicity." *Early Welsh Poetry: Studies in the "Book of Aneirin."* Ed. by Brynley Roberts, 1–16. Cardiff, 1988.

_____. "Gildas and Maelgwn: Problems of Dating." Ed. by David N. Dumville and Michael Lapidge. *Gildas: New Approaches*, 51–9. Woodbridge, 1984.

_____. "The Historical Value of the *Historia Brittonum*." *Arthurian Literature* 6, 1–26. Ed. by Richard Barber. Cambridge, 1986.

_____. "Kingship, Genealogies and Regnal Lists." *Early Medieval Kingship*. Ed. by Peter S. Hayes and Ian N. Wood, 72–104. Leeds, 1977.

_____. "Nennius and the *Historia Brittonum*." *Studia Celtica* 10/11, 78–95. Cardiff, 1976.

_____. "On the North British Section of the *Historia Brittonum*." *Welsh History Review* 8, 345–354. Cardiff, 1977.

_____. *St. Patrick: AD 493–1993*. New York, 1993.

_____. "St. Patrick and Fifth-Century Irish Chronology: The Kings." *St. Patrick: AD 493–1993*. Ed. by David N. Dumville, 45–50. New York, 1993.

_____. "St. Patrick and Fifth-Century Irish Chronology: The Saints." *St. Patrick: AD 493–1993*. Ed. by David N. Dumville, 51–58. New York, 1993.

_____. "Some Aspects of the Chronology of the Historia Brittonum." *Bulletin of the Board of Celtic Studies* 25, 439–45. Cardiff, 1974.

_____. "Sub-Roman Britain: History and Legend." *History* 62, 173–92. London, 1977.

_____. "Verba Militibus Mittenda Corotici. An Analysis of St Patrick's Tract on the Crimes of Coroticus." *St. Patrick: AD 493–1993*. Ed. by David N. Dumville, 117–128. New York, 1993.

Ekwall, Eilert. *The Concise Dictionary of English Place-Names*. Oxford, 1936.

Evison, Vera Ivy. "Distribution Map of England in the First Two Phases." *Angles, Saxons and Jutes: Essays Presented to J.N.L. Myres*, 126–167. Ed. by Vera I. Evison. London, 1981.

_____, ed. *Angles, Saxons and Jutes: Essays Presented to J.N.L. Myres*. London, 1981.

Falkenstein, Adam, Franz Marius Theodor

de Liagre Böhl, Heinrich Otten, and Peter Calmeyer. "Gilgamesh." *Reallexikon der Assyriologie und vorderasiatishen Archäologie* 3, no. 5, 357–74. Berlin, 1968.

Finberg, Herbert Patrick Reginald. "St. Patrick and Glastonbury." *The Irish Ecclesiastical Record* 107. Dublin, 1967.

Foot, Sarah. "Glastonbury's Early Abbots." *The Archaeology and History of Glastonbury Abbey: Essays in Honour of the Ninetieth Birthday of C.A. Ralegh Radford*. Ed. by Lesley Abrams and James P. Carley, 163–190. Woodbridge, 1991.

Foster, Sir Idris. "*Culhwch ac Olwen* and Rhonabwy's Dream." *Arthurian Literature in the Middle Ages*, 31–43. Ed. by Roger S. Loomis. Oxford, 1959.

Frayne, Douglas R. "The Birth of Gilgamesh in Ancient Mesopotamian Art." *The Canadian Society of Mesopotamian Studies Bulletin* 34, 39–49. Toronto, 1999.

Frere, Shepard Sutherland, Mark W.C. Hassall, and Roger S.O. Tomlin, "Roman Britain in 1987." *Britannia* 19, 436–7. Stroud, 1988.

_____. "Roman Britain in 1989." *Britannia* 21, 303–78. Stroud, 1990.

George, Andrew. "What's New in the Gilgamesh Epic." *The Canadian Society of Mesopotamian Studies Bulletin* 34, 51–8. Toronto, 1999.

Gill, Christopher, and Timothy Peter Wiseman. *Lies and Fiction in the Ancient World*. Exeter, 1993.

Goetinck, Glenys. *Peredur: A Study of Welsh Tradition in the Grail Legends*. Cardiff, 1975.

Goodrich, Norma Lorre. *King Arthur*. New York, 1985.

Gowans, Linda. *Cei and the Arthurian Legend*. Cambridge, 1988.

Grant, Robert McQueen. *The Earliest Lives of Jesus*. New York, 1961.

_____. *The Letter and the Spirit*. London, 1957.

Greene, David. "The Chariot as Described in Irish Literature." *The Iron Age in the Irish Sea Province*, 59–73. Ed. by Charles Thomas. London, 1972.

Griscom, Acton. *The Historia Regum Britanniae of Geoffrey of Monmouth*. London, 1929.

Gruffydd, R. Geraint. "From Gododdin to Gwynedd: Reflections of the Story of Cunedda." *Studia Celtica* 24/25, 1–14. Cambridge, 1989–1990.

Güterbock, Hans Gustav. "Die historiche Tradition und thre literarische Gestalung bei Babyloniern und Hethitern bis 1200." *Zeitschrift für Assyriologie* 42, 1–91. Berlin, 1934.

_____. "Die historiche Tradition und thre literarische Gestalung bei Babyloniem und Hethitem bis 1200." *Zeitschrift für Assyriologie* 44, 45–149. Berlin, 1938.

_____. "Sargon of Akkad Mentioned by Hattusili I or Hatti." *Journal of Cuneiform Studies* 18, 1–6. Cambridge, MA, 1964.

Haycock, Marged. "'Preiddeu Annwn' and the figure of Taliesin." *Studia Celtica* 14/15, 52–77. Cardiff, 1984.

Heidel, Alexander. *The Gilgamesh Epic and Old Testament Parallels*. Chicago, 1949.

Higham, Nicholas. *An English Empire*. Leicester, 1996.

_____. *Gildas and the Fifth Century*. Leicester, 1994.

_____. *King Arthur: Mythmaking and History*. New York, 2002.

_____. *The Northern Counties to AD 1000*. London, 1986.

Hodges, E. Richmond. *Cory's Ancient Fragments of the Phoenician, Carthaginian, Babylonian, Egyptian and other Authors*. London, 1876.

Hughes, Kathleen. "The Welsh Latin Chronicles: *Annales Cambriae* and Related Texts." *Proceedings of the British Academy* 59, 233–259. London, 1975.

Jackson, Anthony. *The Symbol Stones of Scotland*. Stromness, 1984.

Jackson, Kenneth Hurlstone. "Arthur in Early Welsh Verse." *Arthurian Literature in the Middle Ages*, 12–19. Ed. by Roger S. Loomis. Chicago, 1959.

_____. "The Arthur of History." *Arthurian Literature in the Middle Ages*, 1–11. Ed. by Roger S. Loomis. Chicago, 1959.

_____. "Brigomaglos and St. Briog." *AA* 10, 61–68. Newcastle upon Tyne, 1982.

_____. "The Britons in Southern Scotland." *Antiquity* 29, 77–88. Gloucester, 1955.

_____. *The International Popular Tale*. Cardiff, 1961.

_____. *Language and History in Early Britain: A Chronological Survey of the British Language 1st to 12th c. A.D.* Edinburgh, 1953.

_____. "On the North British Section of the *Historia Brittonum*." *Celt and Saxon: Studies in the Early British Border*, 20–62. Ed. by Nora K. Chadwick. Cambridge, 1963.

_____. "Once Again Arthur's Battles." *Modern Philology* 43, 44–57. Chicago, 1945.

_____. "The Site of Mount Badon." *Journal of Celtic Studies* 2, 152–155. Cardiff, 1958.

Jacobsen, Thorkild. "Early Political Development in Mesopotairnia." *Zeitschriftfiir Assyriologie* 52, 91–140. Berlin, 1957.

Jarman, Alfred Owen Hughes. "The Arthurian Allusions in the *Black Book of Carmarthen*." *The Legend of Arthur in the Middle Ages*, 99–112. Ed. by P.B. Grout, R.A. Lodge, C.E. Pickford, and E.K.C. Varty. Cambridge, 1983.

_____, and Gwilym Rees Jones, eds. *A Guide to Welsh Literature*. 4 vols. Cardiff, 1976.

Johnson, Flint. *Gwrtheyrn, Hengest, and the Fifth Century. Relative and Absolute Chronology in Britain, AD 400–700*. Forthcoming.

_____. *Origins of Arthurian Romance: Early Sources for the Legends of Tristan, the Grail and the Abduction of the Queen*. Forthcoming.

Jones, Michael E., and John Casey. "The Gallic Chronicle Restored: A Chronology for the Anglo-Saxon Invasions and the End of Roman Britain." *Britannia* 19, 367–398. Stroud, 1978.

Jones, Thomas. "Datblygiadau Cynnar Chwedl Arthur." Trans. by Gerald Morgan. "The Early Evolution of Arthur." *Nottingham Mediaeval Studies* 8, 3–21. Nottingham, 1964.

Keevil, Graham D., David Collin Arthur Shotter, and Michael Robin McCarthy. "A Solidus of Valentinian 11 from Scotch Street, Carlisle." *Britannia* 20, 254–255. Stroud, 1989.

Kent, J.P.C. "The End of Roman Britain, the literary and numismatic evidence reviewed." *The End of Roman Britain*, 15–28. Ed. by P. John Casey. Oxford, 1979.

_____. "From Roman Britain to Saxon England." *Anglo-Saxon Coins*, 1–22. Ed. by Reginald H.M. Dolley. London, 1961.

Ker, William P. *Epic and Romance: Essays on Medieval Literature*. Woodbridge, 1896.

Kirby, David P. "Problems of Early West Saxon History." *English Historical Review* 80, 10–29. London, 1965.

_____. "Vortigern." *Bulletin of the Board of Celtic Studies* 23, 37–59. Cardiff, 1970.

Kramer, Samuel Noah. "Heroes of Sumer: A New Heroic Age in World History and Literature." *Proceedings of the American Philosophical Society* 90, 120–130. Philadelphia, 1946.

_____. *History Begins at Sumer: Twenty-Seven "Firsts" in Man's Recorded History*. Garden City, 1959.

_____. "Sumerian Literature, A General Survey." *The Bible and the Ancient Near East: Essays in Honor of William Foxwell Albright*. Ed. by G. Ernest Wright. Garden City, 1961.

_____. *The Sumerians: Their History, Culture, and Character*. Chicago, 1959.

Lacy, Norris J., Geoffrey Ashe, Sandra Ness Ihle, Marianne Kalinke, and Raymond H. Thompson, eds. *The Arthurian Encyclopedia*. London, 1986.

Laing, Lloyd. "Archaeological Notes on some Scottish Early Christian Stones." *Proceedings of the Society of Antiquaries of Scotland* 114, 277–87. Darking, 1985.

_____. *Celtic Britain*. New York, 1979.

Laistner, Max Ludwig Wolfram. *Thought and Letters in Western Europe AD 500–900*. Ithaca, 1957.

Lapidge, Michael. "Gildas' Education and the Latin Culture of Sub-Roman Britain." *Gildas: New Approaches*. Ed. by Michael Lapidge and David N. Dumville, 11–50. Woodbridge, 1984.

_____, and David N. Dumville, eds. *Gildas: New Approaches*. Woodbridge, 1984.

_____. *The Anglo-Saxon Library*. Oxford, 2006.

Lewis, Ceri W. "The Historical Background of Early Welsh Verse." *A Guide to Welsh Literature*. Vol. 1. Ed. by Alfred O.H. Jarman and Gwilym R. Hughes, 11–50. Swansea, 1976.

Lloyd, John Edward. *The History of Wales:*

From the Earliest Times to the Edwardian Conquest. London, 1939.

Lloyd-Jones, John. *The Court Poets of the Welsh Princes.* London, 1948.

Loomis, Laura Hibbard. "Gawain and the Green Knight." *Arthurian Literature in the Middle Ages,* 528–540. Ed. by Roger S. Loomis. Oxford, 1959.

Loomis, Roger Sherman. *Arthurian Tradition and Chrétien de Troyes.* New York, 1949.

_____. "By What Route did the Romantic Tradition of Arthur Reach the French?" *Modern Philology* 33.3, 225–238. Chicago, 1936.

_____. "Calogrenanz and Crestien's Originality." *Modern Language Notes* 43, 215–222. Baltimore, 1928.

_____. "Discussions: Cause or Coincidence, a Reply to Monsieur Ferdinand Lot." *Romania* 54, 515–526. Paris, 1928.

_____. "Edward I, Arthurian Admirer." *Speculum* 28, 114–127. Cambridge, 1953.

_____. *The Grail: From Celtic Myth to Christian Symbol.* Cardiff, 1963.

_____. "The Spoils of Annwfn: An Early Arthurian Poem." *Publications of the Modern Language Association* 56, 887–936. Menasha, 1941.

_____. "The Strange History of Caradoc of Vannes." *Franciplegius: Medieval Studies in Honor of Francis Peabody Magaun, Jr.* Ed. by Jess B. Bessinger and Robert P. Creed. New York, 1965.

_____. *Wales and the Arthurian Legend.* Cardiff, 1956.

_____, ed. *Arthurian Literature in the Middle Ages.* New York, 1959.

_____, ed. *Medieval Studies in Memory of Gertrude Schoepperle Loomis.* New York, 1927b.

Mackreth, Donald F. "Roman Public Buildings." *Urban Archaeology in Britain,* 133–146. Ed. by J. Schoefield and R.H. Leech. London, 1987.

MacMullen, Ramsay. *Christianity and Paganism in the Fourth to Eighth Centuries.* New Haven, 1997.

MacNeill, Eoin. "The Irish Law of Dynastic Succession." *Studies* 8, 376–382, 640–53. Dublin, 1919.

Margary, Ivan D. *Roman Roads in Britain.* London, rev. 1967.

Maxwell, G.S. "Review of *The British Heroic Age* by Nora Chadwick." *Britannia* 8, 492–494. Stroud, 1977.

McCarthy, Michael Robin. "Carlisle." *Current Archaeology* 116, 368–372. Friary, 1989.

_____. *A Roman, Anglian and Medieval Site at Black Friar's Street, Carlisle,* 368–372. Kendal, 1990.

_____. "Thomas, Chadwick, and Post-Roman Carlisle." *The Early Church in Western Britain and Ireland,* 241–256. Ed. by Susan M. Pierce. Oxford, 1982.

Meaney, Audrey. *A Gazeteer of Early Anglo-Saxon Burial Sites.* London, 1964.

Miket, Roger. "A Re-statement of Evidence for Bernician Anglo-Saxon Burials." *Anglo-Saxon Cemeteries 1979,* 289–305. Ed. by Philip A. Rahtz. London, 1980.

Miller, Molly. "Bede's Use of Gildas." *English Historical Review* 91, 241–261. London, 1976c.

_____. "The Commanders of Arthuret." *Transactions of the Cumberland and Westmorland Antiquarian and Archaeological Society* 75, 96–117. Kendall, 1975.

_____. "Date-guessing and Dyfed." *Studia Celtica* 12, 33–61. Cardiff, 1977.

_____. "Date-guessing and pedigrees." *Studia Celtica* 11, 96–109. Cardiff, 1976d.

_____. "The Disputed Historical Horizon of the Pictish King-Lists." *Bulletin of the Board of Celtic Studies* 28, 1–34. Cardiff, 1978.

_____. "Historicity and the Pedigrees of the Northcountrymen." *Bulletin of the Board of Celtic Studies* 26, 255–280. Cardiff, 1976b.

_____. "The Last British Entry in the 'Gallic Chronicles.'" *Britannia* 9, 315–318. Stroud, 1978b.

_____. "Relative and Absolute Publication Dates of Gildas' De Excidio in Medieval Scholarship." *Bulletin of the Board of Celtic Studies* 26, 169–174. Cardiff, 1976a.

Morris, John. *The Age of Arthur.* London, 1973.

_____. *Arthurian Period Sources.* Vol. 3. *Persons: Ecclesiastics and Laypeople.* Chichester, 1995.

Nash-Williams, Victor Erle. *The Early Christian Monuments of Wales.* Cardiff, 1950.

Newell, Arthur. "Arthurian Notes." *Modern*

Language Notes 17, 277–8. Baltimore, 1902.

Nitze, William A. "Arthurian Names: Arthur." *Publications of the Modern Language Association* 64, 585. Menasha, 1949.

Noth, Martin. *Überlieferungsgeschichliche Studien* 1. Halle, 1943.

Ó Corráin, Donnchadh. "Irish Regnal Succession: A Reappraisal." *Studia Hibernia* 11, 7–39. Dublin, 1971.

Ó Hogáin, Paul. *Fionn macCumhail: Images of the Celtic Hero*. Dublin, 1988.

Padel, Oliver. "The Cornish Background of the Tristan Stories." *Cambridge Medieval Celtic Studies* 1, 53–82. Cambridge, 1982.

_____. "Geoffrey of Monmouth and Cornwall." *Cambridge Medieval Celtic Studies* 7, 1–28. Cambridge, 1984.

_____. "The Nature of Arthur." *Cambridge Medieval Celtic Studies* 27, 1–32. Cambridge, 1994.

_____. "Some South-Western Sites with Arthurian Connotations." *The Arthur of the Welsh*, 229–248. Ed. by Rachel Bromwich, Brynley F. Roberts, and Alfred O.H. Jarman. Cardiff, 1991.

Page, Denys L. *History and the Homeric Iliad*. California, 1959.

Pallis, Svend Aage. *The Antiquity of Iraq: A Handbook of Assyriology*. Copenhagen, 1956.

Parry, John Jay, and Robert A. Caldwell. "Geoffrey of Monmouth." *Arthurian Literature in the Middle Ages*, 72–93. Ed. by Roger S. Loomis. Oxford, 1959.

Pearce, Susan M., ed. *The Early Church in Western Britain and Ireland*. Oxford, 1982.

Piggott, Stuart. "The Sources of Geoffrey of Monmouth: I The 'Pre-Roman King-List.'" *Antiquity* 15, 269–86. Gloucester, 1941.

_____. "The Sources of Geoffrey of Monmouth: II The Stonehenge Story." *Antiquity* 15, 305–319. Gloucester, 1941.

Rahtz, Philip A. ed. *Anglo-Saxon Cemeteries 1979*. Taunton, 1980.

_____. "Pagan and Christian by the Sevem Sea." *The Archaeology and History of Glastonbury Abbey: Essays in Honour of the Ninetieth Birthday of CA. Ralegh Radford*, 3–38. Ed. by Lesley Abrams and James P. Carley. Woodbridge, 1991.

Ramm, Herman G. "The End of Roman York." *Soldier and Civilian in Roman Yorkshire*, 19–99. Ed. by Ronald M. Butler. York, 1971.

Rhys, Sir John. *Celtic Britain*. London, 1904.

_____. *Celtic Folklore, Welsh and Manx*. Oxford, 1901.

Roberts, Brynley F. "*Culhwch ac Olwen,* the Triads, and Saints' Lives." *The Arthur of the Welsh*, 73–96. Ed. by Rachel Bromwich, Brynley F. Roberts, and Alfred O.H. Jarman. Cardiff, 1991a.

_____. "Geoffrey of Monmouth, *Historia Regum Britanniae* and *Brut y Brenhinedd*." *The Arthur of the Welsh*, 97–116. Ed. by Rachel Bromwich, Brynley F. Roberts, and Alfred O.H. Jarman. Cardiff, 1991b.

_____. "Geoffrey of Monmouth." *Nottingham Mediaeval Studies* 20, 29–40. Nottingham, 1976.

Robinson, J. F. *The Archaeology of Malton and Norton*. York, 1978.

Ross, Anne. *Pagan Celtic Britain*. London, 1967.

Rowland, Jenny. *Early Welsh Saga Poetry: A Study and Edition of the Englynion*. Cambridge, 1990.

Rowley, Harold H. *From Joseph to Joshua: Biblical Traditions in the Light of Archaeology*. London, 1950.

Schoefield, J. and R.H. Leech. eds. *Urban Archaeology in Britain*. London, 1987.

Selkirk, Andrew. "Birdoswald: Dark Age Halls in a Roman Fort." *Current Archaeology* 101, 172–177. Friary, 1986.

_____. "Birdoswald. Dark Age Halls in a Roman Fort." *Current Archaeology* 116, 288–91. Friary, 1989.

Sims-Williams, Patrick. "The Early Welsh Arthurian Poems." *The Arthur of the Welsh*, 33–72. Ed. by Rachel Bromwich, Brynley F. Roberts, and Alfred O.H. Jarman. Cardiff, 1991.

_____. "Gildas and the Anglo-Saxons." *Cambridge Medieval Celtic Studies* 6, 1–30. Cambridge, 1983a.

_____. "Gildas and Vernacular Poetry." *Gildas: New Approaches*, 169–90. Ed. by Michael Lapidge and David N. Dumville. Woodbridge, 1984.

_____. "The Settlement of England in Bede and the *Chronicle.*" *Anglo-Saxon England* 12, 1–41. London, 1983b.

_____. "The Significance of the Irish Personal Names in *Culhwch ac Olwen*." *Bulletin of the Board of Celtic Studies* 29, 600–620. Cardiff, 1982.

Smith, George. *The Chaldean Account of Genesis*. London, 1876.

Swanton, Michael James. *The Spearheads of the Anglo-Saxon Settlements*. London, 1973.

Tatlock, John Strong Perry. *The Legendary History of Britain*. Berkeley, 1950.

Thomas, Charles. *Christianity in Britain up to 500 A.D.* London, 1981.

_____. "East and West: Tintagel, Mediterranean Imports and the Early Insular Church." *The Early Church in Western Britain and Ireland*, 17–34. Ed. by Susan M. Pearce. Oxford, 1982.

_____. "'Gallici nautae de Gailiarurn provinciis'—A Sixth/Seventh Century Trade with Gaul, Reconsidered." *Medieval Archaeology* 34, 1–26. London, 1990.

_____. *A Provisional List of imported Pottery in Post-Roman Western Britain and Ireland*. Redruth, 1981.

Thomas, Gwyn. *Traddodiad Barddol*. Cardiff, 1976.

Thompson, Edward A. "Gildas and the History of Britain." *Britannia* 10, 203–226. Stroud, 1979.

Thurneysen, Rudolph. "Zimmer, Nennius Vindicatus." *Zeitschrift für Deutsche Philologie* 28, 80–113. Halle, 1896.

Wacher, John S. *The Towns of Roman Britain*. Los Angeles, 1974.

_____. "Yorkshire Towns in the Fifth Century." *Soldier and Civilian in Roman Yorkshire*, 165–177. Ed. by Ronald M. Butler. York, 1971.

Wenham, Leslie P. *Derventio (Malton) Roman Fort and Civilian Settlement*. York, 1974.

West, Geoffrey D. *An Index of Proper Names in French Arthurian Prose Romances*. Toronto, 1978.

_____. *An Index of Proper Names in French Arthurian Verse Romances, 1150–1300*. Toronto, 1969.

Wilhelm, James J., ed. *The Romance of Arthur*. New York, 1984.

Williams, Griffith John, and E.J. Jones. *Gramadegau'r Penceirddiaid*. Aberystwyth, 1934.

Williams, Sir Ifor. *Lectures on Early Welsh Poetry*. Dublin, rep. 1970.

Williams, N.J.A. "Llywarch Hen and the Finn Cycle." *Astudiaethau ar yr Hengerdd*, 234–265. Ed. by Rachel Bromwich and R. Brinley Jones. Cardiff, 1978.

Wiseman, Timothy Peter. *Remus: A Roman Myth*. Cambridge, 1995.

Wood, Michael. *In Search of the Trojan War*. Oxford, 1985.

Wright, Neil. "Gildas' Geographical Perspective: Some Problems." *Gildas: New Approaches*, 85–105. Ed. by Michael Lapidge and David N. Dumville. Woodbridge, 1984.

_____. "Gildas' Prose Style and its Origins." *Gildas: New Approaches*, 107–28. Ed. by Michael Lapidge and David N. Dumville. Woodbridge, 1984.

Index